for Robert, Jessica, Alayna and Riley

Acknowledgements

It was my dear friend Annie Bergen, who kept insisting that I could write a book. You were right. Thank you Annie, for your devout friendship as you lovingly watched me attempt to keep my family intact. I found my bravery when my friend Diana Persson, encouraged me to take a creative risk and helped me to believe I could tell my story on my terms. Thank you Diana, for saying so and pushing me to become who I've always wanted to be, a writer.

Thank you Ryan Carney, Jessica Feser, and the team at Friesen Press, who kept me going and allowed me to change my mind too many times to count.

Thank you Tanya Guenther, Dr. Gary Malenchak, Jared Hildebrand and Dennis Fehr, for keeping my mind, body and soul healthy along the way.

Peter Cantelon read my very first draft and offered me amazing insight. Thank you for letting me know that I had a story to tell. Thanks to my good friend and medical guide, Barb Dyck, for reading the manuscript with the perspective of a neurology nurse and as one who has known our family's private struggles and triumphs. And thanks, Rob, for finding the courage to trudge through the manuscript and relive our good and bad days.

Jessica, Alayna and Riley, thank you for your forgiveness when I didn't get it right and thank you for letting me know when I did. You are awesome people.

1
Typical Days

The traffic light turned red, giving Joanna the chance to scan her list one more time. Pick up chips, pretzels, hot dog buns and candy. Done. Grabbing the pen, she crossed off, get more beer. Sighing, she shoved the paper back into her purse. Joanna Kornelson did love a plan. She even loved her dependence for annoying lists. With three kids and a husband to manage, lists were her lifeline to keeping organized and getting through busy days. Days like today, when she had to stay on track of where she needed to go and all she needed to do. Joanna took a long drink from the water bottle kept in the console of her Jeep.

It was the start of summer vacation. A time when families slowed down for camping, beaching and road trips. Meals became simpler and happy, outdoor fun was always the objective for the day. But for Joanna it was not turning out so idyllic. Since the last day of school she had been nagging Ally, Jack and Lydia to clean up their old school supplies they dumped and abandoned in their rooms. And yet, she found herself caving into their whining demands, like driving them around as if she was the chauffeur. Whatever happened to the idea of getting on their bikes? The new bikes they got them for Christmas that now sat in the garage, always in her way.

Joanna took in a deep breath and let out a familiar sigh. The light turned green and Joanna hit the gas pedal. Summer had no vacation days for her. She still had three more loads of laundry waiting. She had to pack her husband's overnight bag and then see if the kids had plans after supper. Oh right, supper.

Although she had her share of headaches trying to keep her clan content and occupied, Joanna loved being a mom. She saw them off every morning and was there when they got home at the end of a school day. It was important to be available for her family. Even though she was often left emotionally drained, enduring the repetitive monotony of daily life while her efforts were not always appreciated, she was glad to have the choice of putting her career on hold to raise her family. Graham, her husband of nearly twenty years, was a successful lawyer, allowing her financial freedom. Joanna was grateful and never took for granted what she considered blessings.

With the first week of July behind them, Joanna believed with a bit more patience from her and a fair amount of compromise from the kids, they were going to survive the next two months. She was careful not to over schedule fourteen year old Ally, and twelve year old twins Jack and Lydia, especially in the summer. She liked the idea of kids hanging out with their friends at the local parks and riding their bikes to the beach. But they always reminded her that these weren't the olden days and kids didn't want to "play" outside like she did when she was growing up in Mountain City. Her rebuttal was always the same, she was not about to let her kids hibernate indoors all summer while bingeing on Rice Crispy cake and Netflix. They could call her old fashioned, but no amount of complaining lessened her resistance when it came to the expectations of her kids. That wasn't totally true; they did wear her down more often than she cared to admit. She drove them around too much, let them stay up too late and sleep in until mid morning. But it was summer, she justified, so she let her rules slide, slightly.

Joanna waved to her neighbour, Hannah, who was going for a walk. Joanna hoped to get in her daily run before Graham left for their *cabin* with his younger brother, Todd, later today. Their task was to DIY the old deck on the family cottage. It would be their first drive to Lake of the Woods since their father, Ed, unexpectedly passed away this past winter. The cabin had been in the Kornelson family for three generations and it was the place their children would spend their summers yet to come. It was where Graham and Joanna got married. The cabin was where they celebrated birthdays, milestones and family events. It was their home, their getaway, their history.

Joanna tapped her fingers to the easy rhythm playing on the radio. This would be a great summer. It had to be.

Losing Graham's dad to cancer had been the most difficult experience the Kornelson family had endured. Just before Christmas, Ed, complained about feeling tired and then, by the end of February, he was gone. Peacefully and sadly, her husband's father who had guided and led this family was no longer a part of their daily lives. As each day passed without him, they slowly began to find strength in the bonds of their family and rebuilt an unfamiliar everyday without Ed. Graham had been shaken to the core losing his dad so suddenly. So Joanna did what she could for her husband to ease him back from the heavy grief that buried him for weeks.

Adding to their stress this past year was Ally, who had become difficult to manage. At fourteen, their oldest daughter struggled with her first year of high school. Changing schools had brought on changing friendships. Ally always had a difficult time with transitions and as she got older it was not getting any easier. Ally had been unusually disrespectful towards her teachers, which was not like her. She was their strong willed one growing up, who was not afraid to challenge anyone when she wanted something. But intentionally disrespecting those in authority was not how she was raised. Joanna explained to her teachers that it was a rather trying year of changes for Ally. With the stress of high school, and her goal to become a concert pianist would have been enough pressures. But then her beloved grandfather, affectionately known as, Papa, passing away had been a lot for Ally to handle. They had hoped it was just a teenage phase she would outgrow.

Ally had always lived under the expectations of being the best. Even at a very young age, they noticed Ally could carry a tune on pitch and keep a steady beat. Ally continued to excel musically and now showed promise of becoming a very gifted pianist. But her strong willed nature made her strive for perfection causing much tension as she practiced the piano for hours at a time, ensuring each piece was mastered.

Jack was scheduled for hockey camp next week and was registered to start soccer the third week of August. At twelve he was consumed with sports and competition. He hoped that he would grow this summer and planned to pass at least two levels of swimming lessons. Lydia, at age twelve going on seventeen, hated anything Joanna wanted her to do. The only way Lydia had agreed to take swimming lessons again depended on her mother buying her a new bathing suit. Lydia loved fashion and clothes and knew everything about how to be popular. Joanna realized she was in trouble with that one; and it was going to be expensive.

Joanna would have to keep her mothering skills sharp over the next few years. She couldn't let Ally's disrespectful attitude get further out of line or her constant quest for musical perfection whenever she practiced; which was all the time. Jack always wanted to over extend his sports schedule. And Lydia's disinterest in everything that remotely interested the other two kids was getting tiresome. It was an unpredictable changing dance for Joanna to know her kids and to make sure they stayed on the right path. She didn't want perfect kids. She wanted her kids to become amazing adults. And she would make sure every opportunity would be given to them, no matter what it took out of her.

Joanna pulled onto the driveway of their century old Queen Anne Revival home she had restored and beautifully decorated over the past fifteen years. As a former interior decorator, design was her passion, but creating a home for her family was always her objective. As Joanna opened the car door, Bentley, their most loved family possession came running out to greet her as she gathered shopping bags from the back of the Jeep. Jack followed Bentley from the backyard.

"Did you buy anything good?" he asked, looking in the bags. "Chips? Doritos?" he listed off, digging through one more bag. "M&M's and chocolate covered almonds? You hardly ever buy junk food for us!"

"And I didn't buy it for you this time either. It's for Dad and Uncle Todd while they're at the cabin rebuilding the deck this weekend," she explained, keeping Bentley from hopping into the trunk.

"Oh, and I guess the beer is for them too?" Jack added sarcastically.

"No, that I bought for you. To get you through the family reunion this weekend," Joanna joked, hoping the humour would soften the reminder.

Jack put the bags down. "What do you mean family reunion this weekend? I thought you were kidding about going to that gathering of strangers. You were kidding, right?"

Unfortunately for Joanna and the kids, she was not kidding. Bowing down to the pressures of the generation before her, Joanna agreed to show up for this extended family event that happened every three years.

"It will be fun. Your cousins will be there." Joanna headed towards the kitchen door at the back of the house. At least she *thought* his cousins would be there. This was a gathering of her mother's side, the Shapansky family. So Joanna presumed her sisters succumbed to the pressure as well and would show up. She reminded herself to call Laura, her older sister, just to be on the safe side. Joanna had decided to make the best of the weekend and continued to convince herself it would be good to catch up with vaguely familiar distant relatives. At least she didn't have to cook all weekend and she promised the kids they would come home for night instead of staying in the private school dormitories where the reunion was going to take place.

Lydia was sitting on the counter eating a banana smeared with peanut butter. Jack followed his mother inside plunking down the snacks that weren't for him. "Lydia," Jack said full of annoyance, "did you know that we were going to the strange reunion this weekend, all weekend?"

His twin gasped, followed by a look of horror. "What?"

Joanna added the beer into the cooler. "Not all weekend, just Saturday and Sunday."

"That's practically the whole weekend, Mom," Lydia emphatically exclaimed, licking the gooey mess off her fingers.

Joanna turned her attention to her distraught twins. "Look, it's only for a couple of days. And we're going swimming at the pool." She paused. "And Grandpa and Grandma will be there."

"Swimming? Jack questioned. "Where are we going?"

7

"I told you the reunion is in Gretna," Joanna said quickly, as she found the hot dogs in the freezer and added them to the cooler.

"Gretna?" Lydia shrieked dramatically.

Joanna rolled her eyes. "There's a very nice swimming pool in Altona. It will be fun," she reminded them and herself again.

"Who's going to Gretna?" Ally asked, as she sauntered into the kitchen looking down at her phone.

"You are, you moron," Jack quipped, digging his finger into the jar of peanut butter.

"Jack," Joanna scolded, wondering if she was going to get that run in today.

"Ah no, I'm not going to Gretna, idiot. I've made plans already," Ally announced, still not taking her eyes off the phone.

"How come everyone is acting like you didn't know about this reunion?" Joanna asked with growing frustration. "I told you about it months ago and I said we were going. So we're leaving tomorrow morning. Bring your bathing suits. End of discussion."

Like well tuned instruments of torture, they all began bellowing complaints and whining in unison. Joanna closed her eyes feeling the harassing pressure getting the better of her. She had to go for that run if she was going to keep her sanity. "Look, it's important to your grandparents that we're there so they can show you off. At least you can go swimming and you'll get to meet your second cousins."

"Who cares? I don't want to meet them. We don't want to go. This is lame," Ally said on their behalf.

Joanna crossed her arms with equal defiance. "Well, you're going and I'm going and that's final. I already registered and paid for us to go."

"Wait, Dad's not going?" Jack finally surmised while washing his hands. "How come he doesn't have to go?"

Joanna sighed. "This was the only time it worked for Uncle Todd to get away from the hospital. They want to at least start to rebuild the deck at the cabin so that we can enjoy it the rest of the summer."

Graham's brother was a doctor at the local hospital. He and his wife, Sarah, had two little girls, Abigail and Nora, who didn't get to see their daddy a lot on weekends. But going to the cabin for the first time together was important to the Kornelson brothers, and time allowances had to be made.

Bentley heard the familiar sound of the Graham's car pulling up the driveway, and begged to be let out to greet his master.

Lydia opened the door, went to meet her dad, and started the rant before Graham could get out of the car. He took in a deep breath. "Hello Bentley," he said, petting his dog. "How come you don't greet me all excited anymore, Lyd?"

"Dad!" Lydia whined as Bentley raced back to the kitchen door. "Mom is making us go to some lame weekend in Gretna and now our whole summer is ruined," she lamented, as they walked back into the house. "And none of us want to go and she's making us go anyway!"

"Where is this mean mother of yours?" Graham teased, walking into the kitchen. "All the way to Gretna. You poor, poor kids."

"And Altona," added Jack, throwing the towel into the sink.

"Yeah, well I'm not going," Ally declared.

"Just in time, I see," Joanna said, coming from the butler's pantry. "I can't find the beer holders."

"I think we left them at the cabin last summer. Got all the stuff I need?" he asked, taking off his tie and tossing it over Lydia's shoulder.

"Dad, don't make us go to this," she pleaded, taking the tie and pretending to choke herself.

"And why can't I go with you and Uncle Todd to rebuild the deck?" Jack asked.

Graham paused before looking innocently at Joanna. "I don't know?" he began, looking for the answer in her eyes. "Because that's what Mom said." Graham knew full well that it was his decision to go with just his brother.

"Really, you're a lawyer and you defend people's points of view all day and that's how you defend mine? 'Because that's what Mom said!'" Joanna repeated. She ran her hands through her long, straight pony tail in complete frustration. "Look, you three and I are going to go and love spending the next two days in Gretna. Your father and uncle are going back to the cabin that their grandfather built and get it ready for us so we can enjoy it for the rest of summer. Dad will be back late Saturday night and then he will join us on Sunday. Now I'm going to get ready for my run that I've been putting off all day because I've been shopping and doing everything for you guys, all day." She looked at her family staring back at her with vacant expressions on their sun kissed cheeks. She loved these people, but every time they didn't get their way they acted like the world was falling apart.

"Mom's right, it's only a couple of days. Stop giving her a hard time about it. Go and enjoy yourself." Graham picked up his briefcase and headed towards his office down the hall from the kitchen.

"That's nice for you to say, Dad," Ally piped up before he left the room. "You get to go to the lake while we have to be with a bunch of people we don't know."

Graham leaned against the frame of the doorway. He did not want to go around with his teenage daughter who hated backing down as much as he did. "Ally, just drop it, okay. That's enough from all of you. You're acting like this will be the worst weekend of your lives. Family is important and don't forget it."

He felt a sharp twinge of loss at his own statement. This would be the first time returning to the family cabin since his dad had died, he remembered. Family was important because once they were gone, it was forever. He looked at the floor as the unexpected grief tampered with his emotions once again. "Now stop giving your mom a hard time about this and let her go have her run." He pushed himself off the door jam and walked out of the kitchen and into the sanctuary of his office, where he could shake off his battle of emotions in private.

"Fine," Ally spewed with defiance, stomping out of the room. Lydia continued the drama as she too left the kitchen, slamming the swinging door behind her. Ally began playing a dramatic Bach Fugue to get her frustration out. Pounding out each note as it solidified her intensity with each musical phrase.

Joanna sighed.

Jack grabbed the basketball from the back porch and headed outside with Bentley to blow off steam on the basketball hoop.

Alone in the kitchen, Joanna reminded herself that this stage of life would soon pass and one day she would look back fondly on these tender years; but not today. The decision to go to the family reunion had a fragile consensus and she would take it. She headed upstairs to change into her running clothes, grabbing her last opportunity to run away, at least for a little while.

2
Family Connection

The Shapansky Reunion turned out to be what the kids reluctantly called, 'an okay time.' Joanna watched as they finally mingled with new found family members that ended up to be not that strange after all. At first Jack sat with his grandpa and listened to embellished stories of yesteryear. Lydia found comfort in joining Grandma and her sisters walk through the gardens of the private school campus. Ally followed her mom around as Joanna reconnected with cousins and great aunts, paging through dated photo albums reminiscing of times gone by; and yet it truly only felt like yesterday. Joanna hated clichés about time passing by, but how they all rang true as story after story was shared over potato salad and cold cuts.

In the afternoon a group was organized to drive the short distance to the neighbouring community of Altona, and enjoy the town's outdoor pool.

Hopefully they will start mingling with the other kids, Joanna thought, loading a few of them into her Jeep. After a few quiet moments it didn't take long before small connections and conversations started between these unknown cousins during the quick drive to the pool.

Once they were all changed and into the water, Joanna could finally enjoy the afternoon of simply wading in the shallow end of the pool, while watching the kids interact with each other in the water park.

Laura slipped off her sandals and joined her little sister in the refreshing water. "At last, everyone is happy," Laura said, while they watched Jack jump off the diving board.

Joanna sighed. "Yeah, I know. I'm actually glad we made the effort to come." She readjusted her sun hat. "Well, at least most of us did." Joanna was referring to their frequently absent oldest sister, Pauline.

Laura, the middle sister had three boys, who all adored their cousin, Jack. Harry, Laura's playful husband, got the job of tossing the boys into the water. He was the biggest kid of them all.

Joanna suddenly missed Graham and now wished he was here too. But she knew he needed this time with his own brother, who was his best friend. How lucky he was to come from an amazing family. How blessed she was to be a part of his family, who was nothing like her own. Standing beside her sister, Joanna felt like she was standing next to a distant relative.

"Pauline said she was going to try and make it. But I guess..." Laura started to say but trailed off, "it doesn't matter, it's her decision," she added, tucking her bobbed hair behind her ears.

The oldest sister of the three often found somewhere else to be when it came to their family. Since they were kids, Pauline was never around and when she was, she loved to be the boss. If Pauline did come, they always showed up last and always the first to leave. It was hard not to take it personally, Joanna and Laura had said one day, when Pauline missed another family birthday.

"So, Graham is at the cabin? That must be nice to have a place to go to all summer," Laura casually stated, crossing her arms.

Joanna tried to ignore the hint of resentment in Laura's comment. When Joanna married the wealthy, charming and successful, Graham Kornelson, everything changed between her and her family. Everyone knew Graham had come from a privileged family, which now had set Joanna apart. They all liked Graham and he never flaunted his family's affluence in front of Joanna's family, but something had changed. Joanna had become a Kornelson.

Then there was Laura's husband, Harry, who was a goofy kid stuck in an overgrown man's body. He didn't take life or responsibilities all that seriously. He played with his boys like they were his buddies. He worked at a local hardware store, mostly for the coffee breaks and the opportunities to talk with other guys about guy stuff. A few years earlier he opened up a bike repair shop that had struggled and limped along. Graham was able to help them out of the dismal situation with some legal advice, barely keeping them out of bankruptcy. Laura worked as a school secretary in one of the middle schools and in the summer she filled in at the school division office to help make ends meet. Laura and Harry did have enough, but Graham and

Joanna always had more than enough. And the many differences did not go unnoticed by the two older sisters.

"Todd and Graham are rebuilding the deck. Todd had to be back at the hospital for tomorrow so they didn't have a lot of time this weekend. The bathroom needs some work too. Hopefully it will get done before the summer is over," Joanna explained, dabbing cool water on her neck. "This is the first time they've gone to the cabin since Ed died. I hope they're doing okay," she added, staring into the distance.

Laura nodded like she had been paying attention. Joanna had always sensed Laura's touches of jealousy over the years. Especially when Joanna came home from university and announced she was dating Graham Kornelson. Always considered the prettiest of the sisters, Joanna lit up a room with her big, brown eyes and wavy, chestnut brown hair.

They had all grown up in Mountain City, a bustling community just an hour north of the American border in Southern Manitoba. Although Joanna and Graham had attended different high schools and had casually met a few times at sporting events and through mutual friends. But they reconnected during their years while at university, both feeling overwhelmed by the big city of Winnipeg. After Joanna and Graham were married and Graham had finished law school, they moved back home and into one of the most well established neighbourhoods and coveted historic homes in Mountain City.

The lack of common ground between her and Laura had grown wider as the obvious economic differences became apparent. Laura had to work to keep her family afloat while Joanna had chosen to stay home full time when Ally was born.

While growing up their mother, Susan, had made the brazen choice to work outside the home while raising her three daughters, placing them in the local day care. Their liberated mother of the 1970s insisted that she had her own career as Head Librarian of the regional library. Joanna had always resented those years in her childhood and vowed to have a different life for her children.

Joanna's life had turned out exactly how she had imagined it would be. Perhaps she was blinded by her own happiness, that she didn't see how it was hard for Laura and Harry to watch Joanna and Graham climb the ladder of success; always achieving and buying up life like it had no price tag. Joanna didn't know that it was difficult for Harry and Laura to put presents under their Christmas tree or that it was not possible have a new outfit for each occasion. They just didn't talk about things like that. The sisters connections were shallow and tepid. They tried to get along when necessary, but never tried to go beyond the surface.

"Nice dive, Jack!" Joanna called out as her son hinged himself into a perfect pike off the five meter diving board.

"Great, now he'll probably want to join the diving team. That kid wants to do it all," Joanna said. She bent down to splash the refreshing water over her legs and arms.

"Is that a problem?" Laura asked, turning towards Joanna. "He seems to be in everything else."

"That's the problem. He's too involved." She sighed. "And Ally has piano, we can't get her to stop playing."

Laura faced her sister more directly. "So where is the problem, Joanna? We can't get our boys off the couch for anything and they refuse to practice guitar. We can't afford to pay for lessons they don't even care about. So we made them quit. When is having dedicated kids such a problem?"

"Well, it's Lydia. The other two have found their 'thing', but Lydia wants nothing to do with anything they're doing. She just looks at Pinterest all day; that is if I'd let her." Joanna took a long drink from her water bottle then watched Jack make another perfect dive, this time catching the attention of others. *Perfect*, she thought. *Just what he needs, an adoring audience.*

"She'll find her 'thing'," Laura reassured. "Some kids just need a little longer to figure it out, while for others it just all comes so easily."

Joanna took another sip of water, wondering exactly what her big sister's direct comment meant. Laura didn't know the trouble they were having with Ally's attitude and disrespectful outbursts this past year. Ally appeared perfect on the outside. She was talented, pretty and had so many friends. She was breezing through school, although the added pressure on herself to be perfect made her impossible to live with. But Ally desperately wanted to fit in and be one of 'those' girls, making Joanna concerned that her daughter was trying so hard to be something she was not. Perhaps that's why she had been coming undone at the seams. The expectation she put on herself was taking its toll.

Harry, dripping wet with a smile under his big beard and mop of hair came walking up towards his wife and sister-in-law. Once close enough, he shook like a wet dog and gave his wife a big, sloppy kiss.

"Harry, you got us all wet!" Laura shrieked, playfully pushing him away.

"You two made of sugar? No one's gonna believe you came to the pool. You didn't even get in," he said, grabbing a towel from the nearby chair, drying off his beer gut. "What time do we have to get back to the wonderful world of Gretna?" he asked, shaking out his hair again.

The sisters shrieked. "Now!" Laura said, finding a towel for her and Joanna. "Go call the boys. They'll listen to you sooner than me anyway."

Slowly the cousins gathered up their kids, wet towels and coolers and headed back for the barbecue supper with the older generation who had stayed back at the school.

"So, Ally, has it been all bad today?" Joanna asked, ringing out her daughter's long wet hair.

She answered nonchalantly with a shrug of her shoulders. "I guess not. Those cousins from BC or Alberta or wherever are kinda cool."

Joanna noticed over lunch the eventual, timid conversations between Ally and what would be her third cousins from Abbottsford, British Columbia.

"But when are we going home?" Ally asked quietly, with that familiar tone of annoyance.

"You just said you were having fun. We still have dinner and then we can go home," Joanna explained, gathering up the last tote bag.

She was answered with a rolling of the eyes and a 'fine', as Ally walked away without carrying anything, leaving it all for her frustrated mother. Joanna sighed deeply.

Lydia was talking with her new found cousin as she approached Joanna looking for her flip flops. "Here, help your momma out and carry something to the car."

Lydia took a tote and some towels and kept on walking without stopping for breath, as she was describing what she found on Pinterest last night.

"Mom, I'm going with Uncle Harry," Jack called out at the exit of the pool. Joanna waved in permission and headed towards the car. She was so glad that Graham was coming home to share the load. Just like the bag of heavy wet towels digging into her shoulder, Joanna was tired of carrying the burden of keeping her kids happy.

Joanna walked to the parking lot, thinking about what Laura said about how nice it was to have a cabin. Joanna couldn't imagine her summers without the private family getaway. She wondered if that's what bothered Laura. She had an envious tone in her voice that Joanna had detected before, but now she felt it. Closing the trunk, she took inventory of the kids in her Jeep. Joanna got into the driver's seat, grateful that they caught up, even with a shallow conversation. Laura often seemed so closed off and it was hard to find something to talk about. Growing up, they had never been a close family. But now as adults, something else had changed, causing the crack in their fragile adult relationship to grow wider. Joanna decided it was probably nothing to worry about. They were still family and if this was as good as it was going to get with her sister, she would have to be okay with that.

3
Summer Interrupted

After the barbecued chicken, an array of salads, corn on the cob and the apple pies had disappeared, it was time to say good bye, at least until tomorrow. Sunday morning the Shapansky clan would gather for a morning church service, lunch, and one last family picture.

Joanna and the kids hugged their family members and said good night when Jack asked if Brandon and Tyler, Laura's two older boys could come for the night. The mothers agreed and everyone piled into the cars to make the forty minute journey home. Owen, the youngest nephew, who was only three, made a fuss and wanted to go to Jack's house too. As cute as he was, Joanna was tired and grateful that it was only the older two who were coming. Heading down the highway, a mental list began to add up as Joanna decided what would happen once they got home. She wanted to unpack the pool things and throw the wet towels into the washer. Settle the kids with a snack before bed and then she could enjoy a long shower and sip a glass of wine on the deck.

Graham texted during dinner, telling Joanna he would be home around midnight. They wanted to work as long as they could before losing the sun. Joanna asked how his time had been at the cabin. And in typical Graham fashion, he texted back that it was 'good', but also admitted he was really tired. Hopefully he would share more if she found the energy to stay up until he got back.

Driving home Joanna glanced over, noticing that Ally seemed withdrawn and distant. Perhaps something was really bothering her eldest daughter and she was missing the signs. Ally wasn't one to keep secrets. They did have a good relationship and it wasn't unusual for Ally to confide in her mother. She felt fortunate to have open communication with her teenager. But whatever was bringing on this new attitude, rich with defiance and meanness, Joanna had to know why. Noticing that the boys were chatting it up in the back row, while Lydia was unplugged to the rest of the world by being plugged into her iPod, Joanna decided to make the most of the opportunity with Ally.

"Hey, Ally," Joanna started, "is everything -"

"Mom, quiet, I'm listening to this song," she hastily interrupted, turning up the volume.

Joanna looked at the screen on the dash. Dave Brubeck's, 'Take Five'. "Why do you want to listen to this song, it's not - "

"Shh Mom, I'm listening to the chord progressions," Ally explained, putting her head closer to the speaker.

Joanna stared straight at the road. *How many teenage girls try to pick out chord progressions to classic jazz pieces from 60 years ago?* A slight smile crossed her sun chapped lips. *My daughter, that's who.* They noticed her musical ability when she was just a year and a half. Ally was able to sing all the words to nursery rhymes and loved to dance to all kinds of music. They registered her in music classes when Ally was three. She loved moving to music and learning new songs and excelled as all children do when given the freedom to move to simple tunes. But Joanna saw a special talent in Ally, and she would make sure her daughter was given the opportunity to develop her gifts.

At age seven, Ally began piano lessons with the seasoned sought after piano teacher, Mrs. Buhlin, who was able to draw out Ally's musical talents. On occasion their perfectionist daughter was known to pound on the piano in musical genius frustration, when her fingers didn't always have the skill to play what was singing in her head. But soon her fingers caught up with her brain and she started performing at local festivals and easily passed piano tests. This fall she would be preparing for her grade 9 piano exams. Maybe Ally was nervous about having to take another exam?

"Okay, now you can talk to me." Ally turned down the knob on the console.

"Oh, I just wanted to talk. You know, catch up, see how things are going," Joanna said casually, hoping to spur a conversation. "Looking forward to the rest of the summer?"

Ally played with the seat belt. "Yeah, I guess. Lots of my friends will be gone and I don't want to be bored. Can I get a job? Sally is getting one at the Burger Shack."

"A job? You're barely fourteen, Ally. You have lots of time to get a job. Don't you want to enjoy the summer and go to the beach and bike rides and go to the Burger

Shack for ice cream instead of serving it?" Joanna suggested, slowing down as she pulled into the outskirts Mountain City.

"Mom, this isn't 1986. We text and tweet and catch up on Facebook. Kids are different," Ally explained to her outdated mother.

"Well, I don't believe that. Yes, you have technology we didn't even dream about way, way back in the 80's. Kids will always be kids, no matter what year it is. And hanging out with friends and your family without the Facebook is important too." They hated it when Joanna referred to Facebook like it was a futuristic entity.

They turned the corner to their bay, lined with ancient oak trees and modern fences. Joanna pulled up the driveway and waited for the garage door to open. "I'm just saying, Ally," Joanna continued, "summer is a great time to relax and figure stuff out. I don't want you getting a job or over schedule your days just so you won't be bored. Being bored is okay, sometimes. It helps you to see what's important."

Ally clicked the seat belt. "Whatever."

"Hey, everyone grab something to bring into the house, please," Joanna ordered as they all jumped out of the car.

"And Mom," Ally said as they gathered at the trunk of the car to claim their bags. "Can you at least think about the job idea? Mention it to Dad. He still thinks I'm ten."

Joanna handed a beach bag to Ally as she looked at her daughter who was growing up right before their eyes. She smiled and kissed the top of her head. "Of course I will think about it and talk to Dad when he gets home."

"Thanks Mommy."

***

Running a brush through her hair, Joanna heard Graham roll over and put the pillow over his head. He got home just after midnight. Joanna couldn't manage to stay up much past 10:00. She did wake briefly as he made his way into bed, but quickly drifted off to sleep, happy he was home.

"Do we have to go to this thing?" he complained with muffled dread.

"Oh, don't you start. It's actually kind of fun seeing everyone again," Joanna said, choosing earrings to accessorize her new sundress. She was up early, went for a run, watered the flower garden and the clay pots of begonias and geraniums on the front porch. Then she enjoyed a cup of coffee on the back deck.

"Everything aches," Graham complained once more, finally sitting up and stretching out his arms. "I'm definitely not used to working my muscles like that."

"Get up, we have to be there in about an hour and a half. I made coffee if that's any consolation," Joanna said, leaving the room. "I'm going to check on the kids. I think they're up already. At least I heard noises coming from their rooms. Brandon and Tyler stayed the night, we're taking them back with us."

She walked down the hall and saw Lydia's door was open. She was making her bed, placing all her pillows and animals in their spots. "Good morning sweetie, did you have breakfast already?"

"Not yet, I was going to wait until the boys were done. They're already down there," Lydia said, straightening out the polka dotted pillow.

Joanna walked to Ally's room. She knocked softly on the door. No response. She knocked again. Nothing. "Ally, are you up?" she asked.

"Yes, but don't come in. I'm not dressed!" Ally responded with her usual morning annoyance. The girl was not a morning person unlike her mother and sister.

"Okay, but hurry up and go eat something, we have to leave soon." No response.

Joanna heard Graham calling for her and she turned back towards their bedroom. "What Graham?"

"I forgot to get a towel," he yelled through the shower door.

A minute later she came from the linen closet with a fresh towel. "Here you go. I'm going down for breakfast and your coffee will be waiting."

He simply moaned in fatigue.

Joanna headed for the stairs thinking about what the rest of the day held. By the afternoon they would be home and hopefully be able to spend the rest of this beautiful Sunday together as a family. Those precious times were getting harder to find. And she didn't think it would get any easier to carve out time with Jack's sports and now with Ally wanting a job. Oh yes, the job. Joanna remembered she needed to talk to Graham.

Rounding the corner of the hallway, Joanna noticed something on the floor at the bottom of the staircase. She saw Ally, just lying there, silently.

"Ally, get up. What are you doing on the floor?" Nothing. "Ally, this isn't funny. Get up," she insisted, taking a few steps closer. "Ally, get up," Joanna repeated, running down the staircase.

Ally's body was still. Joanna came closer and noticed the slightest twitch of her hand and arms. Joanna moved Ally's hair from her face. Foamy spit dripped from her mouth. Her skin was grey, turning a sickening blue. Joanna went numb. *This can't be happening; whatever this is, it isn't happening.*

"Ally get up. Wake up, " Joanna screamed again. She touched her daughter's arms, stiff as lumber. "Ally, can you hear me?" Joanna felt the rise of hysterics running through her own body.

Ally began to make gurgling noises, choking and struggling for breath.

"GRAHAM!" Joanna yelled at the top of her lungs. "GRAHAM. GRAHAM!" Lydia came rushing to the staircase with the boys following behind. "Get back," Joanna yelled, "and go get your dad. Now! Quick, hurry!"

She turned back to Ally whose skin continually changed colours. Her lips swelled up and more saliva oozed from her mouth. *My baby is dying*, Joanna thought with unimaginable fear. "My baby is dying," she said out loud. "Ally come back, don't do this. Graham, come here," she pleaded through hysterical tears.

"What going on?" Graham rushed down the stairs, seeing his wife panicking beside his daughter lying lifeless on the floor. "What happened? What happened, did she fall?" he questioned, pulling a shirt over his head.

"I don't know. I just found her here and she's not breathing and she's turning colours," Joanna explained. "I don't know what to do for her. I don't know what to do." Joanna clenched her hands to her face, kneeling beside Ally, begging her to wake up.

Jack came down the stairs with Graham's cell phone. "Here Dad," he timidly said, afraid to look at his sister and watching his strong mother fall apart. But he didn't look away.

"Go back upstairs and stay there, Jack," Joanna demanded through her tears.

"I don't know," Graham said into the phone, "my wife just found her lying at the bottom of the stairs. Is she breathing, Jo?"

"I don't know, I think so. She's making noises but it sounds like she's struggling to get her breath. Please wake up Ally. Wake up," she pleaded.

"They're asking if she fell down the stairs, Joanna. Is she bleeding from her head or anything?"

She took in a quick breath. "No, I don't think so. I didn't hear any falling noises." She moved Ally's hair from her face. "I don't see any swelling or bleeding."

"Okay. We'll bring her down ourselves. Be there in a few minutes." Graham shoved his phone into the pocket of his jeans. "They said we could wait for an ambulance or we could bring her down. It will be quicker if I drive. Help me get her up," Graham demanded, taking control. "She's going to be fine, Jo".

But Joanna didn't move from Ally's side. Graham reached down taking Joanna's arms. "Listen, we have to get her to the hospital. Now get your purse, okay," Graham explained slowly to help calm down his wife.

Joanna went into an organized panic mode. She had to get her purse, make sure the other kids knew they were going to the hospital. The family reunion. Everyone was expecting them. And her nephews. Call Laura.

Joanna yelled up to the kids, "Jack, Lydia, come here." They rushed to the bottom of the stairs as Graham picked up Ally and was heading for the door.

"We're taking Ally to the hospital. I don't know what's wrong but we will let you know. I'm calling Aunt Laura and she can come get you, okay."

Lydia was the first to speak. "What happened to her?"

"I don't know. I just found her at the bottom of the stairs," Joanna said. She could physically feel her emotions shut down keeping her from hysterics.

Brandon spoke up. "I passed her on the stairs when she was coming down and she looked kind of weird and pale."

"Why didn't you get me?" Joanna asked, heading for the front door. She didn't wait for an answer as she grabbed her purse and met Graham at the back door. They managed to get her into the back seat. Ally slumped forward and had gone completely limp with no sign of consciousness. Joanna propped her up and strapped on the seat belt across Ally's lifeless body to keep her from flopping forward. Joanna got into the seat beside her and tried to find a pulse, believing at this one moment that her daughter had now died. A rapid heartbeat was running through Ally's veins. And yet relief did not come to Joanna as Graham sped down the driveway.

Without thought, Joanna grabbed her purse and found her phone. She briefly explained to Laura what had happened and told her to come get the kids. She answered a lot of 'I don't knows' and then hung up. Graham managed to make the ten minute trip to the hospital in about four minutes as he pulled up to the ER doors, finding a stretcher and medical staff waiting.

Joanna wondered if they were all waiting for an emergency on its way to the hospital. A nurse quickly opened the car door and they rushed the stretcher up to Ally, carefully placed her on top, then wheeled her through the open hospital doors.

They were the emergency.

4
Life Undone

Graham was told where he could park the car as Joanna followed the medical entourage into an emergency room. Joanna watched silently as the medical team began monitoring Ally's vital signs. Nurses took blood and inserted an IV line and established oxygen to Ally's limp body. One was writing down numbers as they called out words that Joanna didn't understand. She clung to her purse and stood still wondering how this was possibly happening to them. Ally lay unresponsive. Graham came rushing in and stood beside his wife. Joanna could hear his heavy breathing.

He put an arm around her. "What's happening?" he asked winded.

Joanna swelled up with tears and fear and simply shook her head.

The doctor continued to hold Ally's hand and squeeze it. "So who found her?" he asked.

Joanna licked her lips and swallowed hard. "I did. She was just at the bottom of the stairs. We were going to a family reunion and she was on the floor and she wouldn't get up. What's happening to her? Why won't she wake up?" Joanna held back tears and leaned closer to Graham.

"Has this happened before? Has she ever had loss of consciousness or fainting in the past?" asked the doctor, while continuing the examination.

Graham answered. "No, she's an active teenage girl, who's never had any medical problems before."

More questions were asked with empty, everyday answers. No, there was no history of head injuries. Yes, she eats and gets enough sleep. She plays piano. She has no allergies. She's not on any medication but takes vitamins if she's forced to. No, she doesn't drink or do drugs.

Ally lay unresponsive.

"No," Joanna continued to answer the rapid fire questions, "she hasn't been ill or complaining of headaches.

Ally lay unresponsive.

"When is she going to wake up?" Joanna asked with apprehension. Her cell phone went off. It was Laura.

"We got the kids. What happened, did she fall?" Laura questioned.

"Laura, she's not waking up. I can't talk now but she's not waking up." Joanna stepped away towards the back of the room knocking into a small chair.

Graham took the phone. "Laura, we'll have to call you back. No, we don't know anything yet." He hung up the phone. "Joanna, sit down." He took the chair out for her to sit. She was turning white as snow.

"Okay," the doctor addressed them. "It looks like she had a seizure. We checked her blood pressure, temperature and it's all normal. We are going to check the blood results and get a CT scan of her head."

Joanna stood up. "Why?" she asked. "Why did this happen to her?"

"We will look at the test results. But my guess is that we may not know. People for whatever reason just seizure and we can't always explain why. It probably won't happen again. But what we do know is that she didn't break any bones or anything like that. She did bite her lip so she'll have some swelling and maybe a bruise or two from the fall."

Ally moved her head and Joanna passed the doctor to be at her daughter's side. "Hey Ally, can you hear me?" she asked like Ally was a toddler waking up from a nap. Careful not to disturb the oxygen tubes wrapped around her discoloured face, she brushed Ally's sweaty, messy hair away from her forehead. Graham grabbed his daughter's hand. "Hey, Al, Daddy's here," he said, trying to suppress his tears.

"She's going to come out of it, then I'm going to ask her some questions," the doctor explained.

The nurse conferred with the doctor again as Joanna and Graham stared at their daughter, silently willing her to wake up. Moments later, Ally opened her eyes and looked around with complete confusion. She was lost. She looked at her parents with vacant eyes.

"Hey sweetie, it's Daddy."

"Hi Ally, I thought you were being silly and lying on the floor," Joanna said.

Ally licked her lips and moved her eyes around. Feeling the swollen and bloody taste on her tongue, she cleared her throat. "Are we at a hotel?" she quietly asked.

Graham and Joanna looked at the doctor. "No, Ally, we're at the hospital," Graham answered.

"Why?" she said in a little girl voice.

"Hey Ally, I'm Doctor Alec. Can you squeeze my hand?" he asked, continuing his examination. "Do you remember what happened to you?"

Ally hesitated as her mind tried so hard to make sense of anything. "Did I go swimming at the hotel?"

"We were at a hotel a few weeks ago when she was playing piano at a provincial competition," Joanna answered. "And she went swimming there and she went swimming yesterday too." That seemed so long ago that they were in Altona watching their kids in the pool. Now she was watching her daughter trying to put a sentence together.

"Has she lost any motor skills or anything?" Graham asked. "It looked like she was having a stroke."

"No, her neurological exam is normal. We will do a CT scan just to be cautious, but I think it will be normal," Doctor Alec explained.

"Are we at a hotel?" she asked again.

"No, you are at the hospital. Do you remember what happened?" Doctor Alec repeated.

Ally shook her head.

"Do you know the names of these two people?" he asked.

"Mommy and Daddy," she said with an obvious slur.

Everyone chuckled. It was like she was stone, cold drunk.

"Do you know their names?"

"Graham and Joanna."

"Do you know when your birthday is, Ally?"

Again she hesitated and licked her lips, "April 13th. When can I go back to my home?" she asked innocently unaware.

"We just want you to rest a little bit longer here. Let us know if you have to go to the bathroom and we'll get a nurse to help you."

"I don't want a boy nurse, I want a girl nurse," she managed to say with the swollen lips and tongue.

"We can do that. But the boy nurse went to get you some ice cream and juice."

Ally felt her tongue with her weak hand. "I feel puffy."

"You're going to feel strange for a little while. Do you remember what you had for breakfast?" the doctor asked.

"No. Nothing," she managed to say as clarity slowly kept coming to the surface in her dazed eyes. "When can I go home?" she asked, looking at her parents.

"Soon, sweetie." Joanna could feel her phone buzzing from her purse. Graham told her to ignore it. The nurse arrived with the ice cream.

"This will feel good on your cut lip. I hope you like strawberry," he said, pulling a hospital table up to the bed.

"I wan-ned shocolat," Ally sputtered out. Her hand was too weak to hold the spoon so Joanna offered to feed her.

Graham and the doctor stepped aside as he explained that she might be very tired for the next few hours. He advised them to let her sleep, but watch her closely. The doctor said that this may not ever happen again or it could happen years from now.

Within the hour, Ally's blood work came back normal and eventually the results of the CT of her brain came to the same conclusion, normal. Most of her memory and brain function were slowly returning, allowing her to be discharged.

Graham pulled the car up while Joanna carefully helped Ally into the back seat. Joanna slipped on her own seat belt and they drove away.

Joanna took in a deep breath and sighed looking out the window, still in shock over what had just transpired. As they drove down the familiar residential streets, Joanna saw families going for walks with their dogs, little girls playing with chalk on driveways, families coming home from church. Joanna took out her phone. She had a lot of text messages and phone calls waiting. Graham grabbed her hand. She looked up at him. He kept his eyes on the road.

"We'll deal with that once Ally is settled and we've talked to the twins," he said and turned to see the aching expression of strain and anguish on his wife's face.

She held onto her husband's hand and slowly nodded.

5
Moving On

She placed the cereal bowl into the dishwasher, wiped up the toast crumbs and poured the last of the coffee into her mug. Joanna looked out the kitchen window that was blurred with crying raindrops falling down the glass. She took a sip.

It was September. Back to school, making lunches and signing forms. Back to a normal routine. It had only been a few days and the kids were lamenting that summer was over. And today, it definitely felt over. They had spent the September long weekend at the cabin with Todd, Sarah and their daughters, Abigail and Nora. It was good to get one more weekend at Lake of the Woods before everyone went different directions.

Joanna sipped her coffee thinking about the past few weeks. Remembering how it all started with the unexpected seizure. It had shaken them all for many days. Not knowing if and when it would happen again. It was always in the back of their minds. Every time Ally didn't answer them when they asked her a question. Or if she would sleep a little longer, Joanna felt that panic unsettle her all over again. The only time Joanna felt reassured was hearing Ally play piano; it had always been her happiest place. Ally played everything she could get her hands on. And in summer, when most kids gave up practicing, Ally played familiar classical pieces, then mastered contemporary pianists from Elton John and Billy Joel to Duke Ellington.

Joanna was relieved when Ally's memory came back. Her brain was left without a trace of complication from that awful day. Bumps and bruises from falling soon faded while the swelling of her lips and tongue eventually went down. But the scars of the trauma didn't go away quite so easily for the rest of them.

Life is back to normal, Joanna thought, listening to the sound of the empty, quiet house. She sighed, wishing she could have gone for a run today, but all the same, she really didn't feel like it anyway. Taking her coffee and phone, she walked into Graham's den and sat in one of the chairs that faced the front window overlooking the porch. The rain and wind pounded down hard.

Graham and Joanna had explained the seizure to Jack and Lydia. The twins obviously had questions, but they had few answers. Jack acknowledged that seeing Ally like that had been really scary and how afraid it made them both. But they had reassured their twins that Ally would be fine and life would go on like normal. Nothing would change.

Joanna was concerned that Ally would have more questions. So she spent a lot of time with Ally over the summer, shopping, going for walks at home and at the cabin. Plus, she didn't want her to be alone for a minute. Although they were so different from each other, they grew closer over the past few weeks, and for that, Joanna was grateful. Mother and daughter still had their power struggles that involved a lot of loud discussions because Ally was feeling managed and overprotected by her mother who was always close by, too close. But Joanna needed to keep a close watch on her daughter.

Placing her coffee mug on the side table, Joanna curled her legs underneath her and reached for her phone. She typed in a quick text to Ally, then quickly deleted it tossing the phone on the other chair. Joanna was finding it hard being alone now. She became so comfortable having her kids around all summer, especially Ally. There was no denying it. They still drove her crazy many days with their bickering, complaining and not listening. Joanna didn't want Ally driving her bike or even swimming without supervision, so many allowances were made for her all summer long. Jack and Lydia claimed unfairness all the time, citing that they didn't get the same treatment as their older sister. But it was Joanna who wasn't ready to let Ally go. She still wanted to protect her as long as she could. Picking up her coffee again, Joanna knew she just had to stop thinking about that Sunday morning. It consumed her time with worry.

Once the word got around about what happened to Ally, Joanna was answering phone calls and texts for days. She explained to friends and acquaintances in the grocery store, church and to neighbours on their street. Graham didn't talk about it very much and so he seemed to have moved on from the trauma. But he also didn't feel the burdening responsibility to keep the emotional well being of this family going, the way Joanna did. Joanna knew that Graham loved his kids more than anything and always made himself available to them. He had an easiness about him that she often envied. He didn't have to try hard at anything, it all seemed so simple.

And when he didn't want to talk about something, nothing could draw it out of him. He had grieved when his dad had suddenly passed away, and he didn't often want to talk about it with Joanna or anyone. Graham learned how to be a good husband and dad because he had a great example growing up. He was thoughtful and caring like his father. And in addition to looking after his now widowed mother, he made sure his mom and the estate was taken care of for her. Graham did what was required, and he did it well. He just didn't feel the need to talk about his feelings the way Joanna did. When he was sad he often went for a run or bike ride on his own. Or he retreated into his den, to the very spot Joanna sat.

Joanna stood up and started to straighten out the pillows on the chairs. She headed over to the desk that once belonged to Graham's grandfather, and sorted through some junk mail. Their home was filled with antiques passed down from family members gone by or special discoveries from flea markets. They bought the neglected and outdated house that was at the top of their budget when they moved back to Mountain City. Joanna knew she could make this old place their home, even though money was tight back then.

Years earlier, after earning her degree in Human Ecology, majoring in textiles, Joanna worked in a small interior design company in Winnipeg while Graham was finishing law school. But her first calling and desire was to be a mother. Everything domestic appealed to her. She loved organizing and 'keeping house' as her grandma used to say. She found a love for gardening and cooking and baking. Joanna read cookbooks like novels and always tried out new recipes. Joanna had a reputation for pulling together a dinner party like a caterer. But mostly she loved being able to raise her children. Joanna was so grateful that Graham was supportive when she said she wanted to stay home with Ally after she was born. They had a few lean years until Graham could establish himself in his practice. So many years ago and so much redecorating.

Joanna mentally took a list of all she needed to do today. Laundry, put some of the summer things away and begin to pack up the sun room. Perhaps she should make the effort to give her mother a call, it had been while. Joanna and her mother had so little to talk about. Their conversations usually were about how the kids were doing and coordinating family holidays, which usually fell to Joanna to organize. Susan Schultz had always been practical, logical and showed little capacity to nurture her three daughters. Joanna struggled to come up with a favourite meal that their mother prepared for them that didn't start off from a pre-packaged box. She never volunteered to bake cookies for school picnics like the other mothers did, nor did she get involved in their activities while growing up.

Susan was responsible for managing the regional library. If her mother wasn't working at the library or planning the next fundraiser, she was always reading something

41

and demanded the house be quiet at all times. Joanna's oldest sister Pauline, like her mother, kept her emotional distance. Pauline found friends and school activities to keep her busy and away from their heartless home. So Laura and Joanna often played outside in their backyard as they watched their father care and nurture his garden. Joanna's dad, John, was the principal of the high school which allowed her to see him more than her mother.

During the summers, her dad spent his days in his beloved garden while his wife found companionship in reading and working. Joanna eventually found her place in her family beside her dad as he walked along the lilies and irises. He taught her the names of the shrubs and plants and showed her how to dead head geraniums and how to tell the difference between a weed and a plant. Laura and Joanna would pick vegetables and wash them under the big elm tree in the backyard. She cherished those days working in the garden with her dad that cultivated Joanna's love of gardening.

Joanna walked back to the kitchen and poured the cold coffee in the sink and added the cup to the dishwasher. Taking in a deep breath, she decided to call her mother.

"What Joanna, is everything okay?" Susan answered.

"Hello, Mom. Yes, everything is okay. You don't have to answer the phone like that every time I call you."

Since the seizure, Susan had become skittish and anxious when Joanna's number appeared on the call display.

"Then why are you calling me, I just got to work," her mother hastily responded. Even though Joanna's father had retired ten years earlier, there was no convincing Susan that perhaps it was time to slow down or even retire.

"I just called to see how you were doing and if you and Dad had decided to go away this fall," Joanna replied.

"Oh. We're still talking about it. I'm not sure I can get away. Anyway, how is Ally doing? They're all settled back at school?" she asked, quickly changing the subject.

"Yes, Ally is fine and they're all thrilled to be back at school."

"So no more episodes?"

Joanna hated it when she called the one and only seizure, episodes. "No Mom, I would tell you if anything else would have happened. How's Dad?"

"Oh, he went out for breakfast with some teachers. But I do need to go, dear."

"Okay, we'll talk to you later, Mom. Bye."

Susan hung up without saying good bye. Joanna clicked the phone off and mentally crossed it off her list of things to do - have an engaging conversation with her mother. She was sure that Susan was now going to tell the other librarians about the lovely chat she had with her daughter. Susan loved bragging rights to her family. Just give her the facts about everyone and she would fill in the rest.

Heading into the laundry room just off the kitchen, Joanna started added a load of jeans. Maybe she would bake an apple cake for dessert tonight. She smiled and then laughed at their strained conversation. Her mother felt like a stranger; Joanna had taken such a different direction than everyone had expected. Unlike her mother, Joanna never wanted to share motherhood with a career.

Taking care of Graham and her kids was the only life she wanted. She knew she wasn't living up to her mother's expectations of pursuing a career. It felt like one of many disappointments from her mother over the years.

Starting the washing machine, Joanna smiled finding peace in the decision to enjoy her drudgery. She found the ordinary life of a housewife, just fine for her.

6
Tipping The Balance

With a few weeks of school under their belt, the Kornelson family had found normal again. Their everyday routine started each morning around the breakfast table, except for the early Friday morning choir practices for Ally or meetings for Graham. After school, there was soccer practice for Jack on Mondays and Wednesdays with games on Thursdays and Saturdays. Graham helped coach Jack's soccer team this year. And in between, Jack managed to play for his school's volleyball team. Ally had piano lessons on Wednesdays after school and practiced every morning and evening she could fit in. And Lydia finally agreed to sign up for dance, mostly because the outfits were cool; that took care of Tuesdays after school and Thursdays evenings.

Joanna took a deep breath studying the busy calendar hanging in the mud room. This was just the kids' schedule of events. Never mind Graham's meetings and the volunteer work that Joanna tried to fit in when she could find the time. Joanna often offered her friends decorating advice for their homes or businesses. She didn't mind. In fact, she enjoyed still being asked for her professional opinion.

Life was full for now, but she knew this was a season and soon her three kids would need her less and less. When they were all little, Joanna would plan Friday Family Movie Night; dinner and a movie in the family room. It was so easy to please them, she recalled. Chicken nuggets, a princess movie and life was happy. Now it was hard to find the time where everyone was in the house all at the same time for more than an hour.

Joanna sipped her coffee still staring at the calendar wondering what would happen if she wiped it all away. They needed to find time to just hang out again. Building family relationships would always be important to Joanna. Carving out family time among busy schedules was the way Graham had been raised and it was the way Joanna wished she had been raised; to always put family first.

Graham walked into the kitchen finding his wife studying the calendar in the mudroom. "Are you trying to find a moment in that air-tight schedule for something more?" he asked, standing behind her. He gave her a kiss on top of her head.

"No, I just sometimes wonder how long we're going to be able to manage a schedule like this? Pretty soon they're going to get part-time jobs, and getting their drivers' license and then they'll want to start dating and -"

He playfully covered her mouth with his hand, "No, no, no, let's not get ahead of ourselves, Jo. Let's be grateful that even though they are busy kids, we are still the ones taking them places and being in charge. At least I think we're still in charge."

She took his hand in hers and wrapped it around her waist as she turned to her husband with a smile. "One day, this calendar will no longer be needed and we're going to wonder what are we going to do with all our spare time?"

"The twins are twelve going on thirteen. Find me in about six years and show me what the calendar looks like then. I can't imagine an empty space on it."

Jack came lumbering into the kitchen complaining about his sore calf muscles. Every sport found new muscles. "What's for breakfast, Mom?" he muttered, sitting at the table.

Joanna kissed her husband and headed to the stove to scoop out the healthy egg and veggie mixture she had made earlier. "Pop in the toast, Jack, and you can make yourself a breakfast sandwich. And you have to eat some fruit too.

"That's what juice is for," he said, chugging down a glass of orange juice.

"MOM!" Lydia screamed from upstairs. "Ally's doing it again. She's having a seizure," she yelled, filling the house with unsettled horror.

Joanna and Graham ran up the back set of stairs off the kitchen to find Lydia standing in the hallway, petrified.

"She's in the bathroom," Lydia cried with fear and tears pouring down her face. "She's shaking and making weird noises."

Graham got to her first as Joanna grabbed a towel and put it under Ally's cheek to soften the blows of her face hitting the hard tile floor. "Graham, what do we do?" Joanna screamed.

Jack stood beside Lydia in the hallway not able to take his eyes off the horrific strange angles Ally was lying. Her body was stiff and shaking while saliva leaked from her swelling, blue mouth.

Jack turned off the phone. "I just called the hospital and they said to bring her in or call 911 if you want an ambulance to come."

"Go to your rooms," Joanna screamed out, not realizing her twins were watching the seizure happen. "Ally wake up, wake up."

But Jack and Lydia could not stop watching their sister.

"She can't hear you, Joanna," Graham yelled back. "Lydia, when did you notice her? When did it start?"

Lydia gulped back her tears. "I just heard a banging noise when I was in my room and I opened the bathroom door and found her here. Then I screamed for you to come." She covered her face with her hands.

Once the shaking stopped, they noticed Ally's contorted body relax in slow stages as the seizure released its grip. She lay like she was sleeping, just like when she was a baby, Joanna strangely recalled.

Ally looked calm and peaceful when suddenly she opened her eyes, wide and scared.

"Mommy?" she said weakly.

"I'm right here, honey. Mommy's here." Joanna wiped her wet hair from her face and wiped the blood and saliva that dripped from her lips.

"Is Daddy here too?" she asked, moving her head to look around. But she was so disoriented she didn't know where to look.

"I'm right here, Ally," Graham said, reaching for his phone. "I'm going to call Todd and see if he can meet us at the hospital, if he's not already there."

"Okay," Joanna said softly, watching Ally's changing confusion in her eyes.

Joanna looked up seeing her twins still standing in the hallway looking at their mother, begging with innocent expressions to tell them everything was going to be fine.

"Lydia, everything is fine," she tried to say in a convincing tone. "Can you get my phone for me? It's on my night table," she requested gently. "I'm going to call Nana to come over and then she can take you to school, okay?"

"I don't want to go to school today, Mom," Lydia said, as tears spilled down her face. "I thought she was dying." Awkwardly, Jack put his arm around his sister.

"I'll call Nana, Mom," Jack offered.

"No, Jack, it's okay. I'll do it. Can you go downstairs and open the door and help us get Ally into the car, please?"

The calmness between them felt eerie and rehearsed. So polite and prescribed as they all went about their tasks. Joanna called Graham's mother to come be with the twins. Graham hung up his phone and said Todd was on his way to the hospital to meet them in the ER.

Graham managed to get Ally down the stairs. Jack opened the back kitchen door and then the car door to get Ally inside. Joanna grabbed her purse and like déjà vu, they once again rushed to the hospital, although this time the urgency had slightly diminished. They now knew what to expect. Unfortunately, they knew.

7
All Is Well

Ally heard herself crying. She couldn't stop. She didn't know where she was and her head hurt. People were touching her and asking questions. She cried and wanted her mom.

"It's okay, honey." She heard her mom say in that sweet and gentle voice.

Was she reassured? Ally didn't think so. Everything felt loud and mixed up. Everything was wrong. Everything was so tired and achy. Something was very wrong. She cried some more.

"Daddy?" she wailed out in a question. Where was her dad?

"Hey, baby, Daddy is here. And Mom is here. And Uncle Todd came to visit you too?"

Ally opened her eyes as she felt her mother's touch wipe her face. Strange ladies were standing over her, reaching for her arms and putting something in her ear.

"I'm cold," she managed to say. A warm blanket fell on top of her.

"It's okay, Ally. Just stay still. It's going to be okay." She heard her mother's voice offering soothing comfort. She nodded.

"Hey, Ally, do you know me?" Todd asked.

"You're my Uncle Todd," she meekly answered.

"Do you know where you are right now?"

She hesitated looking around. "I think I'm at the hospital because you're a doctor."

"Very good. Some of my friends are here and they're going to look after you. Do you know what happened to you?"

She waited again as the words from her uncle all sounded so strange to hear. "Did I fall down?" she asked. "My head hurts."

"Do you think you can sit up Ally?" a lady asked. "We can give you some water and a pill to help the headache go away."

Suddenly Ally was sitting upright and the world seemed so confusing. Why was she here? Why did her head hurt so badly and why were her hands stiff yet so very weak. But she saw her parents and Uncle Todd. She saw two other ladies and another man. They were talking to each other while looking at her. The cold water touched her mouth and her lips refused to go around the cup. It all felt puffy. The nurse held the cup and wiped up her mouth like she was a little girl.

Then it all made sense. But it didn't. "Did I have a seizure?" she asked no one.

The room got a little quieter. "Yes, Ally, you had a seizure in the bathroom at home. Do you remember?" Graham said, taking a step closer.

Tears ran from her eyes. "I had another seizure," she repeated. "No, I don't want a seizure," she cried, realizing another layer of clarity came over her like an untimely wave.

Joanna sat down beside her and wished away her daughter's discomfort and anguish. "Oh Ally, you're going to be okay. It's all going to be okay."

But Ally just kept repeating that she had another seizure through tears of deep despair. Joanna embraced her daughter as she tried to comfort Ally.

Todd explained what a seizure does to the brain. "Neurons are specialized cells in the brain. When these neurons generate an abnormal or excessive electrical signal, a seizure can occur." Todd went on, "these abnormal signals can be related to a variety of situations. Perhaps diabetes, brain lesions, brain edema or in many cases all the tests come back completely normal and we don't know why the seizures occur."

"She had her first seizure seven weeks ago," the ER doctor added, reading her chart. "She needs to see your family physician for a follow up appointment. I'm going to suggest that we put her on an anti-seizure medication starting today to control any further seizure activity," he advised, checking her records one more time. "Although her CT was normal, the family doctor might want an EEG and MRI depending on what's found."

Ally's head swirled with the medical words that didn't make any sense to her. She didn't understand and she just wanted to go home where everything felt normal.

"Ally, do you have any questions?" Todd asked. He noticed she was listening intently.

"No." She wanted to ask if this was going to happen again. But she didn't know how to say the words.

"Doctor Phillips is going to get in touch with your family doctor, Connie Strueber, is it?" Todd asked, looking at Ally's chart. "Perfect, she's great."

"What about seeing a specialist or something, Todd?" Joanna asked. "What do we do if this happens again? Will it happen again?"

"Just wait until you've seen Dr. Strueber. She'll run a bunch of tests and then she'll recommend what to do next," he answered.

Doctor Phillips added, "When someone has one seizure, we don't medicate because it often doesn't happen again. But in Ally's case, since this is her second, we consider that epilepsy and adding a drug to help control the seizures is the next step."

He explained possible side effects of the drug could be rash, sedation, blurred vision and irritability. Graham and Joanna looked at Ally who had her eyes closed and lay asleep oblivious to how her life was about to change. How they were all about to change.

"Todd, can you be a part of these decisions about tests and drugs?" Graham asked.

"I can definitely consult with Connie if that's what you want."

"So you're saying Ally has epilepsy?" Joanna asked, not believing what she was hearing.

"If someone has more than one seizure, yes, we consider that epilepsy. But further tests will give us a better understanding."

Joanna couldn't take her eyes from her daughter as she lay so still. She was perfect; even with her lips swollen and bruises darkening her forehead and arms. Her daughter couldn't have a disorder as unpredictable as this. This couldn't be happening. Not to her, not to her family. Ally was going to be a concert pianist. How could all of this be happening? They couldn't be right, this just doesn't happen.

"You can take her home now. Unless you have any further questions. Let her rest and sleep as much as she wants. She can take Tylenol for her headache," Doctor Phillips said, putting the chart down.

"Can she play the piano?" Joanna asked as the emotion got caught in her throat.

"As long as it doesn't bother her headache," he answered. "She can play like she normally would."

But Joanna was asking so much more than that. Is her daughter going to have a normal life? She didn't want to ask the question, not really. She didn't want to hear the answer. Because she already knew.

8
Finding Normal

It was mid morning when they returned home from the hospital. Eleanor was reheating the cold eggs while a fresh pot of coffee was brewing.

"Oh, my poor, dear girl," she cooed, gently embracing her granddaughter in her arms. Eleanor was a slight, small woman with the most tender, loving heart. Always impeccably dressed with pink lipstick and pearl earrings that made her even more endearing. She loved her role as Nana Ellie to her five grandkids and her heart broke when anyone she loved was in pain. Her cure, homemade cookies and hugs for everything that hurt. Eleanor struggled to find herself again after her husband's sudden passing, but her family gave her purpose as she continued to be the best grandma they could have asked for.

"Hi Nana. How come you're here?" Ally asked.

Eleanor looked to Graham and Joanna, not certain what she should say.

Graham answered. "She came to stay with Jack and Lydia while we were at the hospital with you."

"Oh," Ally said with deadpan emotion.

"How are you two doing?" she asked her son. "I've made fresh coffee. Wasn't sure if you had breakfast this morning. But I can make something if you like or do you want to rest?"

"I'm going to settle Ally back into bed," Joanna said, playing with Ally's hair. "Did the other two get off to school?"

Eleanor poured a cup of coffee and passed it to Graham. And in hushed tones she answered, "Jack said he wanted to go but Lydia was really quite distraught, so I made a 'grandma' decision and let her stay here with me. I sat with her on the couch and we just chatted a bit. I think she's in her room now. I hope that was okay."

"That's perfect, Ellie. Thanks for coming over so quickly," Joanna said, giving her mother-in-law a hug. She guided Ally up the back staircase into her room.

Joanna heard Graham beginning to explain to his mother what Todd and the other doctor had said. How many times would they have to be repeating this story? Joanna didn't want to think about it. Not yet. She got Ally back into her bed and pulled the curtains closed.

"Mommy, sit with me a little bit," Ally said quietly.

Joanna noticed her teenage daughter's vulnerability and how childlike and fragile she became after a seizure. She was no longer that girl who offered her looks of annoyance and rolled her eyes at her mother's advice.

She kissed her forehead. "Everything is going to fine, Ally. Whatever is going on with your brain, we're going to figure it out and you're going to be okay. It's all going to be okay."

"This is scary, Mom," Ally stated simply.

Joanna hesitated. "I know it is. It's scary for us too. But you're not alone in this at all. We're a family and we are here for each other, no matter what."

Ally nodded her head in agreement. She noticed Ally's eyes were closing as she began to drift off. Joanna was relieved that sleep came to her so quickly. She slipped out and closed the door as Graham was leaving Lydia's room.

"How is she?" he asked.

"Sleeping."

"I just talked to Lydia," Graham said, running a hand through his hair. He guided his wife farther away from their daughters' bedrooms. "It took a while to get it out of her, but she's afraid this is going to happen to her too."

Closing her eyes, Joanna was not prepared to deal with another daughter. Why didn't Lydia just go to school? One unstable daughter was enough to deal with today. The minute she thought it, she was instantly stabbed with the worst feeling of guilt. Of course this would affect Lydia and of course Joanna would need to talk to her as well. But she just couldn't figure out in this moment what she was going to do. Or how she was going to mother anyone anymore. She didn't know how she was going to manage anything.

"What did you tell her?" she finally asked.

Graham guided Joanna to their bedroom and closed the door. Joanna saw that she hadn't made the bed. He led her to the chairs that sat in front of the decorative fireplace. "I told Lydia that we will wait to hear from the doctor and that they are going to put Ally on medication so this won't happen again. And I tried to tell her that this won't happen to her, but then I stopped myself because did we ever think this would happen to Ally?" He looked at his wife with tears in his eyes.

Joanna clasped her hands together so tightly her knuckles were turning white. Emotions continued to flip around inside of her as she battled the uncertainty, anger and guilt. "Oh Graham, I don't know what to do? How are we going to explain this to everyone else? What does this mean for us now? Epilepsy? Who has epilepsy in our family? Isn't it a genetic thing?"

She stood up, her hands balled up at her side as she was ready to crack wide open. On the fire place mantel held pictures of their family over the years; times spent at the cabin with Papa and Nana. Photos from when they were babies. She began to cry softly seeing the images that were right in front of her, but now it was another life she once knew.

Graham rose and embraced his wife as her shattered dreams for their daughter's normal life was turning into a foreign reality. "I know this is hard to take in. But we're in this together okay, Jo? We'll get through whatever this is. The kids are strong and we've got family and friends to help us figure this out."

"Oh, Graham." She clung to the strength of her husband. "What if Ally's life will never be the same again? What if she can't have a normal life?"

She began to sob. And her husband held her closer.

"We'll figure it out." It was all he kept saying, hoping that Joanna would somehow find comfort in his empty words. He certainly had no idea what was going to happen to his family. But he tried to convince his wife, and himself, otherwise.

***

By the next week Joanna and Graham took Ally to see their family doctor. Dr. Strueber set up an EEG Scan and reviewed her new drug schedule with them. In a few weeks an appointment would be arranged for Ally to see a paediatric neurologist at the Children's Hospital in Winnipeg.

Another week passed as Ally adjusted to life of taking a pill each morning and night. As she increased the medication and was at her optimum level, she was feeling more and more tired and chose not to go out with friends as often. She went to bed earlier and wanted to sleep in late. Eventually the mood swings began and everything and everyone set her off. Lydia and Jack had lost their patience and often lashed out at Ally for being unreasonable and short tempered when it came to doing her share of the chores. Ally pounded the piano and threw her music on the floor if the piece was getting the better of her. Joanna and Graham tried to be patient and help her cope with so many changes that had unexpectedly become part of her every day.

Her friends came over now instead of them all going out; allowing Ally to feel more relaxed at home. They asked her questions about what it was like to have epilepsy. They were understanding and just wanted to be with Ally as if nothing had changed. This group of girls had been friends since kindergarten and it was good for Ally to feel like her old self among them.

It was days before Thanksgiving and Joanna was hosting her family for the big turkey dinner on Sunday afternoon. Ellie was having them all down with Todd and Sarah and their girls on Thanksgiving Monday. It would be the first Thanksgiving without Graham's dad. Nothing about Joanna's favourite holiday was making her feel festive. Her family's gatherings were about getting together because that's what families were supposed to do. While Graham's family dinner would feel like someone was missing from this tight family. And it would be difficult to celebrate without Ed for the very first time.

Joanna grabbed her fall coat and headed to the backyard. A brisk breeze swept across the yard gently blowing colourful leaves to the ground. It felt like fall with the garden nearly bare as most plants had finished their colourful displays. The lawn and the few leaves left on the trees were brown, making the entire yard a beige shade of autumn. There were a few carrots and potatoes left in the vegetable patch, and she had picked what she wanted for her Thanksgiving dinner. She walked over to the shed and found the gardening tools. She cut a variety of chrysanthemums, sedums and hydrangea blossoms that had finished their summer bloom. Adding a few oak branches and dogwood sticks she knew she could come up with a centrepiece or two for the table and entrance.

The sun was shining down as a brief reminder of warm summer days. The evenings brought crisp and glorious sunsets on the prairie town as their world was preparing for a long winter's end to the amazing colours of a Canadian fall.

"Good morning Joanna," Hannah called out, walking down from her back porch to meet Joanna at their fence.

"Hi Hannah," she answered, adding one more twig to her basket.

"That looks lovely, Joanna," she said. "Having the family down for Thanksgiving again this year?"

"Yes, my parents and my sisters' families are all coming on Sunday. Thought I'd pick a few flowers to make an arrangement for the table."

Hannah Scott had been one of Joanna's closest friends since she and her husband Aidan moved in next door just over five years ago.

"Well, that will look nice. You always do such a good job, Joanna," Hannah paused before adding, "and how is Ally doing?"

Joanna knew Hannah was asking not just for information sake, but because she cared. Hannah understood unexpected disappointments. She and Aidan had experienced their third miscarriage this past winter.

"Well, the good part is that she hasn't had a seizure again. The down side is that the medication she's on has been taking a toll on her and on the rest of us. There can be side effects to medications."

"Oh, I know all about that. The hormone shots and other drugs I've had to take is tough to handle," Hannah said, crossing her arms.

"She's getting more headaches and that's manageable with Tylenol. But her mood swings and irritability and she wants to sleep all the time, I don't know what's the drugs and what's normal teenage girl. I don't know if I should get mad at her when she lashes out at us or just let it slide.

And when the other two see that I let her get away with it, they say I'm being unfair."

"Don't be too hard on yourself, Joanna. You're learning along with her how this is all going to get played out. Just be patient with all the kids and especially with yourself. Your family is going through a big adjustment," Hannah reassured.

"It's just so hard to figure her out at the best of times and now adding her condition and the drugs into it, I don't know who she is anymore."

"You will. You're a good mom, Joanna. You don't give up on anything," Hannah said.

"I should be saying that to you, Hannah. Any word on what to do next?" Joanna asked.

Hannah had shared her struggles with infertility since they became friends and neighbours. Joanna hoped and prayed that Hannah could become a mother. She was a kindergarten teacher and loved children. It was so sad to see them struggle with each disappointment. Although through it all, Hannah was so positive and reassuring to others; she inspired Joanna.

"Wait and see, seems to be the answer for everything," Hannah answered, pulling her hoody closer to block out the brisk breeze. "And that's okay, I guess. Like you, we just hope for the best and get prepared for the worst. But who gets to live through a lifetime without any struggles?" she commented.

"That's true. I never thought of it that way before, Hannah. You go through life never thinking bad stuff happens to you and then it does and at least for me, it caught me off guard. I still struggle with accepting that this has affected our family," Joanna said, putting down the basket.

"I know, I thought Aidan and I would have this big old house full of kids by now. But when it happens, it will happen. I hate that saying, but it's true," Hannah added, looking at her large, empty home.

Joanna picked up her basket of fall blooms. "Hey, do you want to come in for coffee and we can chat some more?"

Hannah took out her cell phone. "I can't, I have to get ready for school. I'm teaching in the afternoons now. But let's try another morning, Joanna. It's been a while." They gave each other a quick hug goodbye.

Joanna brought the basket into the mud room off the back entrance of the kitchen. She trimmed the branches and began to create several arrangements that would be placed around the house and dining room table.

Placing a vase on the front entrance table, she took a step back to see that it was perfect. She loved her home; it fit who they were as a family. It was all she had wanted her entire life. Hot dogs in the backyard fire pit or formal gatherings in the dining room and movies in the family room. Their home was a gathering place for all who were in their lives. Joanna loved to entertain. To her, their house didn't feel extravagant or grand, it felt like their home. Unlike the home she had grown up in, it was important to Joanna that she share what she felt so blessed to have, and never took it for granted.

But her perfect home was feeling splintered with Ally's diagnosis and altering medication. Something had changed and it worried Joanna that she was losing control of all she had worked so hard to gain. When the phone rang or she got a text, Joanna always thought the worst, that Ally had another seizure somewhere and she wasn't there for her. It was an odd feeling; one she never expected she would have to face. Always preparing herself for something bad to occur.

Joanna shook off the uncomfortable feelings, looked up at the clock in the living room, and decided to bake a batch of Ally's favourite gingersnap cookies. When Ally and the twins got home from school, the aroma of fresh baked cookies was sure to make any possible bad mood go away. Joanna had a lot to do in the next few days but adding cookies to her list was the least she could do to find normal again.

9
Not Fair

Lydia looked outside her bedroom window, watch-
ing the snow falling to the ground. With every minute the
flakes got larger and more dense. She hugged her pillow,
pulling her knees closer into her chest. Bentley whined
asking to join her on the window bench. Wiping her tears
from her cheeks she motioned for her faithful companion
to sit beside her. Releasing the pillow and another round
of tears coming, Lydia grabbed Bentley and hugged him
close. He passively let her squeeze him as pity and sadness
poured out of the newly anointed teenage girl.

A few weeks ago, on November 29, the twins officially
became teenagers. Over the years they had celebrated their
birthday together with their mutual friends. Even though
Lydia had thought for her thirteenth birthday she would
want her own party with her friends, she was still okay
sharing her big day with her brother. This year they had
asked if they could all go see the latest and at the moment
greatest, super action, super hero, super CGI'd movie in
3D at the theatre as their birthday present. Graham and
Joanna thought that it was a great idea for the first few

days, until Joanna realized that 3D movies were not recommended for epileptics. And since birthday parties included siblings, her parents had hastily decided no 3D movie.

Echoes of yelling 'that's not fair' could still be heard ringing in the house when Jack and Lydia declared unfairness. When Jack eventually relented and agreed to see the movie at the regular theatre, Lydia still felt extremely slighted. But it was no longer just about the birthday disappointment. Ally was always getting her own way. Their time spent playing video games was limited and sometimes taken away depending on Ally. Staying out late suddenly had limitations and Ally always got to sleep in weekend mornings, even getting permission on Sundays to miss church if she was too tired.

Their mother was always in Ally's room talking with her behind closed doors. Their parents were frequently having meetings with the school and Ally's teachers to talk about her condition. And Lydia was constantly being asked by teachers and friends' parents, 'any more seizures?'

Lydia ran her hands through Bentley's soft fur. She hugged him as the last of her tears fell. She turned to her door when she heard Christmas music coming from downstairs. *I guess Mom is fine now*, she thought.

Joanna and Lydia had just finished another huge yelling match. It was late Saturday afternoon and Lydia wanted to go to the mall with her friends for pizza. Rides to get picked up and dropped off had been arranged. But Graham and Joanna were going to a Christmas party and they needed Lydia to stay home with Ally, who was not allowed to be home alone. Jack was at a volleyball tournament and wouldn't be home until late.

"Why can't Nana stay with her?" Lydia pouted to her irrational mother, while they were baking Christmas cookies.

"Because Nana does enough for us and it's snowing out and Dad doesn't want her to drive in this weather," Joanna said, putting the last of the cookies in containers. "Lydia, stop making this so difficult, you can go out with your friends anytime. We need you to be here tonight."

"Are you going to pay me?" she asked with sassy tone.

"Pay you for what?" Joanna asked slowly.

"Babysitting," she spit out, "I'm babysitting my older sister," she yelled back.

Fire burned in Joanna's eyes. Lydia could see she was pushing her mother to her limit, yet again. They had been battling over little and big things for weeks and it was wearing on them both. Joanna threw the metal spatula into the kitchen sink. "I have had more than enough of your sassy, selfish attitude, Lydia. You are thirteen years old and you're acting like you did when you were four and didn't get your way."

"I never get my way," she screamed, trying to keep the tears back.

"It's not about getting your way all the time, Lydia," Joanna said, tearing the floury apron off and throwing it on the counter. "We all need to make changes for everyone around here. And you keep acting like you're such a victim."

Joanna knew she needed to stop talking to Lydia like this, but her nerves with her trying daughter had worn her sensibilities down. She knew Lydia was feeling left out and was tired of always seeing Ally's needs being met above all else. But Joanna didn't know how else to parent right now and she just wanted everyone to keep the peace until she could figure out how to do this better. With Christmas just over a week away and parties and concerts and getting the house ready, Joanna was constantly in a state of being frazzled.

"We need your help tonight, we don't have any other options. You can go out with your friends another time. So could you please stop making such a big deal whenever we ask you to do something."

Lydia, like her mother, hated not having the last word, kept the argument going. "I never get a say. You just always tell me what to do, Mom. I have a life you know."

Joanna rolled her eyes. "You're thirteen, Lydia. I know that you want to always have your own way but that's not how it works around here. We compromise and help each other out."

Graham walked into the kitchen and saw the familiar battle grounds and war wounds across their faces.

Again? he thought. "What's all the yelling about this time?" he asked, grabbing a cookie.

"Mom is so unfair and never lets me do anything. She's making me stay home and babysit Ally, so I can't go out with my friends. Dad, it's not fair!" she stressed, wrapping her arms around her dad and burying her face into his side.

He gently wrapped an arm around his anguished daughter and looked at Joanna, who was obviously just as stressed. He shrugged his shoulder with that pleading look in his eyes that said, 'come on let her go. Ally will be fine on her own.'

"No, Graham," Joanna said, answering her husband's silent request. "We're not leaving Ally alone. We discussed this," she added with a sharper tone.

"Why are you yelling again?" Ally asked as she wandered into the kitchen.

Lydia turned from her dad. "Because Mom is making me babysit you, baby Ally," she yelled in her sister's face.

"LYDIA!" Graham scolded.

Ally pushed her sister away. "Get out of here you, freak. And I don't need a babysitter."

"Ally," Joanna said, simmering down, "that was not necessary."

"Oh sure, I get yelled at and Ally gets, 'that's not necessary,'" Lydia mocked dramatically. She stared down her mother. Lydia saw the hurt she had placed in her mother's deep brown eyes. But she didn't care.

"Lyd, come on," Graham replied.

"Lydia," Joanna said between gritted teeth, "stop being so nasty."

"I'm being nasty?" she reiterated, throwing her arms in the air. "I'm being nasty, what about you, Mom?" Tears sprang to her eyes. "Well......I hate you, Mom. You're so mean and so unfair. I hate my life!" She turned and ran out of the kitchen, up the front staircase and slammed and locked her bedroom door. She dove onto her bed, pounding the mattress over and over again.

Joanna was stung. By her daughter's tone, her words and the intensity of how much hatred came from her angered, young soul. Her first instinct was not to let her get away with that outburst, because it certainly wasn't over. She rounded the island and headed for the swinging door after Lydia. Graham stopped her in her tracks by reaching his arm over the entrance, not allowing his wife to add to the carnage of words with Lydia.

"Graham, I need to go talk to her," she said, ready to take on another round.

"Not yet, Jo. I don't think talking right now is a good idea at all. Let her, and you, calm down first."

"Yeah Mom, it looks like you're going to kill her," Ally added.

"Ally, don't make jokes now," Joanna warned, trying to move past her husband's arm.

"Joanna, no. You're not going to talk to her," Graham said, placing his hands squarely on her shoulders. "Look at me," he said. "You are just as upset as she is and you were not helping the situation."

Joanna looked over to Ally who was intently listening to their exchange. "Graham, please, not in front of Ally."

"What? Do you think that she didn't hear you yelling at Lydia?" That wasn't helpful he realized.

Joanna threw his hands off of her shoulders and took a step back. "Not in front of Ally," she reiterated slowly in a whisper.

"I don't want Lydia staying with me tonight," Ally requested. "She's annoying and I don't need someone with me all the time."

Joanna sighed looking up at the ceiling, knowing that this would be the thousandth time they would be having this conversation. "Ally, this is what we've decided. You cannot be home by yourself until you've been seizure free for one year."

"But Dr. Shaw didn't even say that. That's your rule, and it's dumb," Ally emphatically stated.

Dr. Barbara Shaw was their paediatric neurologist, who had been amazing at guiding them through the changes they were experiencing as their family learned to live with epilepsy. Jack and Lydia met with a neurology nurse who showed them what to do in case Ally was having a seizure. She answered all of their many questions and was very patient and understanding. Graham had eventually agreed with Joanna's idea of keeping Ally with someone at all times for at least a year. But now, it seemed that Joanna's safe guards to keep her family in agreement were cracking.

"Maybe we should let Lydia go and let Ally stay home. We don't have to stay at the party that long and Ally can text us every half hour to let us know she's fine," Graham offered.

"Yeah," Ally said enthusiastically.

"Graham, no!" Joanna spat out. "That is not what we agreed to do. I can't believe this. I keep trying to keep everything as normal as I can for everyone. We put these rules in place to keep Ally safe, and now you just throw it all out."

"Joanna, it's been months and she's fine," Graham placated, reaching out to his wife. She took a step back and grabbed the containers of cookies.

"No, it hasn't Graham, it's barely been eight weeks," she stressed, placing the containers in the freezer. "I don't believe you," she added. "Ally go to your room, please."

No one moved. Ally watched as her parents stared at each other. "Now!" her mother insisted.

Getting up from the stool, Ally leaped up the back staircase as she heard the hushed angry tones from her mom and dad.

"Jo, before you start in on me, listen to -"

"You knowingly cut me down in front of them, Graham. We make these decisions and then you take their side. What kind of credibility do you think I have with the girls?" she shot back like bullets from a gun.

He rubbed his hands over his face in frustration as he had tried times before to get Joanna to compromise when it came to lessening the reins on their family. He could feel they were beginning to choke under her tight grip. Graham leaned against the island and took in a deep breath before responding.

"Jo, it just seems like you want to have control, no, no, let me finish," he added when his wife started to counter argue. "We can't control every second of our kids' lives. We can't prevent Ally from having another seizure. We can't always force them to do what we want them to do when they have minds and opinions of their own. They're growing up, Jo, and we have to help them do that. Not just orchestrate every minute of their day."

She crossed her arms as she took a stance against her husband. "You didn't really answer my question. What kind of credibility do you think I have with the girls if you keep challenging our decisions that we made right in front of them?" she asked again.

Graham was a good lawyer, but his wife would have probably made an even better one. He took in a deep breath and slowly blew it out. "I get what you're saying, but you leave no room for compromise with them."

"We've made rules, Graham," she said with growing anger in her voice. "I am their mother and they need me to give them boundaries and consequences to protect them."

They were quiet for a few minutes as they regrouped for their closing arguments. Joanna turned and started to wipe the counters still dusted with flour.

She hated fighting. She loved her husband and found comfort in his strong arms and voice of reason. But the way he offered to make everyone happy somehow made her so angry with him. She needed him to be her rock and equal when it came to raising these kids. He rarely raised his voice to them and could tenderly relate and understood them long before she did. She was great at meeting their daily needs of lunches, clean clothes and driving them places. But Graham was not only their dad, but their pal and they loved and respected him with such ease. He was better at defusing situations, she knew that. But now she needed him to buy into her philosophy, for structure and guidelines. Why were they struggling so much lately to find the middle ground in all of this?

Joanna felt her husband walk up behind her. He put his hand over hers as she wiped the counter. He threw the cloth into sink and leaned close up against her. They both stared out of the window watching the snow fall heavily to the ground as wintery dusk fell over their home. The snow covered their backyard with another thick, heavy layer of pure white. He wrapped his arms around his wife's slender, fit body. She placed her head on his chest. Joanna closed her eyes and took in the familiar feeling of this place, in her husband's loving arms with his scent of his cologne and even breaths.

Graham loved his wife. He loved her steadfastness and commitment to their family and all of the twists and turns that came with raising teenagers. He loved that she cared so deeply for them and wanted them to be amazing people. He loved that she understood what it took to become an extraordinary family; it took extraordinary parents committed to always being one step ahead of their kids. He loved her talent to make their house a home and this group of people a family. He loved his wife.

"Jo, we have great kids who are going to be kids. I'm grateful that you want to give them all that we can. And that you want to protect them and make sure Ally is safe. I understand that fear you constantly have for her."

Tears sprang to her eyes as she closed them tight, willing away the emotion.

"I was just trying to come up with a compromise; and I should have done that in private, you're right."

She turned in his arms as the tears quietly fell down her cheeks and onto his sweatshirt. "Lydia has just been so difficult lately."

"I know. I'll go talk to her now," he said, kissing her forehead. He gently rubbed her back that was carrying the weight of the world.

He rested his chin on the top of her head. "You know it is snowing pretty hard out there. Makes me want to stay home and build a fire tonight."

"But what about the party at the Wagner's tonight?" Joanna asked.

"Oh yeah, that's what started this whole thing."

She smiled.

"Do we really have to go?" he questioned softly.

It had been a long while since they had an impromptu family night that wasn't on the schedule, Joanna realized. She looked up at Graham. "We could cancel because of the snow. They do live out in the country and the roads may not be that great out there," she justified.

"I know the Jeep could drive through anything, but...." he said smiling. "So why don't we stay home and let Lydia go out with her friends tonight. They'll just be in town and she has to be home by 9:00."

Thinking about it, she really didn't mind staying home on a snowy Saturday night just before Christmas. "Okay, let's stay home. Jack will be home later. Hopefully it's not snowing too bad out by Morris and they won't have trouble on the roads."

"I'll go talk to Lydia," Graham offered, before kissing his wife.

"And I'll call the Wagners."

"I love you, Jo."

She kissed him again. "I love you too, Graham. Thanks for being a good husband." They kissed again.

Graham headed to the back staircase. It was too late for Ally to sneak upstairs as she was caught sitting in the stairwell, listening to her parents from the kitchen.

She held back her own tears. "I'm making a lot of trouble for you and Mom."

Graham sat down on the step and placed his arm around her. "No, Ally. Just keep being a regular teenage girl, okay. We'll figure out the rest of it as it comes."

"But everyone is fighting because of me," she cried, leaning into her dad.

"Hey, every family goes through stuff. It's just our turn now. We're all going to be fine."

"It's so unfair, Dad."

"Hey, it probably is. But that's life. And this is ours."

She wiped her face. "I'm glad you and Mom worked it out. Sorry I caused you guys to get so mad at each other."

"Your mom and I will always get through whatever we're facing. Your mom is way too good to let any of us slip through the cracks."

They heard Dean Martin crooning that it was cold outside. They smiled. Graham kissed his daughter and said they were going to stay home tonight because, "Baby, it's cold out there!" Graham sang along. Ally laughed giving him a hug. "Love you, Daddy."

"Love you too, Al. Now I have to go see if Lydia still loves us too!"

"I'll go help Mom clean up the kitchen," she said and headed back down the stairs.

Graham ran his fingers through his hair and took in a satisfying breath. He knew they would get through today's challenges. He knew as long as he and Joanna could find their middle, they could get through anything. He got up and headed the rest of the way upstairs.

He knocked on Lydia's door. "Lyd, it's Dad. I want to talk to you."

Instantly the door flew open to find his little girl in a mess of tears. "Oh Daddy. I hate feeling this way."

He walked in and was met with Lydia crashing into him, squeezing him tight. He gathered her up and let her cry. "It's going to be fine," he reassured once more, so glad that this was the last female in his household he had to console. But he wouldn't want it any other way.

Lydia decided that she wanted to stay home after all that. And together they had pizza and watched holiday movies in front of the roaring fire place and glistening Christmas tree. Jack got home later than expected but quickly showered and got into his pjs and joined his family for this peaceful and finally silent night, together.

10
New Beginnings

Graham drove down the highway as the wintery, snowy wind blew across Hwy. 3. Even driving in these conditions, late at night, was a welcomed relief as they got further away from his sister-in-law's house. They were so optimistic for their families to gather for the Christmas season. Food and presents, music and more food. Enjoying egg nog and cookies in the decorated living room; cousins playing in another room. It all sounded so festive and wonderful. At least that's what he and Joanna had hoped for again this holiday.

Joanna's oldest sister Pauline had reluctantly offered to host the Christmas gathering. Pauline and her very reserved husband, Russ Watson, lived in an older part of Winnipeg. Their one daughter Tina, who was nineteen, still lived with them and worked in a government office that she never talked about. The Watsons were not exactly forthcoming about their lives making it difficult to have a basic conversation. Pauline had always been private about her life. Russ was just quiet and very hard to get to know. Graham had nothing in common with his brother-in-law and trying to engage in small talk was so difficult, it had become nearly painful.

But now, they could all breathe a sigh of relief that it was over and they were headed back to Mountain City. No amount of snow falling or blowing could have kept them at that gathering.

Graham looked over to Joanna as she just stared straight at the icy windshield. "You can breathe again," he teased.

She chuckled and looked at her husband. "That was so... I don't even know how to describe it."

"Well, you did a great job of holding back. I'm very proud of you."

Joanna scoffed. "Don't remind me." She turned to him, "I still can't believe Pauline questioning me like that. Who does she think she is?"

Pauline, who was an office manager for an insurance company, suddenly had become an expert in curing epilepsy. She had questioned Joanna about Ally's medications while they were getting the Christmas dinner ready in the kitchen. Then Pauline pressed her about what the seizures were like while they gathered around the tiny dining room table. Even though the kids were eating at a separate table set up in the living room, it made for awkward dinner conversation as Graham tried to change the subject. But Pauline didn't take hints very well.

Once the tables were cleared and they were going to gather in the living room to exchange gifts, Pauline had pulled Joanna aside and continued her ranting of unwanted advice. Pauline worked with someone who had a nephew who had seizures. She explained they chose to forego all medications and tried a homeopathic route with vitamins and special juices that cleansed the blood stream. So far this boy was cured.

When their mother joined in the conversation and began her monologue on Ally's situation, Joanna had hit her boiling point. Why did her mother and sister assume that she and Graham were clueless when it came to their daughter's care? Taking in a steady breath, Joanna patiently explained they were satisfied with the treatment and medical advice they were receiving from their family doctor and their pediatric neurologist.

Joanna turned up the heat in the Jeep and recalled the next phase of their conversation from the hallway.

"We are not going to change Ally's routine now, Pauline. She has been fine since September and her body has adjusted well to her medication. We're not going to upset her life with any more changes."

"But have you gotten a second opinion?" Pauline questioned, following Joanna down the hall.

"That's what I keep wondering," Susan chimed in. "I don't know if all your options have been looked at for her."

"Graham's brother, Todd, is an actual doctor," Joanna added sharply. "He has been involved since this all started and he's going to make sure that everything will get done for Ally."

Pauline rolled her eyes, then looked at her mother. "Well, of course, how could I forget that the Kornelson family has an answer for everything."

Pauline's words came out with hurtful carelessness. Joanna hated being on the receiving end of her sister's advice. When Joanna married into the prominent family, it had bothered her sisters. Money and opportunity was never a struggle for the Kornelson family, and the sisters found it hard not to compare her lifestyle to their own. Joanna's shock and disappointment could not be denied as she stood silent in front of Pauline and her mother.

Joanna looked up at her older sister who was tall, gangly and appeared at least ten years older than she really was. She then glanced toward her mother who simply looked down, avoiding the tension.

"Wow, Pauline. Do you think you've said enough? Or is there more you'd like to say to me?"

"No, I think this discussion is over," Graham said, coming behind Joanna and resting his hands on her shoulders. "They want to open the presents now," he said as he guided his wife back into the living room, tenderly kissing the top of her head and whispering something into her ear.

Pauline glared at her mother and huffed in defeat before joining the rest of the family in the compact living room. Everyone knew something was going on in the hallway but Joanna tried to keep her mood light while Pauline sulked in the corner. Laura sat next to Joanna asking what was going on. Joanna just blew it off as if nothing important happened.

The rest of the evening was divided into camps. The six grandchildren headed downstairs to further examine their new Christmas gifts while the women headed back into the kitchen to make coffee and serve the rest of the baking. The men sat in the living room and were grateful that there was always a hockey game to fill up the blank spaces of their forced conversations. Joanna tried to talk to her niece Tina, but she was too involved with her phone. Joanna was so relieved when Graham rose from the couch and suggested they head back home. He winked at his wife and said he would tell the kids.

With superficial good byes and half hearted hugs, the Kornelson family piled into their Jeep for the hour and a half drive back home.

Now reaching the outskirts of Mountain City, Joanna stared out her side window seeing nothing but darkness. Did people really think they were being helpful by asking stupid questions in the disguise as advice? This wasn't the first time Joanna had faced confrontations from well meaning friends. But when Pauline added her bit about Graham's family having an answer for everything, Joanna felt like she was nine years old again and getting bullied by her big, mean sister.

Graham Kornelson was born into a family whose father and his father before him bought up land and developed many of the streets, buildings and even pockets of communities in Mountain City. Everyone knew their family or at least knew of them. Graham's dad, Ed, was a generous man who never hesitated to donate thousands of his hard earned dollars to the senior centre building project, church fundraisers or community parks and town projects. Graham and Todd believed they could grow up to become whatever they wanted. They both excelled in school academically and athletically, and knew their futures were filled with opportunities and unlimited finances. Ed and Eleanor were excellent parents and had raised smart, kind and ambitious men.

Looking from the outside, it appeared Graham and Joanna were just as picture perfect. They had everything that mattered, charming good looks, expensive cars, a cabin and a boat, a beautiful home. The Kornelson family had never been affected by jealous bystanders. They had surrounded themselves with many friends and had their very close knit family. Graham had never been bothered by what other people may have thought of him or his family's wealth and position in the community. He was proud of his father and grandfather for their commitment in teaching them about working hard and always giving back. And with his father passing away nearly a year earlier, it had brought them even closer.

Joanna couldn't let comments slide off quite so easily. She married Graham because of his integrity and character, not because of family prestige. In fact, he really had to pursue Joanna Shultz, as she vowed never to move back to Mountain City. While in university, she was infatuated with a drop out musician who wanted to move to Vancouver. But when Graham's kind heart and determined spirit won her over, she was prepared to take the good with the bad, even if that meant a move back to their idyllic hometown. Joanna worked hard to build a good life for her and her family. And she loved her life, but she was getting tired of trying to justify it, especially to her sisters.

"Mom, are we almost home," Lydia whined from the back seat.

"Yes, sweetie," Joanna answered back, smiling. "Can't wait to get home."

***

January came with snow, bone chilling temperatures and back to school. Ally was preparing for exams at the end of the month while Jack and Lydia slid back into the routine of after school activities and homework.

Joanna was checking the roast in the oven when she heard the front door slam a little harder than necessary. *Who had a bad day now?* she thought. "I'm in the kitchen," she called out.

Ally came stomping in the kitchen, throwing her backpack and jacket on the floor. She sat at the table and burst out. "Guess what happened?" She started to cry.

Joanna's first reaction was always that she had a seizure, but clearly this was something else. "I don't know, Ally?" she said, joining her at the table.

"You know that Emily was going to have a birthday party, right."

Joanna nodded.

"And she was inviting all these girls and it was going to be so much fun. We were all going to go to Youth Group at church on Friday night and then go to her place," Ally said, sniffling before she continued, "and then we were going to do our nails and stuff and then order pizza at midnight," she paused again, "and then have a sleepover."

Joanna saw where this was going. She closed her eyes as she waited for the rest of the story.

"But now Amanda told me that I wasn't allowed to stay for night, but Emily didn't want to tell me. And then Christine told me that Emily told her that she didn't even want me at the party because her mother doesn't want to deal....with me.....if I have a seizure."

Joanna's heart fell out of her chest. Her hand covered her mouth as she tried to hide her own hurtful disappointment.

"Now I don't know what I'm supposed to do. Am I invited or not?" she cried.

Joanna moved her chair closer, as Ally sobbed in her arms. "Oh, Ally, I'm so sorry. Maybe this is just a misunderstanding. Why don't I call Emily's mom and figure this all out."

"No, Mom, you can't," Ally said, sitting up again. "I don't want my friends to think I'm mad or anything."

"But you *are* mad and everything, Al. This isn't fair. She can't invite you and then not invite you. And then get the other girls to tell you. I know Emily's mother, I can call her and straighten it all out."

"No, Mom," Ally said louder. "I'm just not going to go. They're all stupid anyway. They just want to order pizza at midnight because this stupid boy said he worked that night and he would deliver it."

Joanna had to come up with another solution for Ally. These girls have been lifetime friends, and she wouldn't let it end because of the possibility of a seizure. "Ally, not everyone understands seizures and what to do. Have you told them that you've been fine for months?"

"Yes, of course they know that, Mom."

"But maybe if I just explain to Emily's mom that you've been fine and if something were to happen, she could just call me. And that you're taking your meds and everything has been good."

"No!" she said emphatically one more time before getting up. "I'm just a stupid girl who has seizures and no one wants to be my friend." Ally stomped up the back stairs and slammed her bedroom door.

Joanna sat in disbelief. There had to be some misunderstanding. Joanna never wanted to see Ally be singled out for having epilepsy. She had to fix this for Ally.

Lydia came in through the kitchen door. "Hi Mom, what's for dinner? It smells good."

Joanna shook off the horrible feeling. "Roast beef. How was your day?"

"Good. I'm hungry."

"Here, Lydia, can you go hang up Ally's jacket too." Her daughter gave her that look of 'I have to do something for Ally again.'

"Just do it, please, Lyd. Ally had a rough day today," Joanna sighed, seeing that Lydia's eyes got wider. "No not that, just friend trouble."

Lydia took her sister's jacket and went to hang it up. Joanna sliced up a snack of cheese and apples. *This was the way the new year is going to start*? Joanna thought. She wanted new beginnings and not last year's drama. But the residue of the seizures kept coming back to them as people reacted out of ignorance. Most people cared, some were just cruel, while others disguised good intentions through gossip and rumours. But this episode was the worst; it had personally affected Ally. Joanna thought she had protected her daughter from the myriad of questions and opinions. She had made a concerted effort with her teachers to make sure Ally wasn't feeling like that "special" student. Or if she was having dizzy spells, as she did on occasion, she would get understanding and not pity. But having Ally's friends leave her out like this was something that Joanna could not keep from Ally. Joanna's heart sank; not the great new beginning she was hoping for.

11
Believe Me

The night of the birthday party could have been a horrible evening. Joanna didn't know how she was going to compensate for Ally's disappointment of not going to Emily's party. She had hoped that Lydia wouldn't be nasty to her sister today, as Joanna sensed Ally may come home from school dejected and angry.

Joanna was mentally exhausted trying to come up with ways to make up for Ally's new limitations. No more late nights for Ally. They tried to keep small stresses in perspective before they ballooned into insurmountable dilemmas. Taking pills on time had soon become part of their normal. And now, she had to cope with friends who didn't understand what she was going through. Ally didn't always handle the stress that well, Joanna concluded switching loads of laundry. Teens are already stressed, and now adding seizures into her crazy hormones was a recipe for disaster. Ally took Emily's gossipy ways of uninviting her very personally. She was hurt and thought everyone must hate her and not want her around. Joanna was devastated for her and wanted to make it up the best way she could.

But everything she had suggested to Ally came back with a defiant negative response.

Then Sarah had called late Friday afternoon and asked if they wanted to join them at the Chinese Buffet. Ally never said no to seeing her cute little cousins and Joanna knew being with Todd and Sarah was exactly what they all needed. Ally loved these family nights and being with her aunt and uncle; they always showed concern yet didn't treat her like she was different. Todd talked to Ally like she was not a victim of chronic illness and Sarah, once a voice teacher, loved to sing with Ally at the piano.

After the last fortune cookie was read, they all went back to Graham and Joanna's house to watch a classic Hitchcock film that Todd and Graham wanted to see for the hundredth time. Ally cuddled between her dad and her uncle while Abigail and Nora fell asleep on their dad's lap, totally unaware that birds could be so scary.

Ally was feeling somewhat content, mostly forgetting about Emily's party. Deep down she wanted to be like her other friends, like it used to be, she missed her old life. But that had all changed now. The threat of seizures and the drugs had changed her physically and of course mentally, but Ally still grieved who she no longer was. She loved being with her friends when they would just talk about clothes or boys, hang out at the mall or someone's house. It all seemed so shallow now, but she missed those simple moments with her friends when they were all equals, no one with a medical condition to make them different.

They often asked Ally questions about seizures. Ally shrugged and couldn't really answer them because she didn't really know what they wanted to hear. It felt like the seizures happened to somebody else; like it was someone else's life. Some boys had looked up seizures on YouTube and tried showing it to Ally, but she refused to watch it. Seeing a stranger seizure didn't interest her at all. Her mom did explain how she found her at the bottom of the stairs, it was like hearing a story. Ally never had an aura or any warning that a seizure was about to overtake her body. 'It just happened', she explained to curious friends.

So being invited and then uninvited to Emily's party began to set a course of strain on her friendships. Would she ever feel like she fit in again? No one at school wanted to talk about the party in front of Ally, making everyone feel awkward. Friends were also taking sides between Emily and herself. Ally finally told her friends that she just didn't want to talk about Emily or her party anymore.

Ally snuggled closer to her dad as Alfred Hitchcock's birds kept coming and coming and coming, chasing the kids down the road. The birds kept coming, just like her friends did at school, always asking her questions, always wanting to talk about the party. Ally closed her eyes. When will it end? And why did they want to watch this freakish, old movie? It was suddenly all too much for Ally.

"I'm going to bed," Ally said. "I'm tired."

"Did you take your pills?" Joanna asked.

Jack shushed them as everyone was so intrigued by these birds who wouldn't stop their relentless determination to wreck havoc on the little coastal town. The birds always found this innocent family who couldn't hide and escape from their torment. Ally looked away from the TV.

She leapt upstairs wanting to hide away from all the haunting images of the movie and her mind. Ally couldn't stop the barrage of tears that she was holding back. She had fun tonight with her thoughtful and loving family. But she still felt excluded. She was different. She would no longer find peace. Just like the birds in the movie, always swarming around, always coming closer; epilepsy would always find Ally too.

***

"And God's people said," the pastor prayed.

"Amen." The congregation murmured as the church sanctuary slowly began to filter out into the lobby. Groups found each other and began casual conversation. Pastors mingled connecting with their parishioners, asking about the sick and those suffering from life's troubles. Clusters of people talked about vacations and home renovations; about school problems and elderly parents. It was a place to connect with fellow believers and come together as a community of faith in this familiar place.

Joanna headed towards the coat racks when Emily's mother, Cynthia, came walking in front of her. Their eyes met and locked. An awkward lull fell over them. Joanna panicked to find words lodged in her throat.

"Hi Joanna, how are things going?"

Joanna licked her dry lips. "Good, things are good."

They hesitated.

"How did Emily's party go the other night?" Joanna bravely asked. She second guessed asking, but couldn't help but get involved, even if it upset Ally.

"Oh, it was good. Too bad Ally couldn't make it."

"Make it?"

"Yes, Emily told me that Ally was not feeling well and that you thought it best she not come; you know, in case, something happened."

Joanna stared at this woman she had known for years. They were never close friends, but had known each other through volunteering at school and church.

"Oh, that's not exactly how I understood the situation, Cynthia. I really wished you would have talked to me about it. I'm more than willing to talk about Ally's... condition, about epilepsy. Ally wanted to go, but just didn't feel -"

"No, no, Joanna, I think you've misunderstood the whole situation."

Cynthia swallowed and quickly looked down. But Joanna saw the half truths in Cynthia's eyes.

"It's just that, you know, with all those girls and staying up late and I just didn't..... Emily told me that...." Cynthia stammered, stumbling over her version of the truth.

"Cynthia, Ally and Emily have been very good friends for a long time. I just wished you would have been honest with me and asked me what to do, that's all." Joanna felt a tightness in her throat, feeling the tension building between them.

"Joanna, please don't misunderstand me. Believe me, I have nothing against Ally. I just don't know how all the other girls feel about...if something were to happen, how would they react to her? I'm thinking about what's best for Ally."

Joanna tried to smile to cover up her bubbling anger. "Cynthia, that is my concern as her mother too. As far as I know, none of her friends have reacted badly to Ally, until now. I just think a lot of confusion and misunderstanding is beginning to get in the way of things here."

Cynthia mustered up a look of utter shock as she began nervously playing with her necklace. "I'm just protecting my daughter from -"

"From what?" Joanna asked quickly. She tucked her hair back behind her ear, looking around hoping that they looked like everyone else standing around and talking. But Joanna really wanted to do was yell at this woman and cause a scene.

Cynthia's younger son came running up to them and interrupted the tension by begging to go home. "Yes, tell Daddy we're ready to go," she said, eager to walk away from Joanna. She looked from her son and then back to Joanna. "Well, I guess the girls should be the ones to work this out. Emily told me that it was Ally's decision not to come to the party," Cynthia concluded sternly. She straightened her necklace with a nervous hand and walked on with cowardly satisfaction.

Joanna scanned the crowd of people, most of them she had known her entire life. Part of her wanted to exit this building and never come back. And yet, she wanted to scream in this church, at these people who pretended in their Sunday best that they were happy and fine, just like she was doing. It was getting harder to pretend that all was good; that they would get through this. It was difficult to say they were living with epilepsy. She wanted to scream that her family was still normal. They were just trying to cope like every other family. She wanted to be understood that they were struggling and this was hard.

Taking in a much needed breath, Joanna decided she did want to run. Not just run away, but she wanted to run outside in the freezing, cold winter air.

Graham was already standing by their coats. Finding his key fob, he commanded the car to warm up on this cold morning as Joanna met up with him.

A friend of Joanna's, Eve, and the mother of one of Ally's friends, joined her as they found their coats.

"Joanna," Eve said quietly. "I overheard part of your conversation with Cynthia."

"Oh," Joanna muttered, still caught up in silent rage and slight embarrassment.

"I want you to know that Christine missed Ally not being at Emily's party on Friday night." She paused. "Ally is welcome to come to our house anytime. Even for night. Just let me know what I need to know if something were to happen," Eve said with sincerity.

Joanna looked down putting on her gloves; willing the tears to stay away. "Thanks, Eve. That means a lot to hear you say that."

"You know that Clint is a lab technician, if that offers you any measure of comfort." Eve paused before adding one more thought. "My sister got diabetes when we were really young. I think she was twelve. So believe me, I know a little of what it feels like to, you know, adjust your life. I remember that part well."

Joanna touched Eve's arm. "Thank you, Eve. Our life has changed that's for sure. I just hoped for Ally's sake that her friends wouldn't. But I guess I can't control that."

Eve gave her a quick hug. "Nope, you can't. Just hang in there, Joanna. You're a good mom. Ally's lucky to have you, don't forget that. Even when she makes life difficult, remember she's still a teenager."

Joanna laughed and was relieved Eve understood.

"Ready, Jo?" Graham asked, shaking hands with Eve's husband. "Good morning, Clint."

"Yes, I'll be right there," she answered, then turning back to Eve. "Yes, we've had to do a bit of adjusting but everything seems to be back to normal." She paused finding a deeper honesty coming closer to the surface. "And thanks for saying that. I'm glad you found me today."

Eve squeezed Joanna's hand. "We'll have to talk some more. Christine really likes being with Ally, and I don't want that to change."

Joanna nodded and said good bye as she made her way to the church doors, catching up with Graham who got caught talking to someone else. For every shroud of darkness that Joanna was facing, she could see a stream of light shining through. She was grateful that there were people in her corner rooting for her along the way. Feeling alone in her struggles that so few understood, Joanna now knew that perhaps people were placed in her life for a reason. Once again delicate hope would carry Joanna through another day.

12
The Everyday

The bitter and snowy winter was loosening its tight grip that seemed to clamp down on the Canadian prairies harder each year. But the signs of spring promises were coming. The snow was melting, blades of grass were appearing and the sun hung out a little longer each afternoon.

Every day the Kornelsons found they were getting their footing back again, no longer feeling the haunting of seizures lurking around their home. Or perhaps they had found a new normal and peace was restoring. Ally eventually reconnected with her friends at school which was making her a happier person to be around. She had also kept up her dedication to practicing piano as she prepared to play at the Festival of the Performing Arts in a few weeks. Her teacher, Mrs. Buhlin, was so proud of all that Ally had accomplished. She was playing her Mendelssohn piece so well and her Bach was coming along nicely; it would all be ready in time for the festival.

Lydia was enjoying her dance classes and had made a few new friends. Jack had managed to combine multiple sports schedules throughout the winter. And all the Kornelson kids excelled at school.

Joanna and Graham took a week in January and flew to Jamaica. She realized on one particular cold and dark winter day that she and Graham had not been connecting over the past number of months. They talked a lot, all the time in fact, but always about the kids and their schedules and where everyone needed to be. They would catch up on how his mother was getting along and how they continued to struggle with Joanna's relationship with her parents and sisters. Leaving their everyday life behind, they talked about movies and books and topics that used to interest them before their lives were filled with the business of raising a family. They swam in the ocean and read on the beach. They found that place again in their marriage that had brought them together nearly two decades earlier. When they arrived back home, they were tanned, refreshed and ready to get back to the everyday grind.

Ally had asked again if she could get a job at the well known outdoor drive-in restaurant, Burger Shack. Graham and Joanna talked about it and felt that Ally was ready to carry the responsibility of a job. Epilepsy felt like a season of the past. It happened to someone else, another family, but not them. It had been months since her last seizure. Ally faithfully continued to take her medication and everything had become normal again. So she applied, had an interview and would be starting her training in mid April. The Burger Shack was a father/son team who had been running this local institution for over thirty years.

Joanna was going to miss their time as a family at the cabin this summer. It wouldn't be the same anymore. But Graham had assured his wife that this was just another step towards their ever changing lives. Joanna would go to their cabin with Jack and Lydia while Graham and Ally would join them on days when Ally wasn't working. It seemed like a good plan.

***

It was an unusually warm and sunny April Sunday morning on Ally's first day on the new job. She was excited and nervous and so eager to make her own money. Joanna dropped her off, feeling a tugging on her heartstrings. Joanna drove off the parking lot of the Burger Shack and couldn't believe she was taking her baby girl to her first job.

Where has the time gone? she thought, driving home to pick the others up for church. And yet a satisfying smile crossed her lips. She was so happy that Ally had found her stride again. Ally was still excelling in piano. She played one of her best performances at the arts festival and once again was chosen to play at the provincial competition in Winnipeg.

In the last year, they had seen a few rough patches with Graham's dad passing away and Ally's seizure episodes, but they got through it together. They were there to pick each other up when one fell down. Joanna felt good. Her goal was to get Ally over her difficulties and they had done that as a family. Together, through their struggles, they learned how important it was to be a close family. *Life was good again*, Joanna thought, pulling up the driveway.

After church, Jack and Graham wanted to pick up burgers from the Burger Shack, but Joanna had promised Ally no surprise visits on the first day. So they barbecued sausages with fruit salad and cole slaw. Jack had homework to finish, Lydia took Bentley for a walk while Graham and Joanna napped in the sun room.

The phone rang. Graham got up and headed for the kitchen.

"Yep, this is Graham." He walked back into the sunroom. "Yes."

"Who is it?" Joanna asked, sitting up. Her husband had no expression on his face. She stood up.

"Oh, okay. Yes, okay. We'll be right there," he said, with an eerie monotone voice. He clicked off the phone and dropped it on a chair.

"What happened?" Joanna asked. His eyes told her what she already knew.

"Ally had a seizure and they called the ambulance."

"No," Joanna moaned, grasping her hands over her mouth.

"Come on, let's go. They'll keep her at the Burger Shack until we get there."

Graham told Jack and in less than a minute he and Joanna went to get their daughter.

Roger, the owner, was waiting outside. He waved them to come to the back of the building. Graham and Joanna ran inside the restaurant and looked around the crowded commercial kitchen. Young girls with serious and concerned faces kept making ice cream cones and taking orders. They heard the ambulance coming down the highway.

"She's over here," Dean, the co-owner said quickly.

Walking around the corner they saw Ally lying on her right side as she had just finished convulsing. Ketchup and blood covered the side of her face as the saliva dripped from her swollen mouth. This very private, difficult experience was happening outside the safety of their home, Joanna realized staring down at her daughter who no longer looked like herself.

"May I have some napkins or a towel, please?" Joanna calmly asked. One of the young girls passed a cloth to Dean who then gave it to Joanna. She knelt down and began to wipe off her face as Ally now lay still and paralyzed. "It's okay, Ally, Mom is here now. We're here now."

She heard Graham talking to the ambulance attendants. One of them he knew from high school.

Within a few minutes, Ally opened her eyes and looked around, and tried to get up. The first responders came closer wanting to examine Ally. Joanna refused to leave her daughter as she lay in ketchup and broken hamburger buns.

Graham came behind Joanna, reaching for her. "Come on Jo, let them check her."

She shook her head. "No, I need to stay here."

He tried again. "You need to step back. Let them look at Ally, okay. She's going to be fine, but they just need to just make sure - "

"She's bleeding, Graham," Joanna said, knowing she wasn't making sense. She knew she needed to let them examine Ally, but something kept her from moving away. This time she was bleeding. Her head hit the counter, taking down open ketchup bottles she was refilling and several bags of buns.

Graham reached down and gently guided Joanna to his side.

"This isn't happening. This can't be happening," she murmured over and over while looking down as the two EMTs continued their examination.

"Hey Ally, what's going on? Do you know where you are?" one of them asked, as Ally began to look around.

"I don't know," she said, slurring the words around her swollen tongue.

"Mom?"

Joanna came closer, reaching for her hand. "I'm right here."

"She doesn't have any broken bones but she did cut her head when she fell. She must have smacked it on the counter here. We can just tape it up, it doesn't need stitches."

"Did I have a seizure?" Ally asked, looking at her scraped up hand.

"Yeah," Joanna chocked back her tears, "you did, honey. But you're going to be fine. Daddy is here too."

Ally's face contorted, "I don't want to have seizures." She wailed and burst into tears. "I don't like this," she repeated.

"This is all part of the post seizure stage," the other attendant said.

"Yes, we know," Joanna said, more hastily than intended.

"She's just never had a seizure outside our home and it has been a while. We're caught off guard," Graham answered in an apologetic manner.

"I understand. We can take her to the hospital in the ambulance and get her checked out there. Or you can just take her home for now and make an appointment to see your family doctor. Maybe her medication needs to be adjusted again," he suggested.

Joanna got Ally to sit up as she embraced her crying daughter. "We'll just take her home," she decided.

Graham nodded. "We'll take her home."

The attendants agreed. "Okay, just hold her up like that and I'll tape up the cut on her forehead and she'll be good to go."

Roger approached Graham from the front ordering window where business was carrying on as usual. "Does this happen often?" he asked, wiping his hands on his apron.

"Just started last year I guess, but with the medication she's been taking, she's been fine for over six months."

"We were wondering why she didn't tell us she has seizures?"

"Legally she doesn't have to," Graham answered back, realizing he sounded too much like a lawyer and not a dad. He took a deep breath. "But that aside, I guess we should have. It's just that she's been doing so well and it never occurred to us that this was going to keep happening. We thought she had outgrown it and she was fine."

Dean replied, "I know we can not hire someone based on medical conditions but if we would have known we....it just would have prepared us, I guess. We didn't know what to do. But one of the other girls here, Christine, knew your number and so we decided to call you after we had already called the ambulance."

"Okay, all done here. Just need to sign this form saying that you've chosen to take her home," the attendant said as he approached Graham. He signed it and helped Joanna get Ally to her feet.

Dean walked them to their car. "She's going to be a good worker. She's not on the schedule until Thursday. So if she's feeling okay, we will expect to see her at 4:30."

Graham stared at Dean with slight shock. He could have said that she didn't have to come back. Or we'll let you know, with no chance of a call back. But he didn't. He believed in Ally. Graham shook his hand and got into the driver's seat.

They took their daughter home.

13
Days Of Summer

It had not been the summer they were expecting.
Ally continued to have seizures. And Joanna could feel
her world coming undone. They had no choice but to get
Ally a medical bracelet indicating epilepsy on the back
of the silver emblem. Ally knew it was for her own safety
but she felt branded somehow, reminding her that she was
officially different.

The neurologist ordered more tests, including blood
work and a sleep deprived EEG. Weeks later, the results of
the EEG came back abnormal and therefore, their doctor
decided to increase her medication. For the next several
months they continued the increase, causing Ally to have
horrible bouts of irritability and long stretches of fatigue.
She refused to quit her job at her parents prompting, and
Dean and Roger had refused to let her quit even after the
fourth seizure in their busy restaurant.

"She needs to know that people won't give up on her.
She's a good worker and we can adjust her hours and
responsibilities around here, but we're going to make this
work," Roger said to Graham when he had gone down to

the Burger Shack. He and Joanna had discussed it and if they wanted to let Ally go, they wouldn't file a human rights complaint.

Dean added, "I've not always had an easy life, Graham. But I was fortunate to have good people, like your own dad, not give up on me, so we are not giving up on Ally. Everyone deserves a fair chance."

Humbled by their commitment to let Ally keep her job and dignity intact, Graham shook their hands and they came up with a plan for Ally's work schedule.

But the seizures continued, once at their cabin on the boat dock and three more at home. The last seizure happened one morning when Lydia heard a bang from her room but was too tired to get out of bed to see what it was. Jack found Ally as he was walking past her room and called out for his mom. When Lydia later admitted she heard a noise but didn't say anything, Joanna lost her temper.

Lately there had been a lot of yelling. Joanna yelled at everybody about everything that wasn't going right. Ally was crying a lot because of the distress of the seizures and the changing of her medications. Joanna only found peace working in her garden and going for runs. Graham was getting warn out and frustrated trying to put out the heated arguments every evening when he got home from work. Joanna became so controlling over the summer, there was hardly a place for him in any discussions regarding their family. So he too found a place of solace by picking up more miles on his now daily evening runs. Jack and Lydia stayed in their rooms or just left the house when it would get to be too much.

When they'd seen the neurologist in early July, she had agreed that the current medication was no longer working. She felt they should start a medication commonly used for generalized epilepsy and wean Ally off the first drug. With some patients it often took several attempts to find the right drug, Dr. Shaw explained during their appointment.

Ally had turned fifteen in April and as her friends were excited about signing up for drivers' education classes and getting learners' permits, Ally was told by Dr. Shaw that she would not be allowed to drive until she was seizure free for a year. Disappointments continued to plague their family as Ally tried to make sense of why this was happening to her.

One very hot afternoon, Ally slammed her bedroom door with satisfaction as her mother continued her tirade through the door. She was on Ally's case about staying up too late, watching too much TV. She should be eating better and exercising more, she was working too much, not trying to be nice to Lydia and Jack. Her mom wouldn't stop.

"Fine, Ally. I'm going for a run, and I expect that you will think about what you said and we can talk about it when I get back," Joanna ordered.

Always talking, Ally thought to herself. *Why does she need to talk everything through so much?*

"Ally!" Joanna said, with a knowing threat in her tone.

"Fine," she yelled back. She heard her mother run down the stairs and then the kitchen door slammed.

Ally breathed a sigh of relief. She didn't want to talk anymore. Ally knew she was being mean to everyone but she felt mean inside. This horrible illness was thrust upon her and now she was supposed to act her age, be patient, learn to find a new normal. She hated all those expressions. She wanted to scream. She wanted to feel like her old normal, not look for a new one. Ally walked to her bed, grabbed a pillow and tried to rip it apart. She threw all her blankets on the floor and pounded the bed. She yelled into her pillow, but nothing was easing her discomfort. No one understood her pain and sadness. No one felt her anxiety and fear of the future. No one saw the darkness that was encircling her soul inching closer and getting darker every day.

Everyone just wanted to talk about the seizures and what to do if the next one happened. Ally felt so left out of her own disease. It wasn't really happening to her anymore, it was about everyone else. She just wanted to be left alone for the rest of the summer. This disease was scary and so out of control, even with the medications. She felt like everything was making her crazy. Who would win the battle within her, the illness or the medication? Ally didn't know.

Ally got up from the bed and went to the one place where her world never changed. She went downstairs to the back room. She closed the big sliding doors and sat down in front of the piano. She breathed deeply and placed her fingers on the keyboard. Closing her eyes, she imagined peace and in perfect harmony, music filled the room and then her soul. Ally loved to play hymns, an appreciation she learned from Nana Ellie. 'It Is Well With My Soul', 'How Great Thou Art', and 'Because He Lives', flowed from her heart into her fingers and she captured a peace that passed all understanding. She didn't know all the words, but something about their timeless healing found refuge with Ally. For over an hour, she held a concert for herself and continued to play Bach and Chopin, Billy Joel and Disney hits. She played everything she could find in her collection of music books stacked beside the grand piano. The world was feeling normal again.

Joanna met Graham pulling up on the driveway just as she was about to pop in her ear buds and run as long and fast as she could to the beat of her playlist and the anger in her heart. He was home earlier than she expected. Or maybe he told her that he would be home sooner today. She couldn't remember since all her days felt like they were drifting into one another.

"I thought you ran this morning," Graham questioned, getting out of the car and reaching for his briefcase in the back seat.

"I need to run again," she said plainly, looking at her beautiful home filled with unhappy children.

"What's up? Not a good day?"

Joanna looked down. The harder she tried to get her kids to see they all needed to be kinder to each other, the meaner she got. They didn't care anymore. Ally was making life impossible for all of them, and the twins gave up trying to be patient and understanding. "Just the same fighting like every day. They don't get it."

He reached out and touched her arm. "Come on Jo, they're kids. Brother and sisters. They are going to fight. It's summer holidays and they're probably getting bored and need to get back to school."

"It's more than that Graham. Ally is not just a bored teenager. And the twins don't seem to care or want to understand what she's going through. I'm exhausted trying to get everyone to understand -"

"I know, Jo. You're always trying, too much."

She looked directly at her husband and flipped her sunglasses on top of her head. "Really?" she said with sardonic tone. "I will not let this family fall apart, Graham."

"Since when is it falling apart? Why do you have to be so dramatic, Joanna? Families go through stuff and we'll get through this." He leaned against the car, taking off his sunglasses and rubbing his eyes. They had gone through this discussion too many times to count, all summer long. Joanna was trying so hard to fill in everyone's emptiness that there was no room for anyone else's thoughts.

"Don't act like this is nothing. I'm trying my best to get us all through this," she said, getting heated with every word. "You always try to downplay my feelings or what's been happening here. Our daughter is falling apart and you think it's just going to get better. It doesn't work that way, Graham." She took in a deep breath and let it out. "Look, I need to go for a quick run. Ally and I need some space away from each other. I'll start dinner when I get back."

"I can hear her playing piano. She's found her therapy. And I refuse, Joanna, to get caught up in another discussion about this. Give yourself a break or you're going to drive yourself crazy." He could feel the tensions getting higher and that's not what he wanted.

He took in a quick breath. "What's for dinner?"

"I have pork chops marinating," she answered with little emotion. She was exhausted and she hadn't even taken a step.

Graham reached out to her and kissed her on the forehead. "Go for a run and I'll start dinner, okay."

She nodded putting her glasses over her eyes to hide the flood of tears that were about to spill. Graham always saw everything simpler, leaving her frustrated by her efforts to hold life together. She headed down the driveway and onto the sidewalk as tears came streaming down her face. She forgot about her playlist and ran to the quick beat of her aching heart.

***

Graham loosened his tie and unbuttoned his dress shirt as he made his way upstairs. He too wanted to go for a run tonight. But he would see how everyone was before he left Joanna alone with the kids. He admired his wife for wanting to be at home full time. She was a great designer who had a lot of potential. But her heart was set on being a mother first. Joanna grew up with babysitters and day care. Years ago, when they were talking about starting a family, Joanna vowed that her children would not feel that sense of abandonment that her and her sisters felt everyday when their mother impatiently left them behind for someone else to raise.

Hanging up his suit, Graham thought again about how everything was changing in his once easygoing family. Ally's epilepsy was precarious to manage and Joanna was becoming very controlling. But she was the lioness trying to protect her cubs from the evils of the world. And no matter how hard he tried to get her to ease up on her protection over her litter, he became the invader. Joanna was losing herself in her efforts to be the perfect mother in an imperfect circumstance and he was lost on how to help her to see it.

Changing into a T-shirt and shorts, Graham checked each of the kids' rooms. He heard a standard swing tune coming from the piano so he knew where Ally was. He peeked into Jack's room which was scattered with sporting equipment and car magazines. He wondered how many times Joanna asked him to clean up this mess today? Next he opened Lydia's room and found her stuff all put away neat and tidy, just like Joanna would have done it herself. They were so similar. Lydia was sitting at her desk plugged into some sort of electronic device while bobbing her head and mouthing the words. He walked in getting her attention.

"What?" she said.

"Just coming to say Daddy's home," he said, kissing her on top of her head. "Come help me get dinner started, Lyd."

She unplugged herself and followed her dad. "Where's Mom?"

"Running."

They walked into the kitchen to see a salad half started and cut up potatoes and carrots in foil ready for the barbecue.

"Good, Mom was really mean to Ally today."

Graham turned to face Lydia. "Don't talk about your mother like that."

"Sorry, but it's true, Dad. She really yelled at her a lot."

"Why?" he asked, washing his hands before finding a beer in the fridge.

"Ally was screaming and complaining about how much she hates her life and that she can't do anything like her friends." Lydia grabbed a cucumber and started chomping on the end of it. "And Mom tried to calm her down and talk to her, but Ally wouldn't listen and then Mom just got mad and kept trying to get her to see another side and they just kept yelling at each other."

"Why don't you cut up that cucumber for the salad instead of just eating it," Graham said, taking a long sip of the cold refreshing beer. "Then what happened?" he asked, leaning on the counter.

"I'm not sure, I went outside with Bentley because I was sick of them constantly hollering at each other," she added with teenage attitude. She began slicing the cucumber and adding it to the bowl of lettuce.

"You know Lydia, Mom is under a lot of strain. We're trying to get Ally balanced again on a new medication and that's hard on her system. Mom is trying to get Ally to stay positive and that's been harder than we thought it would be. And it doesn't help if you and Jack just give up and don't make special allowances for Ally right now." He took another swig from the beer bottle and set it down.

"Then what about Jack and me? What about how we feel?" She shot back eating a carrot. "Mom is just all about Ally, all the time. She doesn't ask me about anything anymore. And the only time she notices Jack is when he's playing some sport. And then she's always on her phone instead of watching his game. It's not fair."

Graham took a second before responding. He found the meat marinating in the fridge and placed it on the counter. "I know it seems really unfair to you guys. And like I've told you, it is. But right now Ally is going through a lot and we all need to get through this. But it's her we need to focus on now." He grabbed his daughter's hands in his and leaned on the counter in front of her. "And we will get through this together. We're a family, we won't leave anyone behind, okay?"

She looked into her dad's eyes, feeling his calming spirit and reassurance. He was the rock of their family and Lydia knew nothing would let them fall apart as long as her dad kept them together.

Jack walked in hot, red and sweaty with Bentley following behind. "I'm going to die!" he moaned reaching for his dad's beer. "I'm so thirsty."

"Nice try, Jack," he said, grabbing the bottle back. "Water is in the fridge. Where were you?" he asked, finishing off the beer.

"I went to the park with Bentley and shot some hoops with some other guys who showed up. What's for supper, I'm starving," Jack said, catching his breath in between chugging down two glasses of water.

Jack had grown nearly six inches in the last six months and was getting close to being as tall as his father. He was a good kid and so much like Graham had been at that age. Nothing seemed to bother him and everything just worked out. Ally's condition had definitely affected Jack, but it had made him capable and independent. And more than anything, he wanted to see his family get back to normal again.

"I saw Mom running, she should be home soon. I think she didn't have a good day today, " he added. "She seemed stressed. I tried to help, but it wasn't helping, so I took off."

Graham took in a deep breath and went to start the barbecue. He tossed on the foil wrapped potatoes and came back into the kitchen. "Maybe we should take off to the cabin this weekend. I think this family needs a little holiday." He took out his phone to text Todd and check if they were going up there this weekend.

Ally came into the kitchen looking tired and yet relaxed; the way she did when she finished playing piano. "I'm working this weekend. I can't go to the cabin."

"Can't you trade a shift or something. Your mom really needs a break, I think."

"Well, I need a break from her this weekend."

"Ally," Graham scolded. "Don't talk that way. What's the deal with you and her?"

She looked at her dad and was sorry the instant she said the words. But she wasn't giving in to her mother's pity anymore. "Sorry if that's a mean thing to say. But she wants to talk my head off and I can't handle her constant nagging at me. I'm fifteen."

"Exactly you're fifteen, Ally. She's trying her best. She never had a close relationship with her mom and she wants to make sure you guys do."

"Tell her to just calm down then," Ally said, grabbing a slice of cucumber off the salad. "She panics whenever she hears a noise or if I sleep too long. She wants me to see my friends but then she won't let me stay out late. I want to make some of my own decisions too. I can still think for myself even though my brain is getting fried on drugs."

"At least she can't be mad that you're on drugs," Lydia said, sprinkling green onion over the salad.

Ally started to laugh at her little sister's comment. She laughed harder when Lydia realized what she said. Jack joined in. Graham was relieved to see his family laugh again. As he was bringing the meat to the patio, Joanna came jogging into the backyard. She heard laughing coming from inside the house.

"What's going on?" she asked, wiping the sweat from her forehead.

"Lydia made a joke about Ally being on drugs. They thought it was funny."

"Oh. Are you sure it was meant as a joke and they're not just being mean?"

Graham noticed the concern on her face. "Yes, Jo, it was funny. Go and shower. Chops will be done in fifteen minutes."

She smiled briefly, finding a sliver of relief settle into her aching soul. Her entire run was consumed with the familiar guilt that she couldn't run away from, no matter how hard she tried. It always caught up with her. She saw the neglect through Lydia's behaviour and sarcastic answers. And she knew that Jack would rather be any-where else than at home. Joanna got the message from her twins that their lives didn't matter to her as much as Ally's did. The haunting feeling of not being good enough for her children was devastating. And what bothered Joanna even more was the belief that she didn't really know how to make it better.

But for now her children were laughing and her husband was cooking pork chops. She took in a deep breath bounding up the stairs to clean up before supper. Perhaps things were going to get better, again.

14
Fall

Joanna sat on the window seat in her bedroom as the night breeze slipped through the open crack. Taking a sip of wine, she toasted to another horrible experience that interrupted what could have been a lovely summer day. After enjoying a weekend at the cabin a few weeks earlier, trouble found them again when Ally endured more seizures and ultimately more drug changes. The day after they got back from the cabin, Ally had a seizure in the kitchen. Over the weekend, she was complaining about feeling dizzy. Ally loved to water ski at the lake, but now the reflection on the water was bothering her and suddenly skiing made her nervous.

Today they were in Winnipeg at another neurology appointment. It was late August and the kids were getting prepared to head back to school. Ally in grade 10, and the twins finishing their last year of middle school were beginning grade 8. Their family should be stressing over buying school supplies and back packs. They should be reminiscing about their summer. They should be discussing Ally's future plans when she's finished high school. But none of those discussions were taking place around their dinner table. Joanna and Graham weren't looking forward to the future with great anticipation and expectations like other families they knew. Their conversations were surrounded by medical updates and seizure information and asking unanswerable questions. Around and around these words went, circling in the rooms of their neat and tidy home. Talking privately behind closed doors about fear and wonder for their future. Words of encouragement in the kitchen and hallways as someone in their home always needed reassurance. Expressing deep disappointments in the backyard as plans were always being adjusted for Ally.

During the appointment, the neurologist discussed with them that Ally's blood drug level was high and since her current dosage was not controlling the seizure activity, Dr. Shaw wanted to change her anti-epileptic medication again. Dr. Shaw explained the possible range of side effects, as Ally tried to tune out the list of changes her body and mind would have to endure.

Leaving the hospital, Ally's anger grew with each step down the long hallways. She was upset and distraught with the thought of more side effects, that when they got to their car in the parkade, she burst into tears. And then Ally had another seizure as they pulled out of the hospital parkade and into busy traffic. Graham pulled over into the nearest turnoff. They managed the seizure and then silently and bitterly, made the long drive back to Mountain City.

When Ally had fallen asleep on the way home from Winnipeg, Joanna and Graham discussed their rapidly changing future. Their discussions, like so many in recent weeks, were not going well. Graham could no longer placate Joanna and soothe her into believing everything was going to turn out fine. Even Graham knew that his words were becoming less convincing as he said them. They wondered how she would continue into her adult life; what would happen with her piano ambitions? There were no more good answers or hopeful clichés that convinced Graham and Joanna as they drove home the rest of the way in silence.

Emotionally exhausted from the appointment and long journey home, they picked up a pizza for supper. Lydia was at Nana's house for night and Jack was at hockey conditioning camp for the week. Joanna was secretly relieved that the twins were not around tonight. Opening a bottle of wine, she sipped away her guilt. After the pizza, Ally played piano, watched a few home decorating shows with Joanna and then went to bed.

When Ally had gone upstairs, Joanna wanted to rehash with Graham their disjointed discussion they had in the car. But Graham said he was going for a run, giving him an excuse to avoid his wife. It was just after 9:00 and getting dark when he left the house, giving Joanna the silent treatment. She put away the left over pizza and called Lydia at Eleanor's to say good night and decided not to tell her about the seizure in the car. Lydia was having such a good time sewing and watching old movies that she didn't want to upset her.

Joanna checked on Ally one more time. Sneaking into her room, Joanna opened the door. Ally turned to see who was coming in. "Dad?"

"No, it's me." Joanna sat on her bed.

"Where's Dad? I heard someone leave."

"He went for a run. He'll be back soon."

"Is he mad?"

Was he mad? Joanna asked herself. She guessed he was upset with her constant persistence. She guessed he was mad that his family was suffering like this and it felt like no one could help them. Was he mad?

"No, honey, why do you think he's mad?" she asked, smoothing out Ally's long brown hair.

"Because I woke up in the car when we were coming home and he seemed mad when he was talking to you. And then he was really quiet when we got home and he drank two beers in a row."

Joanna twisted her lips not sure how to answer. "You know, sweetie, when we became parents we had no idea what we were doing. All I know is that I wanted to be great at it. And your dad is amazing and I really thought this was going to be easy. And it was, even with having twins. I loved it when you were all little and we did crafts or bake together."

"I remember doing that," Ally recalled.

"And we would go on picnics and when you got older I took you shopping and lunch. I learned along the way how to be your mother. And then," she paused. "and then when you got epilepsy, I've tried to protect you three from all this trauma and craziness. I thought I could do it too. I really didn't want to mess this up. But I have no one to turn to who understands what our family is going through." Joanna paused with emotion building up in her chest. "I'm sorry if I've failed trying to help you get through this. Because it feels like I have."

"Oh, Mom, you haven't failed," Ally said, sitting up.

Joanna held herself together. "But I've realized that... we have nothing to get through. It's here. We live in it, not through it." She paused again seeing Ally's concern. "I just want to help you, Ally. I just want it all to go away." She burst into tears as daughter held mother, and let her cry.

"Don't cry, Mom. This has been hard on you too. I'm sorry."

"Oh, Ally, don't you apologize, this isn't your fault or something you've done wrong. This is part of our lives now. I need to accept it and help you cope instead of asking why you?"

"You ask that?"

"Of course, I ask, 'God, why is this happening to my daughter?'"

"Any answers?" she asked with a slight smile. "Because He hasn't answered me yet."

Joanna smiled. "I don't want this for you. And I just want to make it better for you. Please be patient because I am trying to figure out how to do that for you and for everyone else."

She lay back down on the bed. "I know." Ally closed her eyes. "I know, Mom," she repeated.

Joanna wiped her eyes dry and took in a deep breath as relief entered her battered spirit. Her daughter did understand how tough this was for them. To admit her shortcomings wasn't easy, but how freeing it was to let go, even a little bit. "I'll let you get some sleep, let's put this day away so we can wake up to a new one."

She kissed her forehead, told Ally she loved her and left her room.

15
Unspoken Escape

Joanna washed her face, brushed her teeth and moisturized with an expensive lotion that promised eternal youth. She put on her pyjamas and brushed her shoulder length hair noticing a few more greys creeping in between the chestnut brown. She looked at herself a second longer. She always thought she was pretty enough. Not glamorous or beautiful, just enough to call herself attractive. Time was playing with the lines on her face and the circles under her eyes. But she wasn't overly concerned. She loved that she took care of her health and tried to always be her best self. To her, that meant more than stressing over aging and dressing like a twenty year old to feel young. Joanna turned off the bathroom light and noticed that Graham had been gone for over an hour.

She caught herself looking into the full length mirror, wondering if she had lost weight. Not that she needed or wanted to. Joanna was stressed. Some women turned to food for relief, but Joanna had turned to running. Perhaps she was using it as an escape, but didn't she deserve something for herself? Grabbing the glass of wine she left on the night stand, she took a sip and made her way to the window bench. She took another sip; it was crisp and inviting. Looking at the glass, she wondered if perhaps this had become a vice too?

Opening the window just a crack, a warm summer breeze blew across her bare legs. She took in a deep breath and leaned back against the wall as she looked outside into the darkness. Only the solar lights lit up the backyard and garden. *Okay, her flowers and vegetables, that was a good escape*, she thought smiling.

Joanna tried so hard to think about something else besides Ally's health concerns and the issues facing her family. Everything was being consumed and turning into something she didn't recognize. Discussions turned into arguments. What really needed to be said was lost in words of blame, words of uncertainty. Words that each of them wanted to hear, but didn't say. But what could be said to make this all go away? Joanna closed her eyes to the familiar pain. Something deep within told her this was not going to get better; more heartache was yet to come. Ally was not doing well, the voice told her.

"God," she whispered out loud. "I can't take anymore. I really can't keep watching her fall apart."

With every seizure, Ally had changed a little bit each time. She was becoming less than herself. She was becoming introverted and staying in her room. Ally's only companion was the piano, playing constantly. They finally had to limit her practicing because she wouldn't stop on her own. She too had found her escape.

Oh God, where did our normal go; where is our middle ground? she wondered. *Who had her family become?* They were strangers under one roof trying to escape the tension and the unknown of when the next seizure would alter who they all were.

Joanna opened her eyes when she heard the back door open and close. Graham came up the back staircase and walked into their bedroom, straight into the bathroom without a glance. He's probably tired. She looked out the window. Just the glow of the cloudy moon shone through the bedroom window. She knew he was exhausted. Working more than he should and then coming home at the end of each day to their strained home life had changed him too. She missed him.

The shower went on for a few minutes and then off again. Moments later, Graham turned off the bathroom light as he walked towards their bed noticing his wife wasn't there.

"I'm over here," she offered, taking another sip of wine.

"Oh," he responded, secretly hoping that she was already asleep. "Come to bed, Jo. It's been a day."

She didn't move. She took another sip and stared out the window. "I had a good talk with Ally before, if that makes things any brighter."

"How is she doing?" he asked, placing his hands on his hips.

Joanna shrugged her shoulders. "I think she's doing, alright, considering. She actually comforted me tonight and not the other way around for a change." She let out a nervous laugh.

Graham walked over and slowly took a seat on the other side of the window seat. "What happened?" he asked.

She shrugged again. "Nothing happened. I just went to check on her and I told her I was trying. It might look like I'm failing, but I'm doing my best to -"

Graham ran a hand through his damp hair with fatigued frustration. "We all know that, Jo. Stop beating yourself up about this. How does anybody prepare to have a kid with a .... brain disorder?"

"Please don't say that everything is going to be fine again, Graham," she said in a dark, crisp whisper. "Because it is not. It's not just going to be fine and we both know it. So stop pretending that every bad thing just goes away and good people get a happy ending. Life's not like that. Real life isn't like that." Tears sprang to her eyes, so she took another gulp of the wine feeling its numbing comfort.

Graham clamped his jaw tight as fatigue and anger collided, swearing softly under his breath. He spoke from a careless heart. He looked up to the ceiling, "Is there anything I can say that you won't rip apart, Joanna? Ripping me apart? Is there any soothing you, anymore?"

Joanna knew she needed to stop talking and apologize. It was not like Graham to swear, but lines were being crossed. She didn't want him soothing her. She wanted him to see and feel her rage as she wanted to blame something or somebody for taking her family down this horrible road.

"Is that what you think I need, soothing?" she questioned, staring him down.

"You know what I mean." He leaned his elbows onto his knees and buried his face in his hands. "Joanna, can we *not* talk about this now? We're both exhausted and not exactly ourselves, are we?" He sat up and took the empty wine glass from Joanna's hands, raising his eyebrows in judgment.

He stood up, towering over her. She stood up, offering him a defiant look. "I'm going to check on Ally." She turned on her heel and left their room, closing the door behind her.

She walked down the hallway and looked back at their bedroom door. They had never walked out on each other. They had never gone to bed angry before. She felt chilled and lonely as she wrapped her bare arms around herself. How do they undo what was said? Joanna couldn't go back in there. So she waited to see if Graham would come for her. She heard him closing the curtains. He wasn't coming to pursue her. The bedside lamp went click, everything was dark. Her head fell foreword as she walked to Ally's room. She opened the door and found her fast asleep, perfectly content, perfectly normal. Stepping inside, Joanna came closer to Ally's bed and straightened out her blankets before kneeling on the floor.

Tears and prayers flowed from her soul. *Please make this all go away. Please make it all better. Please God, can't You help us find happiness and peace again.* The requests poured out like her silent tears. And when she was spent, Joanna got up and crawled back into her bed beside her husband who lay there fast asleep. She wanted to touch his shoulder, yet didn't want to wake him. She wanted him to turn to her and tell her everything was going to be okay as long as they were together. Joanna needed his comfort and that safe feeling she got when he took her in his strong arms. But Graham lay still and silent. Even if their lives did get worse they would still stay together, right? They had to. Joanna knew that she couldn't lose her family over this. Closing her eyes, exhaustion and questions of doubt drifted her off to sleep.

16
Family Gatherings

By the end of September, the Kornelsons eventu-ally found a fragile truce amongst each other. Jack was busy with hockey and volleyball. Lydia decided to join dance again and this year she made the jazz choir at school. Ally was finishing the last of the summer shifts at the Burger Shack. She loved her job as she easily found a camaraderie with the staff and the two owners, who made the effort to make her one of the girls. It made her feel normal. She did find the shifts tiring but they were only going to be open one more week before closing for the winter. Ally was going to miss it.

In school, Ally asked if she could be the accompanist instead of singing in the choir. She was feeling awkward about having to stand in front of people and wanted the security of her familiar piano. Her medications were still making her tired enough to go to bed early each night. But each day Ally was finding it easier to make it through the day and find connections with her friends. She also noticed that her parents had found a tenuous common ground, most days. At least that's what they were trying to portray.

Their conversations were much shorter than usual. Her dad wasn't home as much, either going for runs or back to the office in the evenings, sometimes missing dinner with the family. Her mom ran in the mornings but was always home in time to make them breakfast. The silent tension was better than the yelling that happened all summer long. Sometimes she still heard her parents argue at night behind their closed bedroom door. Now everything just felt stiff and moderately polite.

It was Thursday morning and Ally walked into the kitchen for breakfast. Her dad said something to her mom who was staring out the kitchen window drinking her coffee. Her mom closed her eyes to his words and then placed the coffee mug on the counter with a little too much effort. Crossing her arms over her chest, she turned to Ally. "Good morning Al, did you sleep well?" she asked with a pasted smile.

Ally watched her dad who was looking down in contemplation. "Yep." Looking at the table she decided on yogurt with a banana and granola sprinkled on top.

Graham walked over to Ally at the breakfast table. He kissed her on the top of her head, "Have a good day, sweetheart." And he turned to leave.

"Bye Dad, are you going to be home for supper tonight?" she asked, the question catching her dad's expression of surprise. Yes, she had noticed his absence.

He added a casual shrug. "Of course," he glanced to his wife. "I'll see you tonight." He walked out the door.

Joanna took in a deep breath. "So we are going to Grandpa's birthday party this weekend at Uncle Harry and Aunt Laura's. Are you working Saturday?"

"Unfortunately no," she murmured, dipping her spoon into the creamy, thick yogurt.

Joanna felt her sentiments. No one seemed in the mood for much company these days. The hovering tension was easier to manage in the privacy of their home, but in public, it felt like pretending to be that family everyone assumed perfect.

On Saturday the five Kornelsons piled into their Jeep and drove across Mountain City to Laura's house. It was an average, older bi-level, similar to the one Joanna grew up in. She was grateful that Laura offered to host the party this time. Joanna knew she wasn't feeling like a great wife and mother, let alone a hostess.

Joanna had brought a pear and goat cheese salad on a bed of lettuce with a balsamic vinaigrette dressing. Pauline's comment about how expensive goat cheese was didn't go unnoticed by Joanna, but she let it go. Russ, her husband, didn't want to try it because he had never heard of goats making cheese before. Joanna acted like she didn't hear that comment either.

The kids ate downstairs around the TV. Ally welcomed the distraction so she didn't have to talk with her cousin Tina, who ignored her most of the time. But that also meant there were no kids to distract the adults from their awkward conversations around the crowded dining room table.

Joanna's dad, John, asked Harry if things were busy at the hardware store. Harry loved his job and talked about local building projects. He could talk for hours about nail guns and table saws. Usually it was annoying, but tonight it was a relief to let Harry dominate the conversation. Pauline and Russ sat like they were mostly uninterested until Graham mentioned to Harry the repairs and projects he and Todd had done on their cabin over the past year.

"Stairs, all the way to the boat house," Harry repeated. "That must come in handy carrying beer down to your boat." He laughed harder and louder than necessary. "How big is your boat?" he asked Graham, buttering another slice of bread.

"Must be nice," Pauline interjected to no one in particular.

Joanna took the bait. "What must be nice, Pauline?"

She toyed with the left over vinaigrette soaked pears left on her plate. "Well, to have a cabin by a lake. But then again, the time and expense of keeping it up must be stressful. And the upkeep of a boat, too."

Joanna squeezed the napkin on her lap. "It is nice, Pauline, and no its not stressful actually. It's been good to go there with Todd and Sarah and fix it up. We always have fun when we go."

She felt Graham place his arm around her chair. She wasn't sure if it was because they were so packed around the small table or as a show of support. She didn't care, she was happy he did it.

"Harry's boss has a cabin at Victoria Beach. He lets staff use it from time to time," Laura offered, filling in the awkward gap. "We're hoping we'll be able to go there next year."

"Yeah, it's a beauty, I've seen pictures," Harry added with genuine excitement. "It has a deck that overlooks a lake and an open loft. It's a log cabin. He got it built by one of those log house building outfits. Of course the hardware store supplied what it could. Even some of our guys got to go up there to put it together."

Harry kept talking about his boss's cabin like it was his own; going on like everyone cared. Joanna privately looked down at her watch. It wasn't even 7:00, she was ready to go home.

"So Graham, where is your cabin again?" Pauline asked, knowing full well where it was located. "It's on Lake of the Woods, right? I think we've only been there the one time, so I keep forgetting."

Pauline was referring to Joanna and Graham's wedding day at the cabin. That was the first and last time her family had been to their private oasis.

"Right on the lake, if I remember," Harry said, cleaning off his plate. "Is there more scalloped potatoes and ham?"

Graham took a sip of the sweet tangy punch, wishing he had something stronger. He passed the casserole. "Yes, Harry, the back of the cabin overlooks the lake side."

Russ decided to chime in. "I hear that those lots out there go for half a million dollars. Can you believe it? At least that's what someone in my office told me."

"What!" Pauline gasped. "You spent half a million dollars on your cabin and you live in that huge house across town."

Graham squeezed Joanna's shoulder that was covered by her long hair.

"No Pauline," Joanna answered. "The cabin and land have been in Graham's family for generations." She paused wondering why she was bothering. "And what difference does it make if we spent a million dollars on it? Everyone needs to stop counting other people's money. I don't judge you on what you own."

"That's because we don't own anything compared to you," Pauline blurted out. The room stayed quiet. Russ looked like he wanted to melt into the floor over his wife's bitter comment.

"Are you kidding me, Pauline," Joanna said, tossing her napkin over her plate. "You know, it's not just about what you own in life that makes you happy."

"That's what rich people say because they have it all," Harry said laughing, hoping to cut the mood. But he was unsuccessful as Laura glared at her husband. He really thought he had made a good joke. Harry finished off his second helping. Graham and Joanna sat quietly.

"Why the sudden interest about the cabin anyway?" Joanna asked, with rising annoyance creeping into her voice.

"Oh Joanna, don't be so dramatic," her mother chimed in. "Pauline was just trying to make conversation. No one cares about anybody's stuff anyway." Susan placed her hands on her lap. "You all have good paying jobs and can provide for your families, that's what's important." Then she looked at Joanna who caught her eye. "Or you married someone with a good income, that's good too."

Graham rubbed the back of Joanna's neck that was getting really warm.

He cleared his throat. "Well, we're not here to talk about that, this is about John. How does it feel to be another year older?" Graham asked, trying hard to change the topic.

John smiled and was happy for the diversion. "Oh, I don't know," he said. "When you get to be my age, you're glad your family is gathering for a birthday celebration and not your funeral."

Graham's face went still, instantly thinking about his own dad who never got to see another birthday. Joanna caught the shock in her husband's eyes. Even though he didn't talk about it, she knew that he still missed his dad. John didn't mean to be insensitive, but right now, everything felt sensitive to the Kornelsons.

Laura stood up. "Why don't we clear the table and I'll get the birthday cake and we can give Dad his presents in the living room. Harry, can you call the kids upstairs?"

"That's a good idea," Susan reiterated. "By the way, how is Ally doing Joanna?" she asked, piling up the plates.

"She's good Mom, thanks for asking. They've put her on a new - "

"I'm glad to hear it," Susan said, politely interrupting. "It would be so nice if they could get her under control," she added, walking to the kitchen sink.

Joanna hesitated carrying dishes to the kitchen. Did she care to hear the details about Ally at all? Did anyone in this house care about how her family was struggling or did they just enjoy judging them? The kids rushed upstairs when they heard that cake was being served.

Graham noticed that Ally looked really sad and wasn't looking up. He walked over to her. "You okay, kiddo?"

"I'm not feeling good and I need to take my pills," she answered, putting her arms around her dad.

"Are they in Mom's purse?" he asked, pulling her closer.

She started to cry softly. "Can we go home, Dad?"

Graham guided her into his in-law's bedroom. "Hey, what's going on, Ally?"

She shrugged, clinging to her dad's waist, not letting go. She had overhead most of the adult conversation around the table upstairs and it made her sad. Where had her safe world gone? Why were her aunts and uncles being like that to her parents? She feared that her dad was going to leave. She was petrified that her life was falling apart and it was her fault. Ally loved her family and wanted everything to go back the way it was before the seizures, before all the medication and tests and doctors appointments. She grieved her old life and the happiness her parents once shared.

"Daddy, I just want to go home. I don't want to be here. I have nothing to do. Tina is just on Facebook and doesn't talk to me and everyone is watching stupid shows. I just want you to take me home. Can we go home? I'm not feeling good, I'm feeling dizzy."

He lead her to the bed and hoped for Joanna to come. He was relieved when she opened the bedroom door.

"What's going on?" Joanna asked, walking into the room. "Harry said he saw Ally come up and then -"

"She wants to go home. She says she's feeling dizzy," Graham said, sitting down beside Ally, holding her tight. "She needs to take her pills and they're in your purse."

Joanna sat on the other side of Ally and touched her forehead to see if she had a fever. She so hoped that she was coming down with a cold and nothing more. Not here. Not now. Not again.

"We can go if you want. Let me get my purse and you can take your pills first, okay?" She kissed her on the forehead and headed to the kitchen.

"Is everything okay?" Laura asked.

"Is she having a seizure?" Susan asked, with great intensity. Pauline over heard and walked to her sisters.

"No, she's just not feeling well. Where's my purse?" Joanna asked Laura. "She needs to take her pills now."

"She takes pills when she's feeling dizzy or does the medications stop a seizure?" Pauline questioned with disguised interest.

Laura went to the front entrance and brought Joanna her purse. "No, Pauline. Ally takes pills three times a day."

"Is it the pills that makes her dizzy?" she asked annoyingly.

Joanna held her breath, thinking that it was this evening that was making them all feel dizzy. "No, but yes. Her body has to adjust every time they increase or decrease a drug. This is our life, Pauline. Just trying to manage an illness that refuses to be managed. So a big house, a cabin, who cares? We're just a family living with epilepsy."

Laura gave Joanna a glass of water. She turned and walked away hearing Pauline mutter a comeback.

Ally took her pills and wanted to lay down for a while. Graham lay with her, feeling more than awkward about lying on Harry and Laura's bed, but Ally didn't want him to go. Joanna headed back into the living room to join the rest of the family to watch their dad open his birthday presents and share the store bought marble cake that her mother brought. Joanna had given her dad a $100 gift card to the local gardening centre and a coffee table book about the Queen's English gardens. She couldn't ignore Pauline's eye rolling at the expense of the gift compared to her present of a charming garden gnome.

When Ally and Graham finally came into the living room, Joanna sighed with relief. Graham indicated that he would take her home but Joanna insisted they all leave together. Everyone wished Ally well and hoped she would feel better soon, as if she had caught the sniffles. They offered birthday wishes and apologies for leaving early and were out the door.

Once they arrived back into the safety of their own walls, Jack and Lydia both headed for their rooms to finish homework while Ally said she just wanted to go to bed. But if she slept now she'd be up and awake by midnight. Trying to regulate her sleep amongst her drug induced brain had become a scheduling nightmare.

"I want to go for a quick run, Ally. Why don't you bike beside me," Graham offered, heading up the back staircase. Reluctantly, she finally agreed.

"Is that a good idea?" Joanna challenged. "If she's dizzy, should she be on a bike?" she asked Graham, following him up to their bedroom.

"She'll wear a helmet and I'll be right there. I won't listen to music. She'll be fine." He unbuttoned his shirt and tossed it on the bed. "Plus it will keep her up and the fresh air will be good. For both of us," he added flatly.

Joanna picked up his shirt and went to hang it up in the closet. "Sorry about that horrible dinner," she said quietly.

"It's not your fault your family is so shallow and say stupid things," he said, hastily digging around his sock drawer.

Joanna felt slapped as she closed the closet door. She knew she could never make an acceptable excuse for how her family treated them. But Graham's words were harsh and mean. It was not like him to talk that way, even about her family.

"They mean well, they just don't understand, us," she offered, leaning against the wall.

"Mean well," he spat out. "What is so hard to understand? I can't believe the idiotic crap they say. Do they know how stupid they all sound?" His words were covered with such bitterness, Joanna didn't recognize her husband anymore.

"Graham, that's enough. Sorry they aren't sophisticated like your family, but they are still my family and we have to accept them no differently than they have to accept us."

"Your dad's comment about feeling so fortunate to have a party instead of a funeral on his birthday," Graham said sharply, standing a foot away from his wife. "Really? My dad died way before he was supposed to, Joanna, and he says that to me."

"He didn't mean anything by it," Joanna said, feeling torn between who she really needed to defend.

"He knew he shouldn't have said it and then he didn't have the guts to apologize. No one in your family has the integrity to stand up for what they really mean. They just spew their stupid opinions hoping no one will notice what idiots they are."

He turned to leave, but she reached for his arm, stopping him a second longer. "Hey, listen to me. I said I was sorry for what was said."

He scoffed. "And why are you sorry and want to cover for their f-"

"Stop it, Graham. You're just being cruel. How is that helping?"

He pulled his arm away. "You're right, I'm not helping. I'll leave that up to you." His gave her a cool peck on the cheek. "Don't wait up," he added, walking away even angrier.

Moments later, Joanna sat on the bathroom floor, crying so hard she had to throw up. If she let go of her control, her family would be in chaos and if she kept controlling everything, her marriage would be over. She wasn't sure where she could find a balance.

"Oh God," she repeated over and over. Why was her life falling apart around her? Why was Graham acting so horribly towards her? Sobbing, tears ran down her cheeks, leaving her empty and weak. She was nothing without Graham. She loved him and the life they built together. Why was he pushing her down and away from him? "God," she prayed. "I can't take anymore."

"Mom, are you okay. I heard you throw up?" Jack asked outside her bathroom door.

She cleared her throat and dried the tears from her face with a towel. She didn't want her son to see her so broken.

"I'm okay, Jack."

She straightened out her hair before opening the door so he could see how strong she was. "I think I may be coming down with something, that's all."

The knowing look in her son's eyes told her that he didn't believe her. He was as tall as she was now and it was hard to hide from his honesty. "Maybe you ate too much of that awful casserole goop Aunt Pauline brought. What was that anyway?"

Joanna laughed as Jack gave her a hug. She willed away more tears that sat at the surface.

He pulled away. "Do you want anything? I can make you tea?"

She nodded. "That would be nice, Jack. Thank you."

He went downstairs and in a few minutes brought his mother tea in her favourite cup. Joanna thanked him as he headed back to his room. He was so much like his father. Or at least how he used to be with her. Graham treated her like a queen, always had. He cared about her morning sickness with Ally and tended to her every need. And when her postpartum got the better of her after the twins were born, he was so patient and generous with his time, he even took a few weeks off to help her adjust to two babies and a toddler. When his father had passed away, he put his own grief aside and was a constant source of comfort for his mother.

Graham was a handsome younger man. He was getting even more attractive as he aged. He had an easy charm and class about him without really trying. He had a kindness and generosity, making Joanna feel safe and cared for. Joanna was so grateful that he chose to love her. She felt blessed all these years to have such an amazing husband and now in a heartbeat, he had become a stranger. She wanted her husband back, she wanted her solid marriage again.

Sitting alone on the window bench, sipping her tea, she wondered about his time spent away from the family. Was she becoming such an awful person that he found it better to be away from her? Suddenly she let her tired mind roam dangerously; fear gripped her as every horrible scenario ran through her head. Was he becoming a workaholic? Was his law practice in trouble? Was he having an affair? Her tea turned cold as she tried to erase these questions that danced mockingly in her mind. He talked so little these days she didn't know where to begin tearing down the wall building higher between them.

She heard Graham and Ally come through the kitchen door. They were laughing and joking. It made Joanna sad somehow. She heard Ally go to the bathroom, flush the toilet and then brush her teeth. Then her bedroom door closed. Graham did not come up.

Taking her tea cup into the kitchen, she noticed Graham was not there either. All the lights were turned off, except for in his den. He was talking softly to someone. Quietly, she walked down the hall and stared into the room. He just clicked his cell phone and reached for the bottle of scotch and poured himself a drink.

Joanna swallowed hard. Which way does she turn? Confront him, or turn away? She decided to take a step back to hide the pain in her eyes.

"Hey Graham, coming to bed?" she asked with a strained casualness in her voice. She swallowed hard when he didn't respond. "Who were you talking to?"

Joanna gulped down what she hoped would be the truth. He gulped down the burning, peaty scotch and placed the glass back on the counter. "My mom. I just wanted to talk to my mom," he answered, quietly without moving.

Joanna believed him and breathed a sigh of relief. "Okay, well I'm going to bed now. Coming?"

He poured a bit more. "Yeah, in a minute." She leaned closer, watching him take a small sip as he stared out the picture window into the dark street, seeing nothing at all. She saw his reflection in the window as his eyes were filled with tears. Joanna turned and went to bed alone.

17
Thread Bare

A week later, Joanna received a family email sug-gesting that she host Thanksgiving this year since Laura had everyone over for their dad's birthday. Joanna shook her head as she finished reading the email. That's not how this was supposed to work. They were to take turns between Easter, Thanksgiving and Christmas and it was Laura's turn to do Thanksgiving. Joanna knew that Laura, Pauline and her mother hated hosting family events and tried to persuade their little sister to have it at her house, always reminding Joanna that she had the space and time to prepare a big dinner.

Joanna ran her hands through her hair. She closed her iPad in defeat and frustration deciding to respond later. Maybe she would ask Graham about it. Then again, maybe not. They had not spoken about the birthday party fiasco since the night it happened. How would she tell him her family would be in their home for Thanksgiving which was just over a week away.

They managed to find an unsettled, fragile line of peace between them. He had made efforts to come home for dinner and offered to pick up the kids from their school and church activities. Joanna still oversaw their schedules: hockey, dance, piano, school dances, homework, she was on top of it all. Her family was her priority and she would keep it together no matter what obstacles stood in the way. She attempted to schedule more family nights. They often included Todd and his family and Graham's mom. Family friends from church would come over for chilli and board games. They felt settled when entertaining, but in reality it helped them to avoid each other.

Joanna needed to finish decorating the house for Thanksgiving. She got some pumpkins from the Farmer's Market Store, and placed them around the terra cotta pots of orange and red chrysanthemums that graced her front porch. She stood on the sidewalk in front of her house admiring her humble display. She was pleased. She waved to a few familiar passersby and neighbours going on mid morning walks. They would chat, ask about Ally and move on.

A car honked and Joanna turned around thinking it might be Hannah heading off to school. It was Clark Banman, a local realtor and one of Graham's golfing buddies. He pulled up in front of Joanna and got out of his car. Shades, a brown leather jacket and he looked like a cologne model. He was good looking and he knew it, which made him less appealing than he gave himself credit for.

He leaned up against the open car door. "So it looks like your staging the house to sell?" he joked.

"Nope, just getting a few things ready for Thanksgiving," she answered, shading her eyes from the sun.

Clark closed the car door, came around and stood beside Joanna on the sidewalk. "You know my offer still stands about the job. I could really use you to stage and prep houses for selling. We're just about to get the condos downtown ready for some open houses. And you've got the touch, Joanna."

Joanna looked back at her home. Clark was a charmer. He could sell anything, especially using his charm and debonair style to his full advantage. For years he had been reminding Joanna that he wanted her on his team and wouldn't stop until he got what he wanted. It all seemed so innocent. Then.

"I've got a pretty full life. I can't imagine going back to work right now."

"Yeah, that's right." He touched her shoulder in caring response. "How's Ally doing? Graham mentioned her seizures a few times at The Club."

"We're managing. Figuring things out as we go," she answered, crossing her arms to the brisk fall wind.

"Sounds like it's been pretty difficult. On all of you, not just Ally."

And how would he know that? Joanna thought. It doesn't sound like something Graham would have shared casually with his golfing buddies on the 16th green.

"I suppose any major life change on a family would make it pretty challenging. You never know when life is going turn everything upside down," Joanna answered truthfully.

He touched her lightly again. "You're right. How do you prepare yourself for life's big storms? I can't imagine that it's been easy. But it looks like you're keeping things together."

Joanna brushed away the hair that blew across her face. "Oh, I'm trying to."

Unexpected tears sprang to her eyes. She looked down.

"I'm sorry, I didn't mean to upset you," he said with deep sincerity.

She kept it together. "No, no, sorry Clark, I'm okay. It's just that it has been really hard on all of us. Never knowing if and when she'll ever seizure again. All the drugs she's on and how it's changed her. Changed us all." Why was she opening up to this man? "But I don't want to keep you from anything," she said, stepping away towards the sidewalk leading up to the house.

"No, don't apologize, Joanna. I just drove by and saw you here, by yourself, so I thought I would come say hi." He stared directly at her for a second too long. "Do you want to go grab a cup of coffee with me. We could talk... about...life. Me, hiring you." He smiled with that charming grin that was on his for sale signs.

"I can't. I'm looking all frumpy and -"

"You look great, Joanna. You could never pull off frumpy. Come on, one cup."

Joanna licked her lips and looked away from Clark. How quickly she wanted to go and continue to be wooed and told how wonderful she was. But she knew his wife, Marie. And he was Graham's friend from The Club. Then she looked at her house, her home. Inside it was getting thread bare as her family was trying so hard to regroup.

It had been so difficult and she was so weary from all the trying. But they were all still here, trying.

She looked at Clark and took a half step closer. "I can't Clark. But thank you. I really appreciate your thoughtfulness, it means a great deal to me. But I need to go."

"Hey, I said I would never give up, didn't I," he said, accepting his loss as he slowly walked back to his car. "And, if you need anything, or someone to, well, just call me."

"Have a good day," she offered and quickly made her way up the walkway, up the front steps and into the safety behind the wooden door. Closing her eyes and leaning against the wall, she told herself to breath. That was no job offer. She hated to admit how much she missed the attention for being something other than a housewife. She felt noticed and recognized, even in frumpy sweats and an old hoody. The only problem was, the attention came from the wrong man.

***

A few days later Joanna was prepping the turkey dinner and tried to forget her chance meeting with Clark. She reminded herself that it was nothing; he was a mere acquaintance who happened to stop by.

Joanna sautéed the onions and celery for the stuffing, adding her usual spice blend of fresh sage, parsley, thyme, salt and pepper. Stirring it together in the melted butter, Joanna thought about what she really wanted for her life. Perhaps getting a job again was the diversion she needed. Deep down, she was living the life she had always wanted and she was happy being a wife and mother. It was all she had ever wanted. It had always been enough.

She turned back to the frying pan as the aroma filled the kitchen with the smell of Thanksgiving. An unexpected smile crept up on her, she was happy with her life. It wasn't perfect as they continued to muddle their way through this trying time, but Joanna was making dinner for her family in the home of her dreams. She resolved to make the best of this Thanksgiving weekend and find a place in her heart to be thankful.

But on the Friday night of the holiday weekend, the faint and familiar sounds of Ally having a seizure came crashing in on Joanna's good intentions. Ally was in the piano room looking for her music when she fell to the ground, knocking her head of the side of the bench. Surrounding her, Joanna, Graham, Jack and Lydia, managed to rally around Ally.

With hopes dashed, Joanna didn't have any reserves left to create the perfect Thanksgiving that she had planned. When she was crying in her room after everyone had gone to bed, Graham found her sitting on the window bench. He held Joanna in his arms as tears of desperation for her daughter ran down her face. His arms felt secure and loving again. Joanna sobbed freely. There was no need for words or explanations or the endless unanswered questions that gave her no peace. She just needed him.

They managed to get through the holiday with the extended family. Ally kept it together to join them for dinner, but quickly found solace in her room. Graham and Joanna let her escape from the dining room to avoid the artificial conversation around the table. On Monday as they were preparing to go to Nana Ellie's for Thanksgiving dinner, Ally felt miserable. She was emotionally spent from getting over another seizure and she didn't want to get out of bed. She loved her dad's side of the family, but not even they were motivation enough to leave the sanctuary of her room.

Graham called his mom to let her know they wouldn't be coming. Ally needed them at home and they didn't want to push her right now. This seizure had effected Ally in a different way and they knew they had to be patient with her. Eleanor understood their decision, even though she was sad for her precious granddaughter.

The twins were in the kitchen with Joanna when Graham hung up the phone with his mother. They were quiet and contemplative. Joanna looked at Jack and Lydia who were obviously lost in their own emotional upheavals. Graham started unloading the dishwasher.

"Hey, I just want everyone to know something," Joanna announced, gaining their attention. "We're going to make it. I know watching Ally go through this is really hard on us all. But above all, we are a family who is going to stick together and we will be strong, together." Joanna looked at them. "I know we've had a hard time trying to make sense out of this. But I believe that for whatever reason Ally has epilepsy, there is a bigger purpose for us all." She wiped away a single tear that ran down her face.

"Why her, Mom? Why did God give Ally epilepsy?" Lydia asked after a moment.

"I don't know how to answer that for you, honey. I don't. Come here," she answered, holding her daughter close.

Graham walked around the island and stood beside Joanna. "You know, I don't ask 'why her' anymore, kiddo. Stuff happens and this is what's happening to her, to us. And your mom is right, we are still a family who will stick together." He wrapped his arm around his wife and pulled her in close.

Jack thought before he spoke. "Thanks, Dad. I think we needed to know that." He looked at Lydia and she nodded cuddled up next to her mom.

The door bell rang. "Who's that?" Graham asked, heading to the front door.

But the door was already opened. "We're barging in, Graham," Todd said, walking into the front foyer carrying a box of food with Nora and Abigail trailing behind. Sarah was carrying a roaster and Nana Ellie was holding a pie in each hand.

"We started eating dinner and it just didn't feel like Thanksgiving. So we packed it all up and here we are," Sarah explained.

Eleanor looked at her son. "Now it's Thanksgiving," she managed to say with tears in her eyes. Jack took the pies to the kitchen so she could hug Graham.

"Thanks, Mom."

Todd brought the box of side dishes to the kitchen and announced he would check on Ally to see if she wanted to come down and join them.

"What's going on?" Joanna said, following Todd from the kitchen and watched him bound up the stairs for Ally's room.

"It's Thanksgiving, Jo," Graham said, picking up Nora in his arms. Todd and Ally came walking down the stairs.

"Come on, I've got a half eaten turkey leg somewhere in there," Todd said as everyone headed back into the kitchen.

Joanna handed out the plates and cutlery as they began digging into the box, finding bowls of stuffing, potatoes, gravy, carrots and cranberry sauce. Graham carved the rest of the turkey as everyone found a spot around the table and island. With grateful hearts, they dug into the best meal they had ever shared together.

"This is Thanksgiving," Ally whispered to Nana with a smile.

She hugged her granddaughter, sitting beside her. "Yes it is, Ally. This is what it's all about."

18
Reclaiming Life

Winter had descended early with snow storms hitting the Canadian Prairies by mid November. Layers of icy snow coated the streets and highways in and around Mountain City. It was definitely going to be a white Christmas this year. And along with that would be a cold winter to endure.

Joanna found the last plastic bin of winter gear stored in the attic. The third floor of their house had become an unusable storage room for all their off season, outgrown and forgotten collections over the years. From cribs to toys, outgrown clothes and Graham's law text books, it was up there lost in the abyss of stuff.

Opening the lid she found ski goggles and extra toques, gloves and one boot that fit Jack when he was five. The winter wind howled loudly way up on the abandoned third floor as Joanna looked out the window. There was nothing to see but a layer of ice crystals that caked to the panes of glass. She sighed deeply hating the mess that lived up here, but not having the interest to do anything about it.

The holidays were just over six weeks away and already Joanna and her sisters were trying to figure out who would host, who would bring what dish, and who would organize the awful round of the nasty Santa gift exchange. Then there was the dilemma of buying their parents the, 'this is from your three daughters', Christmas present. It usually ended in deflated joy after John and Susan opened the gift and would insist that they all shouldn't have, and then exchange it for something else in January. January, maybe she would finally organize this mess after Christmas. Christmas, Joanna's head fell forward in defeat as she sat on an old wooden trunk that was filled with forgotten items from someone's past.

She picked up that one single ski boot and remembered their vacations to Banff when the kids were little and recalled how quickly Jack took to skiing down the bunny hill, while Lydia just wanted to make snow angels. Graham and Joanna were able to ski with Ally on the bigger hills before they would all meet at the lodge and spend their evenings in front of the roaring fire place eating chilli on a bun, Jack's favourite. She tossed the boot back into the bin wondering where its mate had disappeared.

Looking around she saw a margarita glass brought back from one of their other winter vacations. Every winter they planned a trip away, just the two of them. Another gust of wind slammed against the walls. She picked up the glass remembering their week in Cozumel, feeling like the hot Mexican sun was only a dream faint in her memories. She looked at the lonely ski boot. The kids were growing up so fast. Ally would be leaving for university in a couple of years. Although her future seemed so uncertain at times.

It felt premature to think that one day Ally could be seizure free and move out and start her life without their constant, watchful eye. That thought played out in Joanna's mind from time to time. What was it like before Ally was diagnosed with epilepsy? Before all the drugs and blood work and brain scans and specialist appointments. Before the medical bracelet and having to fill out so much more paperwork for school trips, many that included her as chaperone. What was it like before every conversation at church, or the grocery store, or in the hockey rink, always came back to how Ally was doing? Chronic illness was something she never imagined would become a familiar topic of conversation wherever she went.

Joanna sighed, feeling overwhelmed by the memorabilia that told the story of who this family once was. They were like everyone else who had a dream for their family, filled with promises of vacations and memories. But their life had taken a turn that always seemed to have another bend in the road, never knowing if and when another seizure would stand in the way of their happiness. Joanna got up and resigned to the fact that she was only reliving their history of a life they once knew, not finding lost winter gear. She put the margarita glass down and closed the door to their past.

*   *   *

"Hello, Jo, where are you?" Graham asked, walking into the kitchen. He took off his coat and hung it on the hook by the back door and saw no sign of anyone at home. He glanced at the calendar. Jack had hockey practise tonight. That was it. Then he smelt the chilli simmering on the stove and walked over to give it a quick stir.

"Hey family, anyone here?" he called out again, taking a quick spoonful before anyone walked in. Life had found a sliver of happiness since their difficult Thanksgiving weekend and Ally's last seizure. If one thing was becoming clear about their family, they were finding a place of coming together when life had thrown them sideways. It wasn't what Graham had wanted nor expected, but he was reconciling that their life would always be different.

Graham had always found life to be so simple. Nothing was ever too difficult. He survived university, passed the bar and worked hard to achieve his goal, always knowing it would happen. Finding Joanna and convincing her to become his wife fit right into the life he wanted. Then the house and kids came just as scheduled. Although the twins were an unplanned joy, they were grateful for a son and a sister for Ally.

The cancer diagnosis and sudden death of his father had rocked Graham's foundation. His dad was his pillar. They spent time together on the golf course, talking business over lunch at The Club or tinkering on the boat together at the cabin.

Within months of getting over his dad being gone, life knocked him down again when Ally's illness changed them all. He and Joanna were great together when life was easy and manageable. But they had a hard transition dealing with Ed's death and Ally having seizures all within a year. They turned on each other with vicious words and blame in the face of adversity. Thankfully, little by little, they were finding the peace between them that they once knew. And each day, as they sorted out their feelings and circumstances, he and Joanna were finding confidence in their marriage and family again.

"Hey, Joanna," he called again, taking one more mouthful of the spicy chilli. He loosened his tie and took off his suit jacket and walked into his den with his brief-case. He had a few client files to review for tomorrow's set of meetings.

"Here you are, why didn't you answer? Where is every-one?" he asked, kissing his wife on the top of her head. "What's this?" He looked at the computer screen Joanna was intently reading.

"Graham, please say yes," she begged, turning around in his leather office chair.

He stepped closer and looked at the screen a little closer. "Cuba?"

"I've been looking at resorts in Mexico, Jamaica and Cuba and figuring out which weeks are cheapest. Graham, the week of Christmas would be the best deal. That means we wouldn't be around for family gatherings but -"

Graham raised his eyebrows with playful interest. "Really? When can we pack? And what does cheapest mean to you, Joanna? What would we do with the kids over the holidays? That doesn't seem like you to leave the kids over Christmas."

He scanned her face again, seeing the hopeful anticipation.

"Oh, you want to go as a family and leave the "rest" of the family behind. I get you now."

He looked at the screen again and saw sexy, bikini clad women and sun bathing couples sauntering effortlessly along the empty sandy beaches of Varadero. He knew it never really looked that empty and serene as many pasty, white Canadians flooded these resorts all winter long. He too was not looking forward to another long and awkward Christmas day spent with her family. *A break from all that tension would be nice*, he thought, reading the rest of the screen.

"Graham, I realized today that in a few short years the kids are going to be gone and it's not going to be so easy to take family vacations anymore. Even with Ally working in summer we can hardly find time to go to the cabin together. Can we do this instead of our week away in January?"

Graham scrolled down the screen to see the final damage to his bank account. He took in a deep breath and clicked the icon that would be submitting and processing their request to fly out to Cuba for one week of family fun.

Joanna looked at the screen and let out a burst of excitement, hugging and kissing her husband. "Let's go tell the kids. I think their watching TV."

Graham hugged his wife. "No, let's not. Let's surprise them. On the day we leave, we'll pack their suitcases and secretly hide it in the car, and then we'll tell them we're going to Pauline's place, but then we go to the airport instead and surprise them."

Joanna took a step back. "No, we can't do that anymore, Graham. You know that Ally doesn't react well to surprises. She needs to plan and know ahead of time. I don't want to risk another seizure just before we board the plane."

"But they love surprises," he pleaded. And he loved surprising his kids.

"No, we can't. Not anymore," she resigned, crossing her arms. "Ally needs time to process. She gets so anxious if things just get sprung on her, it's not fair. Why can't we tell them now?"

He knew that this was part of their new normal for his family. Ally's seizures affected her frontal lobe which in turn compromised her long term thinking and ability to plan. She did need time to think things through and found herself in a state of panic if she didn't know what was happening in advance.

"Okay, how about we wait until just before Christmas, when they start complaining about having to go to family gatherings?"

Joanna stared at her husband, "Okay, deal!" She kissed him and headed to the kitchen yelling at the kids that it was time for dinner. Graham smiled, following his wife.

***

The week in Cuba was the paradise they had hoped it would be. And making it perfect, Nana Ellie, Todd and Sarah, Abigail and Nora joined them. When Graham told his family their Christmas plans, they asked if it could become an extended family holiday. It was a natural and easy decision to all fly down together. They were more than family, they were friends.

Days were spent playing and swimming at the beach where Lydia and Ally made sand castles with their little cousins. Jack, Todd and Graham rented everything that moved in the water, while Sarah and Joanna sat on beach loungers enjoying long chats or reading, while being served margaritas all day long. Nana Ellie didn't care for that much sun, so her afternoons were spent doing activities in the common rooms in the resort. In the evenings, they gathered again at one of the amazing restaurants and took in late night shows while Nana Ellie offered to watch the grandkids.

It did feel strange to be celebrating Christmas in bikinis and sunglasses surrounded by palm trees and sunshine. Joanna thought about her family gathering at her parents' house without them. Twinges of regret occasionally found its way in, interrupting Joanna's relaxation while sipping her mojito. She wished her family would be different. More than anything she wanted their acceptance. Trying so hard to make things right with her mom and sisters had proved to be futile over the years. Joanna felt like the outcast, always the odd one out. She wanted a life that was different from how she grew up. And somehow, it became interpreted that she wanted a life of excess and better and expensive.

Leaning back in her lounger, Joanna let the fresh layer of sunscreen soak in her bronzed skin. What she knew for sure was that her goal was never about having more than anyone else, especially her sisters. She wanted a life where she could raise her kids. She wanted a husband who was caring and loving. She wanted the life she was living. Joanna was blessed and she knew it. No one had to tell her.

"What are you smiling about?" Sarah asked, reaching for her icy drink.

"Oh, just thinking about my family back home, enjoying Christmas without us."

"And that makes you smile?" Sarah said, scanning the beach for her girls.

Joanna sipped the last of her drink. "My sisters lives are very different from ours and it makes it... awkward."

She placed her sunglasses on top of her head and looked at Sarah, wondering how much to say. "I know that I am in an enviable position with a lot of my friends and my sisters. I know that sounds brag-y and elitist, but that's not what I mean at all." Joanna paused, weighing her words carefully. "Working is an option for me. We have a cabin and a nice home and we get to travel. But I don't want to be envied or despised because of it. This is my life and I am so grateful."

"Why do you care so much about what other people think?" Sarah questioned, adding lotion to her arms.

Joanna looked at her sister-in-law. "And you don't? I don't believe you, Sarah."

Sarah shook her head. "No, I don't. I don't care about what others think about me at all, ever. What a waste of my time to dwell on 'what ifs and maybes'. I think you have a happy, good life because you put energy into what's important to you. You love your home and use it for your family and friends. You love your family and want to create a great childhood full of memories for them. It's not about what you can give them, it's about how you've raised them that matters."

Sarah took another sip of her drink. "All week your kids have been so thankful that you took them on this trip.

167

They're not spoiled, rotten, rich kids demanding more. You care about people and making everyone feel that they are welcome into your life and that they matter to you. You make it look easy and natural."

Joanna laughed. "Well, thank you, but it's not easy." She thought about what Sarah said. "I do want my kids to become amazing adults. But with Ally... and then the twins feeling neglected." Joanna recalled what they had all gone through since the first seizure.

She took in a deep breath. "Graham and I were having some troubles a little while ago."

Sarah sat up on the lounger. "I'm not that surprised, Joanna. I absolutely saw the stress you were under with Ally and everything. But you and Graham, you guys are that rock solid couple. I can't imagine how tough it must have been for all of you."

Joanna looked out onto the beach landscape seeing her family running and laughing in the water. "Ally's seizures and drug changes and all her appointments really has taken a toll on us. Graham and I didn't always agree or manage everything the same way."

"And how are things now? You guys look fine."

She turned to Sarah. "It's good, right now. But this whole thing has made us feel vulnerable, as a couple, as a family. It's like we all fell down into this place of unknown when Ally got diagnosed. And it's so unpredictable. We just never know when the next fall out will be."

"Oh Joanna, I never thought of it that way. I'm sorry, I know how difficult this was for all of you. But it looked like you were handling everything so well."

"And we were, and then we weren't and now we know that we take it as it comes. But I don't want to go around saying how awful our lives are when everyone looks at us and sees our nice house and Graham is a successful lawyer from this great family. No one understands that 'life' happens to everyone, why should we be set apart?"

Sarah took another sip of her watered down margarita. "One thing I've learned from being a doctor's wife is that no illness or accident happens to one type of person. Rich and poor people get cancer and young and old people get into accidents. Life doesn't pick favourites when it's handing out bad circumstances."

"Isn't that the truth. Epilepsy is so random, at least that's what it feels like to me, anyway. We've asked a thousand why questions and we will never know."

"You and Graham have made such a good life for yourselves and I don't mean just financial. I mean you are connected with your kids, they respect you guys. Your every-days mean something to you and you definitely don't take your life for granted." She reached out and touched Joanna's oily arm. "Be grateful, Joanna. You've made it this far, you'll make it the rest of the way. You've done a great job and you've worked hard to have these amazing kids. That just doesn't happen without a great mother."

"Thanks Sarah," Joanna said, with a sense of relief.

"And stop caring about what your sisters or friends or gossipy people say or think about you! Take it from me, my father was a politician. I know all about having to let that negative talk go."

"Mommy!" Abigail called out, running to the loungers. Immediately Joanna sat up with alarm.

"Ally made a big castle for me!"

Relieved that the excitement about Ally was good this time, Joanna and Sarah got up and walked down to the edge of the water as Graham, Todd and Jack joined in, making them a mote and river from the castle. Ally looked up at her mom with a huge smile that Joanna had not seen in a long while. Then Abigail gave her cousin a big hug. The four year old was so excited to have a sand castle, not realizing it would be swept back into the ocean in a few short hours.

Joanna went back to the loungers and got her camera, snapping pictures of her family enjoying December 24th in the Cuban sunshine. It had been too long since she had seen her family this happy. Joanna needed these memories captured. She knew that one day she may need to look back and remember these good days when life wouldn't being so kind.

19
Harmony & Understanding

Joanna couldn't help herself as she browsed through a gardening magazine she noticed in the drug store. Spring felt like a lifetime away as she stood in the checkout line to purchase Ally's medications. Joanna looked at the time on her phone. She was meeting some friends for lunch on this very cold, mid February day. It definitely did not look like spring was only a few more weeks away when the wind-chill read -43C this morning.

But at least her fading tan was a reminder of their amazing week in Cuba. The time away was what they all needed. Not only did it give them a break from the winter, but they found each other again. The beachside conversation with Sarah gave Joanna the confidence she lacked. Joanna often got caught up in other people's opinions and too many times it affected her with negative thoughts and self-loathing. She needed to change the conversations she was having with herself.

Joanna finished her errands and drove to meet a group of women whom she had known over her lifetime living in Mountain City. Karen and Fran were friends from high school. Lori joined the group as one of the mothers they got to know when their kids were all in kindergarten. Grace's husband Ben was Graham's law partner and they became friends when they moved back to Mountain City. Together they had formed a friendship based on raising babies to teens and living with husbands who never understood them. They were meeting at the cafe in the large golf/curling club and banquet hall called The Club. It overlooked the 18 hole golf course that held formal dinners and weddings. In winter it wasn't exactly beautiful but it still offered a great place to meet for lunch.

"So then I asked him, 'why do I need to tell you to shovel the driveway when you can clearly see that the snow is nearly a foot high'," Karen said to Fran as Joanna joined them at the table. "Joanna, do you have to nag Graham to do his part around the house?"

She sat down and stuffed her purse under her chair. "No, not really, I guess. He just does it, or now Jack does a lot of the shovelling and mowing in summer."

She ordered herself a water while Karen continued on with her rant. "Well, I told Cal that if he doesn't start helping with the lawn and the gutters or the pool this summer, I'm hiring a pool boy." Karen giggled like a teenager from a 1950s movie. "And I get to hand pick him myself."

In minutes, Lori and Grace joined them in the quaint cafe that was decorated with whites and feminine accents appealing to the ladies of the community. On the other side of the hall sat a bar and restaurant that was flanked with rich, dark mahogany wood and furnished with deep, red club chairs. Designed on the masculine side, for those reliving each stroke of their golf game or where business meetings took place over drinks. But together each room opened into a grand common foyer. It was a great facility to have in their area and busy throughout the year. Joanna was proud to see her touches in the building as she was part of the team who redecorated The Club a few years earlier.

Joanna and her friends were chatting about recent winter vacations, kids and husbands over soups and the sandwich of the day. They talked about everything from their Pinterest boards to school gossip and life in general. They talked about ordinary things that everyday women talked about, until the inevitable question was asked about how Ally was doing. No one else talked about their kids' medical histories, just Joanna. Grateful for their concern, but always with the feeling of being set apart.

"So Joanna, tell me, how has Ally been doing? Spencer tells me that she's doing great at school and seems to be fine," Lori asked as her coffee was being refilled.

Her son Spencer was a friend of Ally's, although she didn't mention him a lot. "That's good to hear," Joanna replied. "Taking it as it comes," she simply added in a neutral tone.

"So no more seizures then?" Grace asked, fishing for more.

Joanna took a sip of coffee. "Like I said, we just deal with whatever comes our way with Ally or any of our kids for that matter. Has anyone heard how the Roberts boy is doing after that big hit in the game last week. Jack said the team was really shaken up," she stated, trying to derail the conversation.

Fran answered, "I heard he got another concussion and he may be finished for good from all sports." They all shook their heads in pity, sipping their hot beverages. "So tragic when that happens to a young kid with so much potential."

Joanna tried not to read into the comment and debated whether to change the subject again or use this opportunity to share their experiences in dealing with life's interruptions. She cleared the throat. "Actually, it is hard when you think your kid's life is going one way and then something happens and you have to figure it all out again."

"But it's just hockey," Karen answered with slight annoyance. "I mean it's not like his life is over or changed forever. He can still function and drive and whatever, he just can't play hockey."

Joanna felt their gazes. "But how do we know he wasn't destined to play in the NHL? Ally's life isn't over either and she can function. But a lot has changed for us. When something happens to you and you don't have control over it, it changes everything."

No one knew what to say; leaving an awkward silence around the table.

"Sorry," Joanna said, looking down into her coffee. "I didn't mean to sound like a know-it-all. Believe me, I don't know it all. It's hard to deal with unexpected health issues. But you learn to take it one minute at a time, everyday."

Lori chimed in, touching Joanna's arm. "You're very brave, Joanna. You've handled Ally's situation very well. She seems to be doing so well."

They all nodded in agreement.

But no one saw the tantrums and fits Ally had in the privacy of their home. No one saw the tears and the conversations of assurance for a better tomorrow. No one saw the deepening cracks and the fragile healing in her marriage and the constant guilt that raged inside, telling her that Jack and Lydia were being neglected in the middle of this mess. They all saw what Joanna wanted them to see, that she could put back the pieces of their lives and everything would continue to be perfect for the Kornelson family. Their pity made her feel hollow and empty inside.

"Well, if it isn't the ladies who lunch," Clark Banman said as he sauntered up to their table. "So what could possibly be so interesting today?" he asked, standing right behind Joanna, singling her out. Joanna saw the surprised looks on the faces of Fran and Karen, curious by Clark's familiarity with her.

"Hi Clark," Lori answered. "You know girls don't spill the beans to anyone!"

"Especially real estate agents," Karen chimed in, laughing heartily breaking the strange tension.

"Now this one, here," he said, putting his hands lightly on Joanna's shoulders. "I've been after this one for years, to work for me. Do you ladies have any idea how amazing and talented she is? Just look at this place," Clark said, dipping closer to Joanna. She caught the faint smell of whiskey on his breath.

They looked at Joanna, who reached out to grab her bill that was left in the middle of the table, glad to shake off Clark's inappropriate closeness.

"Since when did you want to get into real estate, Joanna?" Fran asked with great interest.

"You've never said anything like that before," Grace added.

"I don't," Joanna said, trying to look casual.

"Stager!" Clark called out a little too loud. "I need a stager and a gal to design my condos." He reached down and grabbed the bill out of Joanna's hand. "No, no let me take care of that for you, Joanna."

She turned around in her chair trying to retrieve the bill. "No, Clark, it's okay."

"No, no this is what it would be like if you were working for me. I'd buy you lunch every day." He tipped the bill in adieu and sauntered to the hostess' counter. Joanna stood up but it was too late. She didn't want to go running after him and make a bigger scene.

"Well, well, well," Karen chirped, pushing her coffee cup forward. "That was interesting."

Joanna shook her head, sitting down. "Oh, that Clark, always a charmer," she said, glancing to see that he was actually leaving.

"Too much of a charmer if you ask me," Fran added leaning in. "You heard that his wife kicked him out," she said in a hushed whisper.

"Really? Marie finally did it?" Lori asked. "I'm not surprised, he's a bit of a shyster if you ask me. I don't buy his good looks and charm for one minute. He's always flirting with all his friends' wives."

Joanna swallowed hard feeling so awful that he bought her lunch, making her feel like his next deal to close.

"And Cal told me that he is all over the beer cart girls when he's golfing," Karen joined in. "So, why his interest in you Joanna?"

"Oh Karen, don't tease her," Grace said, touching Joanna's arm. "She has found her catch with Graham. Clark is just being Clark."

"And I would never work for him, if that's what you're all thinking," Joanna added to clear the air. Although, that's not what the group was thinking at all. "Anyway, I need to get going."

"I guess your lunch is taken care of," Fran teased.

Joanna politely laughed it off as she confirmed their plans of getting together on Saturday night with their husbands. They all hugged and said their kind good byes and headed out into the winter wind. This time the cold air felt refreshing as it stung Joanna's exposed face that was still burning with embarrassment.

***

The back door slammed shut a little harder than usual when Graham walked in at the end of the day. Joanna put the lid back on the potatoes she just finished mashing, then turned to the gravy. Lydia just finished setting the table while Ally was sitting on the counter telling Joanna about how everyone hated the new songs their choir teacher had picked for the Spring Choir Concert.

Graham threw his coat on the chair. "Girls, I need to talk to your mother. Could you go to your rooms, please," he said, holding back something that was about to explode. Joanna turned around suddenly catching his anger. She motioned to Ally and Lydia to leave the room before looking back at Graham. She pursed her lips in concern figuring something awful must have happened for Graham to be this upset.

"But we're hungry," Lydia whined, grabbing a pickle from the dish.

"Now!" he demanded, pointing to the back stairs. Graham wasn't an angry man and managed his emotions well, rarely coming home upset. His daughters knew he wasn't joking and ran up the back stairs. He checked to make sure he heard their bedroom doors close.

Joanna licked the back of the spoon tasting the gravy and added a bit more salt. She tried to act casual, hoping to bring down the tension before facing Graham again. "What happened?"

"What happened?" he asked, now bursting. "What happened? You have to ask? I don't know Joanna, you tell me what happened?" he yelled, standing a foot away from his wife.

She swallowed hard and was suddenly very nervous at the level of his fury. "What are you talking about, Graham?" she asked, turning off the element and crossing her arms.

He stared at her for a second longer than necessary. "I need a drink," he growled, heading down the hall to the den. Taking in a deep breath she waited a second and followed.

He slammed ice cubes into a glass and poured the scotch over top. Swirling it twice, he slammed it down his throat, never feeling the burn. He loosened his tie and looked at Joanna who stood in the entrance like a deer in headlights.

"Close the door." She did.

He reached for the bottle again but Joanna walked over and held onto the decanter before he poured a second glass.

"No more. Would you just please tell me why you're so angry." She swallowed again slowly realizing this was directed at her.

He stared her down placing the glass on the bar counter before walking to the window and rubbing his face roughly with this hands. "Ben told me something rather interesting today." He turned to Joanna, crossing his arms over his chest. "He said that you and Grace had lunch today at The Club."

"Well, in the cafe part, but yes, so?"

"Grace told him that you have an admirer who wouldn't leave you alone." He raised his eyebrows. "Do you think you have something to tell me about that, huh?" He paced the floor.

"Graham, what are you talking -," she stopped in mid sentence. Grace must have gone to the office and told Ben a warped version of..... she sucked in some air. *What a horrible thing to do. Why would Grace do that?*

"What exactly did Ben tell you?" she asked with caution.

"No, no, you don't get to ask any questions here," he said, raising his arms in the air. He sat on the edge of his antique, oak desk. Graham looked up with his demanding eyes glaring at Joanna. "I want you to tell me what happened today because the version I got does not make you or I look very good."

"What did she say?" Joanna exclaimed, taking a step forward. "Graham, it was nothing. Clark just stopped by our table and was teasing me about wanting me to work for him. Then he took my bill and paid for my lunch. But I insisted that he didn't have to do that, but he did anyway. That's all," she said, putting her hands on her hips hoping that would enough to calm him down. But it didn't convince Graham.

"That's all! That's all?" he shouted back to her.

"Graham stop yelling. Why would Grace say anything to Ben when it was all nothing?"

"She said he touched you, and was flirting with you, and you didn't try to stop him."

"What was I supposed to do, slap him?" she shouted back with tears burning her eyes. The deep embarrassment creeped up her face as she rehashed the awful ordeal. This was not how she wanted Graham to find out or to ever find out. Clark was a womanizer and everyone knew it. They would just laugh it off. But now there was no laughing as Graham's anger filled the room.

"Graham, I'm not sure what you exactly heard. But what could have possibly happened in a busy restaurant? You're making it sound like I'm....well I'm not or haven't done anything wrong. He keeps bugging me about working for him and I keep putting him off," she explained, taking a few steps closer. "Graham, come on, Clark is just a jerk and everyone knows he's harmless. You're making far more out of this than -"

"Harmless, really Joanna, how naive are you?" he spewed, heading to the bar to pour himself that second drink. "You tell Marie how harmless he is."

"I just heard they split up."

He turned to her with more anger ready to blow. "So then Ben tells me Clark dropped by the house to pay you a visit."

"No, he didn't," she meekly answered, as the truth ran across her eyes. She looked down remembering. "He did, but that was in fall and - "

"So? What? You were just going to wait until I found out? When were you going to tell me that *that man*, came to *my* house to see *my* wife," he shouted, nearly shaking the windows.

Joanna tried to hold back the tears. "Stop yelling at me and I will tell you what happened. Who told you anyway?"

"Does it really matter who told me, Joanna?" he shouted even louder. "What have you been hiding from me all these months?" he asked, swirling the melting ice in the glass.

Jack tried opening the door. "Why are you yelling? We want to eat."

"Jack, get out and go eat with your sisters," he screamed at his son, who immediately closed the door.

"Graham, do not raise your voice to our kids. Or I will walk out of here and there will be no more explaining, do you hear me? They have nothing to do with this, so keep your voice down," she demanded with a controlled steady tone that matched his steely eyed resistance.

Graham knew she was right. His anger ran so deep in this heated moment that he knew he needed to take a second to gain his composure. He sat down on a chair in front of the window, carefully placing the glass on his knee, thinking cautiously about the next thing to say.

"Ben comes into my office to tell me that Grace told him about Clark stopping by your table while you were having lunch. Then he tells me that he wasn't sure if he should be the one to say anything, but he heard that Clark has been going around town telling people that you and he had a meeting," he said, adding quotation marks with his fingers, "about going into business with him. Clark's been telling people what a great job you've done decorating our house." He leaned forward and glared at Joanna. "How would he know what the inside of my house looks like?" he asked through gritted teeth.

"He's lying. He's lying. He never came into the house. I was working in the front yard back in fall and he drove by. I turned him down flat when he asked me if I wanted to work for him. And then I said no when he asked me out for coffee. I said no, Graham, and he left. I haven't talked or seen him until today. He's lying and you believe him before you believe me."

"That's not what this is," he barked out.

"Really, because that's what it feels like to me, Graham. If you would have believed and trusted me, you wouldn't have come storming in here yelling accusations at me about stupid gossip."

"Why didn't you tell me last fall that he was here?" he said, rising to his feet.

"Because I didn't think of it. Because it wasn't a big deal."

"You didn't think it was a big deal?" he repeated, taking off his tie, suddenly feeling like he was being strangled. "I hear that my wife has been seen with the town playboy and you don't think I'd be angry about that? You didn't think I'd be angry that I have to hear it from people in my office. Do you know how much of an idiot I looked like because I didn't know anything about it?"

"Nothing is going on. And I didn't think you cared about what anyone thought about you." Joanna wiped away the tears with the back of her hand.

"I care when people are gossiping about my wife and I don't know anything about it," he shouted, slamming his hand on his chest like an ape claiming his possession.

"I thought we trusted each other, Graham. I assumed you trusted that I wasn't inviting men into our home while you're at work. Just like I trust that you're not flirting with the beer cart girls at the golf course every Saturday morning," she yelled back with fear and anger, pacing the floor. "I can't believe this. After all that we've been through in the past few years, you would rather believe rumours than me. I thought I knew you better than that."

"Don't twist this and make it about me not trusting you, Joanna. You weren't honest with me."

"Do you want an account of everything I do and every-one I talk to at the end of the day?" she asked angrily. She took in a deep breath and let it out. "The fact that you jumped to a very wrong conclusion about me really, really hurts, Graham. How could you even possibly believe for one second that I would even consider...whatever it is that you think happened with Clark Banman?"

He took in a breath and exhaled slowly, looking up to the ceiling for answers. Is that what he was doing? How could he believe Joanna would step out on him, especially with a guy like that? He was so shocked when Ben came into his office with this horrible story about his own wife. He and Ben usually talked about these kinds of circumstances as they involved their clients, like Marie Banman, who had come to see Graham a few weeks earlier asking how she could get a quick and easy divorce from Clark. Marie could no longer handle all his alleged affairs. Graham now realized that Joanna didn't know that part of the story or about how many other marriages Clark had messed up.

He glanced over to his wife who now stood in front of the door, so deeply hurt by his accusations and assumptions. He absolutely trusted her. But prideful male ego got in the way of truth, allowing anger to come first. He knew they had been on some rocky ground in fall, and now hearing about Clark talking to Joanna, he put together wrong conclusions that seemed to make sensible explanations as to why they were having troubles communicating back then.

Graham looked up at his wife. She was taking calming breaths and wiping away tears. Joanna had dedicated herself to him and their family and he knew she would never do what Graham had been imagining. What was he thinking coming home and acting like a jealous husband? He wasn't that guy. He looked down searching for words that just wouldn't come. What could he possibly say now to excuse what he had just done to her? He caused that hurt in her eyes and that pain across her heart. How could he undo any of it?

"Fine," she said, opening the door. "Don't answer me. I guess we have nothing left to say." She turned to leave closing the door ever so quietly. It would have felt better and deservedly so if she would have slammed it in his face.

Keeping her tears at bay, Joanna went into the kitchen to find Jack eating alone. "Where are your sisters?"

Jack looked down at his plate and toyed with the peas. "What were you and dad yelling about?"

"Dad just had a bad day and.... yeah, just a bad day," she answered, clearing the dirty plates the girls left behind.

"Are you and Dad going to get a divorce?" he asked, putting down his fork and knife. "Aaron Banman's parents are getting a divorce and he's really upset about it." Jack stared at his mother, begging for answers with his watery eyes. Jack was her stable one. He was the mentally tough, disciplined athlete who handled everything so well. Joanna's heart was breaking seeing her son on the edge, watching his family fall apart.

"Oh Jack." She took the chair beside him. "I'm sorry you heard us yelling at each other again. No, we're not going to get a divorce. We have way too much to keep together here." She leaned over and gave him a hug.

"It sounded pretty awful, Mom. Dad is really mad. I've never heard him yell like that before," he said, unable to hold back the tears.

So she wasn't the only one shaken by Graham's out-burst. "I'm sorry, buddy. I really am. Just be patient. We're working through some stuff," she said, hoping it would mask her own pain.

"I need to go," Lydia said walking in with her dance bag. Joanna looked at the time. She stood up relieved for the distraction. "Okay, I'll take you Lydia. And Jack, everything is going to be okay." She took in a deep breath and kissed her son on the forehead. "Do you have homework?"

He nodded.

"Okay, take your plate to the dishwasher and get started on it. I'll be back later." She got her coat and purse and headed outside, feeling that bitter angry cold on her face once again that day. It stung her eyes and she wanted to cry. But Lydia was following her to the garage and now wasn't the time to fall apart. She had to move ahead. Lydia too asked what the yelling was about. Joanna simply explained that Dad had a bad day at the office and it would be fine. She accepted that as they drove in silence to the dance studio.

Joanna decided to stay and watch the rehearsal, mostly to avoid seeing Graham. Joanna parked the car in the studio parking lot, then ran across the street to a popular coffee shop to get herself a dark roast to calm her frazzled nerves. She watched Lydia practice but was lost in her thoughts, Joanna didn't really remember watching a lot of dancing. She was immersed in her own dismal recollection of how Graham came home so angry. Reliving the whole disastrous fight played out over and over, repeating like a nightmare that she couldn't wake up from. She had never seen him so angry in all the years she had known him. Joanna checked her phone. No messages.

When the rehearsal was over Lydia claimed starvation so they went back to the coffee shop for soup and bread. They took their time as Lydia chattered away and laughed at her own stories. Joanna felt guilty knowing that Lydia felt so special to finally have this moment with her mother, who spent so much time with Ally. But Joanna wanted to sit and listen to Lydia, because she didn't want to go home yet and face Graham. Lydia then ordered a piece of chocolate cake. An hour later, Joanna said it was way past her bedtime and they needed to head home.

Pulling up the driveway, she noticed the den light was still on. Joanna took in a deep breath as she pulled into the garage. "Okay, Lydia, no TV. It's a shower and straight to bed. I kept you out later than I expected."

Lydia undid her seatbelt and leaned over giving her mom a hug. "Thanks Mom for staying and then taking me out. That felt nice."

Joanna smiled, hiding her guilt. "It was nice, sweetie. We should do it more often." That part was true.

Entering the house, she looked around the kitchen. The dishwasher had been turned on. All the food was put away and the table and counters wiped. *Did Graham do that?* she wondered, adding it to her guilt. Maybe it was a sign that he was sorry. She peered down the hallway and saw that the door to the den was closed. Hanging up her coat, Joanna followed Lydia up the stairs ready to call it a day.

She knocked on Ally's bedroom door, but there was no response. A slight panic rose in her chest. Maybe she was already asleep? Ally wasn't allowed to lock her door, so Joanna quietly opened it. She saw Ally lying in her bed, in the dark, with her eyes closed. Stepping inside Joanna noticed she was listening to music with her ear buds in. Looking down at the iPod, Joanna saw she was listening to, 'Aquarius' by the 5th Dimension. Joanna knew that Ally had a broad and eclectic range of music but she had never mentioned this song before. She thought it was odd that she had this song playing on repeat. Deciding not to wake her, Joanna quietly left her room.

Joanna got ready for bed and took her iPad from her night table. She found the song and plugged in her ear buds. She listened to the haunting words that spoke to her daughter.

'Harmony and understanding, sympathy and trust abounding. Let the sunshine in, let the sunshine in.'

Joanna was crippled with guilt and frustration. Her kids didn't want to deal with epilepsy but they certainly didn't want two parents who couldn't keep this family on track. For every step forward, she and Graham were taking a giant leap back. For months they were constantly frustrated with each other and just when they found their footing, something seemed to push one of them off the cliff. She crawled under the covers listening to the song over and over until she fell asleep.

Hours later when Graham finally found the courage to join his wife, he thought it was odd that she was listening to 'Aquarius'.

20
It's All An Act

"It was a great party Joanna, like always," Karen said, giving Joanna a prescribed hug as she walked out the door into the bitter cold.

"Yes, thanks again Graham, Joanna," Cal added. "It's always a great time coming here," he said, following his wife.

Ben shook Graham's hand and offered a hesitant kiss on the cheek for Joanna. "Yes, great party you two."

"And Joanna, you must give me that recipe for the hot artichoke dip. It was delicious. Everything you make is so perfect. Is there anything you can't do?" Grace asked, putting on her coat.

Joanna knew Grace didn't need or want a basic dip recipe, especially one that was store bought. She was full of rehearsed compliments all evening. It annoyed Joanna deeply. But she smiled and went along with their group of friends who had come over for wine and nibbles on a typical Saturday night.

Joanna was still in disbelief that Grace had betrayed her trust. Even after Joanna had confronted Grace, she offered no legitimate explanation or even an ounce of remorse for what she did. Joanna often wondered who else was talking about her. What was said by this group of women after she left the cafe? She couldn't trust her life-long friends or her husband right now. Joanna felt lost and it quickly turned into bitterness that lead straight to anger. A seething undercurrent always ran through her thoughts. She hated living like this, so full of rage that she prayed and cried at night for everything to get back to how it used to be. She prayed for a just a break from the heartache. Joanna begged God to grant her the peace she once knew. She begged God to heal her daughter and mend her family. So far, there were no answers from above. Only silence.

Graham placed his hand on the small of Joanna's back as Fran and her husband were next to leave. "Thanks Joanna, yes it was a great party. And you look great by the way. I love that dress on you." She gave Joanna a quick hug. "You two are amazing hosts. So fun."

"Thanks for coming," Graham said, as he closed and locked the door. Joanna turned and headed into the living room determined to clean up the mess left behind. Waiting until everyone had driven away, Graham turned off the outside lights.

Taking his time he headed into the living room, watching his wife's happy, laughing disposition turn into something else. The someone else that he was responsible for creating. Since the day he came home, ten days to be exact, and yelled and screamed at his wife's innocence, nothing had been the same. He had erased all the happiness and joy they had found over Christmas in Cuba with his accusations about her and that awful Clark Banman.

Graham shuddered thinking about him. Clark was not going to give his wife the simple divorce she was after, making it very clear this was a battle he was not about to lose. It also made Graham resolve and promise himself that he and Joanna would never find themselves in that position. But here they were, happy couple among the crowds and strangers both holding onto so much regret and hurt. He watched as Joanna hurried around the living room picking up wine glasses and placing them on a tray ready to take to the kitchen.

"Here, let me do that," he offered, taking the tray from her. She resisted, but relented, moving onto the dishes of leftover cheeses and olives. Graham placed the tray on the kitchen counter. Taking the empty wine bottles he added them to the recycling bin in the mud room. Joanna quickly and silently cleaned up the leftover food.

"It's late. Why don't we leave the rest for tomorrow?" he suggested.

Without stopping her busy hands, Joanna shook her head. "We can't. Jack has a hockey game tomorrow morning and we have to be on the road by 8:00. And don't forget that Ally is playing in the festival Monday afternoon," she added, ready to recite the rest of their week's activities.

He grabbed a lonely olive left on the tray. "Where is the game again, Brandon?"

"Yes," she answered putting the wrapped cheeses in the fridge. Brandon was a two hour drive and with the icy roads, it would probably take longer.

Graham closed the fridge door and reached out for Joanna.

"What?" she asked, resisting his efforts.

"Nothing, I just wanted to say you did a great job with the party, like always."

"I don't know why everyone makes such a big deal about it. It's cheese, crackers and store bought dips. It's not that hard. Even Grace could do it. But none of them hardly do, they just wait until I, or you this time, decide everyone should come over."

Graham chewed on his bottom lip knowing the timing of this gathering couldn't be much worse. Things had been a little tense between this group of friends since Grace placed Joanna in eye of the gossipy storm. Ben and Graham had talked it out and Ben apologized for his wife's interference. But this cocktail party had been decided a month earlier, and Graham didn't want any more suspicious words spread about them if they suddenly canceled the evening. So, Graham and Joanna acted like everything was fine, laughing at everyone's jokes, pretending to be interested in each other's shallow lives. No one seeing the Kornelson's facade while drinking their wine and enjoying the expensive cheese.

"Jo, you do a great job and I just want to say it doesn't go unnoticed, by them or...me," he said.

She crossed her arms and looked at her husband. "Great, I feel so accomplished," she answered with a twist of bitterness and headed back into the living room with the empty tray.

Joanna had been so deeply disappointed in Graham. Their argument always replaying in her mind and never far away. But as each day brought those horrible moments farther and farther away, the wound only got bigger and continued to fester in Joanna's heart. They didn't know what to say to each other or how to say it anymore. They were lost in their own home, in each other's lives as they tried to navigate through another difficult wave.

Unsure if she wanted to be left alone to clean up or if he should follow her around listening to her orders, Graham stood still unable to sense any direction of how to help his wife. Anxious to bring up the topic again, he decided to let it go and hope that it would go away. But this time it wasn't simply going away and his wife was not rebounding like she normally did. He counted on her forgiveness and her understanding. Reluctantly, he decided to stay in the kitchen and load the dishwasher and in uncomfortable silence they managed to make it look like the evening had never happened, cleaning and wiping it all away.

***

The next day they repeated their vacant stares and public politeness at Jack's hockey game in Brandon. It was easy to look happy as Jack managed two goals and an assist. On the quiet, long and dark ride home, they sat unmoved with the three kids sitting in the back plugged into their own thoughts and music.

Monday morning came with a late winter dreariness that followed the Kornelson family to the kitchen for breakfast. Everyone made it to the breakfast table but Ally, who was found in the bathroom going through another seizure. Like a well oiled machine, they all took their places. Timing the episode, reaching for towels to wipe her up and waiting until the violent shaking and jerking and the inhumane noises of gasping for breath were over. And then they knew, it was now the worst part, when Ally's brain would find reality and she would know that another seizure had gripped her family once again. She would cry and cry. She would cling to her mom's body as hers was wracked with fear and deep uncertainty. Graham would comfort Lydia, and Jack would carry on cleaning up the poured cleanser that Ally had dropped.

And then the last stage was determining where the physical damage had taken place. Where the bruises would show up and how badly it would be revealed that Ally had another seizure. This time she hit her chin on the bathroom counter biting the inside of her mouth and bottom lip and losing a small part of her top tooth. Then they would all go back to their routines before the seizure began. Ally got tucked into bed, Jack and Lydia finished their half eaten breakfast and Joanna went to finish making the lunches. How strange and oddly normal it felt.

Graham topped up his cooled coffee. "I'll take the kids to school and then I'll come back and see how she's doing."

Joanna added mustard to Jack's ham sandwich. "Okay," she said. Then she covered it with another slice of bread.

"Ally is supposed to play in the festival this afternoon," Lydia commented, nibbling on her pancake. "Can she still play?"

Joanna looked up and out of the window. She was angry that this disease had turned her family upside down. She was so angry that it had changed who they were supposed to be. But she would never let this disease take away Ally's right to live a normal life. Joanna was tired of her family falling victim to the careless whims of this taunting illness that plagued Ally and was always changing the rest of them. She was fed up and resolved that it would stop today.

"Of course she's playing this afternoon. She'll be fine by then," Joanna said with steely determination.

Graham looked at Joanna as she placed the sandwiches in the brown paper bags. "Shouldn't we wait and see? Or let Ally decide?"

"Nope," she answered curtly. "She's going to do it. She can't think that this is going to beat her. She has to know she cannot let this get in her way."

Taking a long sip of the hot coffee, Graham was ready to rebuttal her argument. But he knew better than to do so in front of the kids. "Okay guys, I'll take you to school. Let's go."

Jack got up and cleared his dishes. "Is Ally going to be okay?"

"Of course she is," Joanna answered too quickly. "She will always get back up." And she walked out of the kitchen and headed upstairs.

Ally was sitting up and touching her mouth as it continued to puff up.

"How are you doing, honey?" Joanna asked tenderly.

"Mom, my jaw hurts."

"I know, you banged it on the counter this time. Does it hurt to move it?"

Ally opened and closed her mouth shaking her head. "No, just the inside of my mouth hurts and my tooth feels weird."

"Yeah, you chipped it a bit. But we'll get that fixed before anyone will notice."

"Okay." Ally hesitated. "I'm supposed to play in the festival today."

"And you still can. Just get some rest this morning. I'll get you something for your headache. And then once you're up you can eat breakfast and maybe practice for a bit. You know your pieces, you'll do fine."

"But Mom," she slurred with her swollen face, "I just had a seizure, I can't play piano today."

"Ally listen to me." Joanna gently rubbed the back of Ally's scratched up hands with her thumb. "You may have seizures the rest of your life and if you let it interfere with what you want to do, you will be crippled by it. And you are too good of a musician and a brilliant young lady to let anything make you less than what you are meant to be."

"But Mom, I'm all puffy and I don't want to play in front of people today," she lisped from her swollen mouth and lips.

"But today you had a seizure and it is today that you have to deal with this. You are not a girl with epilepsy, Ally. You are a determined, resilient person who's not going to let this define her and get in the way of what is important to you."

"I can't do it," she said, crying and falling into her mother's arms.

"Yes, you can Ally. You have to prove to yourself that you are stronger than any seizure," she said, cradling her daughter.

"I wish God would just tell us why this has happened to you or better yet, I wish He would just cure you, Ally. But today, that hasn't happened." Joanna paused. "But He also gave you an incredible talent to create music. You are a very gifted pianist and if you don't play this afternoon, it's like you're letting it win. You're letting it define you and limit you."

She pulled away. "But it does limit me, Mom. All my friends have their learners' or drivers' licences and I don't. All my friends stay out late at parties and I can't. They drive their bikes up to the beach and you won't let me. I am different than them and I'm reminded of that every time I feel dizzy or I have a seizure or I look at this medical bracelet. I am defined, Mom. It says right here, 'epileptic'," she declared, turning over the silver charm on the ID bracelet.

"Ally, we all live with limitations. You just know what yours are because you have a medical condition. You've learned very quickly what it's like to be stopped in your tracks. But believe me, everyone has something they are dealing with or that they will have to deal with. There are kids at your school who have diabetes or have had to deal with cancer." Joanna sat back and looked at her daughter for a second longer. "Sometimes, Ally, you have to act like you're stronger than you believe you are. You just decide you are going to get through the disappointments of not being like your friends or you decide that you are going to play the best Chopin you've ever played before. It will amaze you what the power of believing in the strength that you have deep down inside of you. I know it's there, Ally."

She wiped away her tears streaming down her bruised cheek bone. "But what if I can't do it?"

"And what if you can, Ally? What if you play this afternoon with the feeling that you are going to play your pieces with absolute perfection. That the composers themselves would give you a standing ovation. What if you played and then took a bow and realized that today you won, and the seizure didn't get in your way."

She hugged her mom again. Thinking about what if.

Joanna kissed the top of her head. "Okay, I'm going to get you something for your headache, because your head hurts, right?"

Ally nodded.

"And then, you can sleep for a bit, eat something, go over your pieces and then we'll go to the festival." She stood up. "I'll be right back."

After giving Ally some Tylenol, she closed the door to her room when she heard Graham coming back from taking the twins to school. She did hope the twins were doing all right. She didn't have a chance to see them off.

Graham entered Ally's room to check on her while Joanna headed down to the kitchen to clean up breakfast and call the school to let them know why Ally wouldn't be there today. Just as she got off the phone, Graham came in.

"Going to work now?" she asked, twisting the cap on the orange juice bottle.

"In a minute," he said. "Ally says she's going to try to play at the festival today."

"Yup," she said, drinking the juice.

"Don't you think we should talk about this before we make her do something she may not be ready to do? I mean, does she want to play? Why the panic to make her do this, Joanna?"

She leaned back against the kitchen counter bracing herself for what was inevitably headed for another argument. "Because Graham, I don't want her thinking she can't do something because of epilepsy. I won't let it win over her, over everything she has accomplished. Next year she wants to go to university and she'll have to audition and if I let her cave now, she'll lose confidence and never believe in herself again. She has to do this, Graham."

Graham leaned on the back of the chair he had just tucked under the table, carefully choosing his words. "I understand all that, Jo. But if she is pushed into something that she's not ready for -"

"She's ready. She's been playing those pieces for months."

"That's not what I'm talking about," he clarified, careful not to raise his voice. "I'm suggesting that she has gone through another traumatic seizure and has never had to perform hours later. I'm asking you to consider, is this going to be too much for her, today?"

"No, it's not," she fired back with great confidence. "I will not let this interfere with her life, her goals and who she is, anymore."

Graham stood up straight and was quiet for a moment as he looked at this woman who had become hard and icy in her decisiveness. "Well, okay then. I guess you don't need me to change your mind. I guess you've decided everything on your own." He grabbed his coat, brief case and walked out.

21
Playing For Real

Ally was a heap of emotional tears standing at the back of the church, having lost all confidence and hope. *Why did I agree to do this?* she asked herself over and over again. Even though her mom made arrangements for her to play at the end of the day, explaining their situation to the committee, Ally had felt defeated as she looked at the grand piano way up on the stage. It was daunting and petrifying to go up there and play her pieces for memory.

Mrs. Buhlin hugged Ally, telling her if she wanted to bring her music on stage, she could. She said she was proud of her for even wanting to play today. "Oh Ally, play for yourself today, honey," Mrs. Buhlin said, rubbing her back and leaning close. "That's all you need to do."

When Sarah came in to listen and show her support with Abigail and Nora, she too spoke to her as a performer. "No one has to know what happened this morning. This is your moment, Ally. Your moment to tell your story through music. It's all your story and as a performer you can play how it feels, for you."

Desperation filled Joanna's heart with doubt as she watched her daughter submit to the hopelessness of defeat. She wanted her daughter to feel successful and be determined to overcome life's challenges. But never did she imagine all those years ago when she started taking lessons with Mrs. Buhlin, that epilepsy would be what Ally needed to overcome.

Ally looked over to her mom and in her eyes, she saw possibility; her mother believed that she could do this. Then why couldn't she believe it too? With all the resolve she could find in that moment, Ally took her music books from Mrs. Buhlin and sat on the pew at the front of the church, waiting for the festival volunteer to introduce her.

Graham came in just in time and joined his wife on the church pew. "How's she doing?" he asked in a whisper.

"She's going to do it," she answered.

Joanna held her breath and reached for Graham's hand. He offered her a quick glance before squeezing it a little tighter as Todd and Nana Ellie sat beside them. Even Joanna's dad, John, walked it in at the last minute. Sitting at the back were a group of Ally's friends from school. Ally must have texted and asked them to come, Joanna surmised.

"Allison Kornelson will be performing Ballade, No. 2 in F Major, by Chopin. Allison please."

Rubbing her hands on her legs, Ally stood up leaving her music books on the pew. She sat at the piano staring down at the keyboard. "Whenever you're ready, Allison," the adjudicator said. "Just take your time."

Ally nodded and placed her hands on the keys. It felt right, they belonged on those notes, in that position. Closing her eyes she heard the tender composition playing in her head. Bum-bum, bum-bum. She saw it, as she counted her hands in, they joined the movement of the notes, the music filling her head leaving no room for confusion and falling down. There was just music all around her, just the music telling her story.

Ally listened to the song coming from the piano. *Don't have a seizure, don't have a seizure*, she told herself. She saw the top of the page in her mind's eye. *1,2,3 & 1,2,3, play strong. Okay, bring out the left hand melody. Keep it flowing, keep it even. Now back to the theme. Don't have a seizure. Be confident*, she reminded herself, getting lost in the works of Chopin. *Enjoy the piece*, Ally smiled slightly. *You're doing it, this part is your favourite.*

She closed her eyes lost in the transition of the Chopin Ballade. Up and down the keyboard, her fingers found their rhythm, found their notes, found their music. *Here's the finish, keep it even, don't get lost, oh yeah, middle of the page*, she imagined in her mind. *Almost done, keep it lively, steady, pause, back to the beginning. Even touch, sing the melody, enjoy this moment. That was good. It's done.*

Ally kept her head down and took in a quick breath as she looked up and realized she had really done it. She loved Chopin and wanted to play it perfectly in spite of watching her scratched up hands across the keyboard. Her head still hurt, her bottom lip was swollen and she was getting a black eye. She stood up beside the piano and took a bow. She rose, scanning the small crowd gathered in the church sanctuary, she found her mom.

They looked at each other, Ally standing on stage while Joanna clapped for her daughter's performance. Ally simply mouthed the words to her mom. "I won."

***

Gathering her certificates, Ally thanked the committee members for accommodating her. The adjudicator was fair in assessing Ally's playing like any other student performing. But she took Ally aside and told her she was impressed with her resolve and believed that some of her students at the university couldn't have played like that when faced with a serious medical complication. Ally was happy with her critique but elated that it was over.

Ally headed towards her friends. Joanna watched her daughter acting like a normal kid among them. *How grateful she was to be raising this girl*, she thought, as Ally came running towards her as the sanctuary cleared out.

"Mom, can I go out with my friends? They want to go for pizza."

Joanna's instinct was to say no, she wanted Ally to herself, just a little while longer. "Are you sure? How are you feeling?"

"Like I'm starving," she replied, as her friends followed.

"We won't be too late," Matthew said, standing beside Ally. "I have homework tonight anyway and I have to practice guitar."

"Yes, go," Graham said, stepping in wondering who this tall, blonde kid was standing rather close to his daughter. "Have fun."

"Well, who's driving?" Joanna asked, looking at the crowd. Most of them she had known since kindergarten and now they were old enough to drive.

"I have my mom's car," Matthew answered quickly. "Don't worry I'll have her home... she'll be home... we won't be late," he stuttered, looking nervously down at Ally who was smiling.

"I have my cell with me, I'll be fine. I hopefully can eat with this fat lip," she said, laughing.

She hugged her parents and headed out of the church like nothing had happened, good or bad.

"Well, can I take you out for pizza too?" Graham playfully asked, hoping she couldn't find an excuse to be alone with him.

"I don't think we should go and spy on her. Besides, Jack and Lydia are at home waiting for supper too."

"Oh, you two go out. I haven't seen the twins in a while," Ellie offered. "I'll take them over to my place and give them supper. You can come get them when you're done."

"Are you sure, Mom?" Graham asked, giving his tiny mother a hug.

"Yes, of course I am. Go on a date." She hugged Joanna and Graham again and headed to her car.

"A date!" Joanna said, with tentative playfulness, letting her guard down. She was exhausted being so angry all the time. "I'm over the moon! Where do you take your dates for dinner?"

Graham smiled down at his wife, elated that this awful day found a sliver of joy. He was grateful to see Joanna smile again.

"I know this great little place that serves amazing short ribs. And there is no chance of running into cackles of teenagers," he answered, as they walked to his car. They agreed to pick up her car on the way home.

Joanna got inside the already warm car. "I'm glad Ally's friends came to see her play."

She hesitated. "Who's that boy she went with?"

He pulled out of the parking lot. "I think it's someone we need to be worried about very soon," he answered with a slight smile.

22
Birthday Joy

Just before Ally's sixteenth birthday, Dr. Shaw believed that adding another proven anti-seizure medication to her cocktail of drugs would give her the seizure control they continued to search for. After another round of blood work to check her levels, it was determined that Ally could no longer go up in dosages on either of her current medications since she was already within therapeutic range. Adding another medication seemed to be the best option. But Dr. Shaw assured them other drug options were available to try if they needed to in the future. She explained to Joanna, Graham and Ally that the new drug had possible side effects that could include tiredness, agitation and maybe more mood changes. Dr. Shaw also reiterated that Ally could not get her driver's permit until she was seizure free for a full year. Ally tried hard not to let it all get to her. The goal was to stop having seizures, and if adding another medication would take care of that, then bring it on, Ally concluded, listening to the doctor go on and on about all this medical talk she didn't care about. She had other things to think about now.

Ally was in an unusually good mood since she had finished playing in the festival. She felt accomplished and so proud that she had overcome the adversity of playing hours after a seizure. It also showed her who her real friends were when they came to watch her perform. They continued to offer her rides and made sure that Ally took her pills on time. They didn't make her feel different anymore, they were just her friends and she could be herself.

Before leaving Winnipeg, they decided to go shopping for some new spring clothes. Joanna was even daring enough to pick out some outfits for Lydia, hoping she would like them. They decided to eat at one of their favourite, authentic Italian restaurants in a strip mall that was on their way out of Winnipeg.

Ally took a quick peek at her phone and saw that Matthew had replied to her last text. She smiled, putting her fork down.

Joanna looked over to Graham and smiled. "Ah Ally, just because we're eating in a restaurant, same rules apply about phones at the table. Put it away," she reminded her, mopping up the sauce with a slice of garlic bread.

Ally smiled even bigger while quickly replying. "Fine, just a second."

Graham finished off his beer. "Who is so important?"

She shut off her phone and threw it in her bag. "No one. Just a friend," she casually replied and dove into her pasta Alfredo.

Joanna sipped her wine. "So Ally, have you thought about your birthday, it's only a few weeks away."

Slurping up the creamy sauce, Ally wiped her mouth contemplating. "I don't know, just hang out with my friends I guess."

"But it's your sixteenth birthday, Ally. Let's do something special for you."

"No surprises," she said, nibbling on the garlic toast. "I hate surprises, they totally through me off."

"No surprises," Graham confirmed, pushing his plate of almost finished ravioli aside. "But think about it, Ally. You only get to turn sixteen once."

Ally looked down and twirled the long noodles around in her plate. "You know, I am bummed that I can't drive like all my other friends. Everyday one of them comes to school all excited that they get to drive. It sucks, actually."

Joanna's heart sank. She wanted her daughter to experience what all kids want at her age. As Ally got older it was becoming apparent that her life would always be different.

"But whatever," Ally sighed. "The doctors all promised since I was fourteen that they would figure out the drugs and I could be driving. Yeah, right."

"Sometimes they say stuff like that so you don't lose hope," Graham answered, crossing his arms on the table and looking intently at Ally. "Maybe one day you'll be able to drive."

She hesitated again, then looked at her parents. "Is this new drug going to make me crazy too? I hate changing drugs."

Joanna reached over and gave Ally a quick squeeze. "We'll take it as it comes, just like we've been doing. Now back to your party, I have an idea -"

Ally's phone buzzed again and her attention went straight to her bag where the message lit up. She smiled. "Sorry, can I just answer this one text? You're done eating. It's like dinner is over." Reaching for her phone, the dilemmas about driving and drugs vanished.

Joanna and Graham smiled at each other again. "Teenage girls," Graham mouthed to his wife, smiling. He waved down their waiter to get the check.

***

Joanna did have a great idea for Ally's birthday and just in time. They were starting to see side effects of the newly added medication as Ally was showing signs of impatience and irritation. Everything annoyed her, especially Lydia. Jack knew enough to stay out of her way and avoided his sister. Joanna was at the end of her rope with Ally. Every morning it was a struggle to her get up, eat breakfast and ready for school on time. It was a constant battle until Ally was out the door. And after school, it started all over again until Ally headed for bed, which fortunately she had no problem doing.

A long, white limo pulled up in front of the Kornelson home as Ally and her friends watched from the living room window. All afternoon the girls had primped and curled and dawned fancy dresses and high heels, took selfies and group shots. Joanna made Ally's favourite meal of lasagna, Caesar salad, homemade garlic bread and served them in the formal dining room.

Joanna took a final picture of them all standing in front of the limo posing like super models before they piled into the spacious entry of the grand car. They were being chauffeured to the theatre in the mall to see the opening night of another epic movie sequel based on a best seller. Graham had pulled a few favours with the theatre manager and got tickets and special seats reserved just for them. The girls felt like rock stars.

"Okay girls have fun, we'll see you after the movie," Joanna said, taking a step back.

Ally quickly popped out of the car and gave her mom a big hug. "Thanks Mom. This is so fun. None of us have been in a limo before. This is awesome," Ally said and headed back inside so the limo driver could close the door.

Joanna smiled, so happy for Ally. When the car made the corner of their street, Joanna turned and headed towards the house. Graham and Lydia were watching from the front porch. *So much for happiness,* she thought, noticing the scowl on her younger daughter's face.

Graham tugged on Lydia's ponytail as she angrily pulled away. "Don't," she bitterly spat out.

Joanna put her hands on her hips and took in a deep sigh. "What now, Lydia?"

"How come she gets everything special?" she questioned bitterly, crossing her arms.

"It's her sixteenth birthday, Lydia. Of course we're going to make it special," Joanna replied, coming up the steps.

"A limo? Really? Don't you think that's a little over the top of special?" she questioned, flailing her arms. "Ally gets everything she wants all the time. You never do stuff like this for me. And Jack is so important because he's a boy."

"Really, Lydia," Joanna said, raising her voice. "You know what your sister has been through and if giving her a really, really nice birthday is going to make her feel special instead of different from everybody, then that's what I'll do."

Lydia grunted and folded her arms again.

"I hope you didn't say anything to Ally in front of her friends?" her mother warned.

Graham put his arm around Lydia as she sank into his side. He looked down at his wife and raised his eyebrows with discernment that perhaps threats weren't useful.

Joanna took in a quick breath and clasped her hands together. "Lydia," she started again. "Ally can't drive like her other friends. I thought it would be nice for them to get a limo ride so they all would be equal, just for one night. You've seen how happy she was about this all week."

"In a couple of years you'll be sixteen and it will be your turn to have a special birthday," Graham added.

Lydia rolled her eyes. "Nothing is special about my birthday. I have to share it with Jack. Nothing is special for me, ever," she shouted and walked into the house, slamming the heavy front door.

Joanna rubbed her forehead. Graham put his arm around his wife. "She'll be fine. This was an awesome idea to get a limo for Ally tonight. You did good, Mom."

Joanna didn't feel like she was a successful parent anymore. From one daughter's extreme joy to the other's jealousy.

"Can't Lydia see the struggles Ally has and if I could give her one night out with her friends…." Joanna didn't know what to say. "She should be happy for her sister." She sighed again. "Ally was so excited. I hope she can just forget about all her troubles and disappointments and have a great time tonight."

Graham kissed her forehead. "Come on inside," he said, leading her into the house. "Maybe you could do something with Lydia tonight. I think all she wants is your time."

Joanna knew he was right. She spent so much time with Ally at appointments or helping her to cope with drugs and their effects. Lydia was often left on her own to get her homework done and get herself to bed without her. She thought Jack and Lydia always felt special because they were twins, but she supposed the novelty had worn off by now. Jack was turning into a noted school athlete and had high school coaches asking Graham what his son's plans were for playing sports over the next few years. But Joanna was mentally exhausted trying to parent a sports overachiever, manage Ally's chronic illness and make Lydia feel special. Lydia was losing her place in the family. Joanna knew and understood Lydia all too well.

23

Let The Sun Shine

"Get out of my room," Ally shouted at her sister, this time with even more intensity. "Mom, tell Lydia to get out!"

Lydia refused to budge.

"Get out or I will push you down the stairs. MOM!" Ally hollered again, turning several shades of red.

"What is going on?" Graham demanded, racing into her room. "Stop yelling at her, Ally."

"She took my hoody, so I took it back and now she says it was hers and took it from my room," Ally explained, huffing and puffing in a fit of anger.

"You're so stupid, this is mine," Lydia shot back, holding the hoody up high in victory. "Yours is navy, this one is black. Can't you tell the difference? I put an L on the label so I would know it's mine and so you wouldn't take it."

"You're such a baby, Lydia. Why didn't you tell me that in the first place?" Ally muttered, looking through a pile of clothes on her bed, finding her lost hoody.

"Then say you're sorry," Lydia demanded.

"No way. Now get out of my room."

"Girls, when did you start talking so meanly to each other? You used to play in each other's rooms all the time." Graham said, picking up more clothes from the floor. "I thought sisters shared clothes anyway."

Lydia glanced at the pile of clothes her dad had gathered, and recognized her new shirt that she bought last week. "Ally, you took my shirt. What is wrong with you? Stop taking my stuff," she hollered, and reached for the shirt as Graham tossed it on the bed.

Ally grabbed the shirt first and Lydia lunged for Ally as they tussled on the bed covered with clothes.

"Graham, what is going on? Girls, cut it out," Joanna demanded, separating them and taking the shirt out of their grips.

Graham reached for Ally and held her back. Her heart was racing in her chest. "Hey, calm down, Ally. Would you look at the laundry before you claim it."

"I thought you two could pack yourselves," Joanna spat out. "We're just going to the cabin for the weekend. Why do you have all your clothes on your bed?"

"She keeps stealing my clothes," Lydia announced. "And you always take her side."

"No one is taking sides," Graham clarified.

"Ally you just can't take all the laundry that's in the basket and dump it on your bed. Lydia's clothes were in there too. Now both of you sort through this pile without yelling at each other. And hurry up Ally, you need to get to work soon."

It was the beginning of June and Ally had started working at the Burger Shack again. It was Thursday and she was scheduled to work the evening shift. The next day right after school, they would be taking off to Lake of the Woods for the entire weekend.

Spring had turned out to be unusually warm which beckoned them to their beloved cabin. Graham didn't want to waste the warm temperatures and could hardly wait to get on his boat. Plus, something wonderful happened to their family when they were one with nature. No tech devices were allowed, other than the occasional rainy day movie on TV. Meals were simple, naps were mandatory and hours on the lake a requirement.

A weekend to bust through the tension was necessary since Ally started on her new drug. They were finding it tough to strike a balance between the interactions of the new drug combination. At one point they were overdosing and had to slowly wean her off one to raise the right dosage of the other. It was complicated to figure out and on top of the dance between the medications, they were constantly worried that a seizure would break through. During these changes Ally was making hasty decisions and getting behind at school. She was always asking for extensions on projects and claimed fatigue way too often as her excuse for her bad behaviour at home. They tried to be understanding and accommodating, but they were all losing their patience with Ally.

"Listen to Mom and clean this up and I'll take you to work," Graham said, leaving them to it.

"Actually Ally, just leave out the clothes you want to take along and I'll pack for you tonight," Joanna offered.

"Really, now you're going to pack for her too!" Lydia complained, grabbing her clothes, matching Ally's violent temper.

"Oh grow up, Lydia," Ally shouted.

"That is more than enough. I can't take you two anymore. I'm going to lose my mind if you both don't cut this out," Joanna shrieked. "Everyday you go at it. I am sick and tired of it and if this bickering doesn't stop immediately there will be consequences so huge you will regret ever raising your voices."

They looked at their mother, who like them knew how to engage in a battle of words. Did they dare ask what the consequences were?

Graham stood in silence not sure his wife could or should carry out her threats. He was worried that the repercussions meant not going to the cabin. That was not going to happen. He had been looking forward to this for days. "Okay, girls, listen to Mom and cut out the fighting."

He looked squarely at Joanna. "We don't want to know what her consequences will be. So get 'er done, girls."

Walking out of the room, he headed to see what Jack was up to.

Joanna closed the door behind her. "'Get 'er done?' That's what you had to tell them? Graham I'm at my wits end trying to manage getting a weekend together that you just decided last minute-"

"It was not last minute. We decided...Tuesday."

She sighed. Shopping, prepping food, laundry, packing, breaking up fights and dealing with Ally's endless mood swings had given Joanna a permanent ache in her neck. "Graham, I have so much to do and I've lost patience with them," she said, pointing to the closed door. "I need you to deal with these things when they come up. I can't be the only one who gets in between their arguments all the time."

"You're not. I was right there, Jo, dealing with them," he corrected, placing his hands on his hips.

The door opened and then closed as Lydia stomped off to her own room with an arm full of clothes. She slammed her bedroom door in their faces. Joanna rolled her eyes and wanted to go another round with Lydia. Why didn't she understand the strain of changes Ally was under and just be patient with her?

Graham grabbed her arm. "Don't bother going after her again. Just let her pack and she'll calm down. Ally will be at work tonight and they'll have their space from each other."

It irked Joanna when he wanted to let everything calm down. She never wanted to let anything go. "If I don't get the last word they'll think they can get away with their bad attitudes, Graham," she explained, full of exasperation.

"Sometimes it's okay to leave a few words unsaid and let it work out on its own. How about I get some burgers when I take Ally to work. You can cross off dinner from your list," he offered. "See, I'm helping."

She leaned her aching head into her husband's chest. "Okay, you win," she said. Standing on her toes, she gave him a kiss.

"I'll ask what the kids want and you go down and finish up whatever you were doing in the kitchen."

"Packing food, Graham. So we can eat on the weekend. It doesn't just magically appear when we show up to the cabin," she explained, heading down the back stairs.

"Oh, that's how I thought it happened," he teased, opening Lydia's door. "Hey, I'm picking up burgers when I take Ally to work. What do you want?"

"Nothing if she's making it," she mumbled, tossing flip flops into her bag.

"Okay, one shack burger loaded with raw onions," Graham said, walking away.

"NO! A chicken burger!" Lydia called out.

***

With little delay, Joanna had three kids, food, bags, a husband and a dog all packed up and ready to leave, exactly on schedule. They would get to the cabin in time to unpack, enjoy a late night snack and finally to bed. Joanna loved going to the cabin. But her family had no clue how much effort it took, even for a weekend. Replenishing the kitchen staples, towels, linens, bug spray and sunscreen; it all needed organizing. Between Nana Ellie, Sarah and Joanna, they shared in the tasks of keeping the cabin well stocked. No one had to keep score or complain, it simply worked.

Todd and Sarah would be joining them on Saturday until Sunday. Joanna wasn't sure how she was going to break the news to Ally and Lydia that they would be sharing a room when their aunt and uncle arrived. She wanted the rest of the ride to Lake of the Woods to be quiet and peaceful, as the twins were plugged in watching a movie while Ally fell asleep. She would wait until the morning to tell them, once they all had at least one night of sleep in their own rooms. Joanna could hardly wait to get there.

Graham was the first to wake up the next morning. He made a pot of coffee and took a cup with him to the boat dock he and Todd had built a few summers ago. Bentley followed his master and obediently took his spot at the edge of the dock and lay down. Graham loved these quiet, peaceful and uninterrupted mornings spent with just him and the lake, as the loons and ducks crossed his view of the endless water. Finding the Adirondack chair he put his head back and took in the serenity and memories of this space he had known his whole life.

This land had been in his family since in the early 1930s, when Graham's grandfather, Jacob Kornelson, bought this place so he could go boating and fishing. Graham's father grew up going to the cabin and often had reminisced about fishing with his dad. Grandpa Jacob passed away when he was only sixty-six, and had willed the cabin and land to his oldest son, Ed, in memory of their many years fishing together.

Graham remembered when he was still quite young, coming down to the cabin with his dad and his building crew to add on a new kitchen and the second floor loft. When Graham was in high school, they built on the addition of two bedrooms and a second bathroom. Years later the deck was extended and eventually stairs built on leading to the boat dock.

Graham took a sip of the steaming black coffee, remembering the awful day when Ed told them that he had cancer. During that meeting, Ed also said he wanted his boys to share the cabin and to pass it down to their children. He made them promise to keep his father's land and cabin in the Kornelson family. Graham took care of the legalities to ensure his father's wishes. Within a few weeks of signing the papers, they watched him fade away as the cancer cells took the heart and then the soul of the man they didn't want to live without.

Graham took in a deep breath and slowly let it out. He missed his dad everyday and could see him right now sitting beside him on the dock with that crazy, old straw hat he wore, only at the cabin. It still hung in the boat house.

Graham took another sip wondering what his dad would say about how he was doing. He wanted to ask him so often, especially since Ally was diagnosed with epilepsy. He second guessed his parenting these days, especially because Joanna seemed so sure of her decisions. She would tell him about the new medications and treatments she had researched. Joanna wanted to know everything about this strange illness that came unannounced into their family. And she talked so intelligently about it; like she had become an expert where he was the mere student. His wife also believed she knew what Ally needed every minute of the hour. Her parenting style had become so intense over the past year. He became a spectator in raising his children when Joanna decided she was the coach and general manager of their family. Where did he belong anymore? To him, he always thought they were good at co-parenting and proved that especially when the twins were born. They became officially outnumbered and had to find extra limbs and patience when handling a toddler and two babies.

Graham smiled remembering the mornings he would take one of the twins with him down to the dock and let them sleep on his chest while he listened to them breathe in contentment. But now, the breathing had become heated and destructive between his daughters, and Joanna was sucked into it every time. She also didn't want to hear his opinions anymore.

Finishing the coffee he placed the mug on the arm of the chair and crossed his arms over his chest. Closing his eyes, he asked himself what would his dad tell him to do? Would he offer advice or just chuckle and shake his head to say, *Good luck, son. Not always as easy as it looks, is it?*

Graham sat up and leaned forward staring into the water. He knew what his dad would tell him. He would tell Graham that your kids didn't choose you nor did you choose them. You were brought together, now figure it out. Graham laughed softly. His dad loved family. He adored and cherished his wife of nearly five decades and was so proud of his sons. How come it seemed so simple for his dad? He wondered if he and his mom argued or disagreed because Graham couldn't recall when his dad raised his voice at his mother, to him or Todd. He was an aggressive and shrewd businessman, but when it came to family, he was generous and patient.

Leaning back again, Graham thought about how it used to be between him and Joanna. Nothing was so horrible that they couldn't talk it through, without anger and yelling. When did Joanna become a yeller anyway? When did they become the couple who avoided conflict and each other? It was easier just to let Joanna have her way, so they could all live in peace. She used to need him and valued his input. He relied on her instincts and trusted her judgments. Now they were skeptical and demanding towards one another. On the surface they managed, but deep down, something was broken.

He saw a small group of ducks float by the boat dock. *Life has always been just that effortless,* he thought, watching them glide by. With two perfect parents, a brother who was his best friend and a life filled with comfort and accommodation in every respect. He had no need to want or complain and yet he never felt entitled. Graham felt blessed.

He loved Joanna Schultz from the moment he saw her while they were students at university. Winning her over to see what a great guy he was proved to be a welcomed challenge. But soon their lives blended and their life of home and family became a reality and a dream they shared together. He loved his kids from the minute he knew they were coming into their lives. He remembered holding them in his arms the second they were born, passing them over to Joanna as they shared their elation of having a family. He loved the house they could finally afford to buy and how it became their home.

The ducks glided around the bend and disappeared. Graham sank further into the chair and hoped and prayed that his family would survive the next turn around the corner. It all seemed so tentative now, never knowing if a seizure would take them all down again. There was a constant level of anxiety in their home. How do they get back to what they once had as a family? Could he and Joanna ever figure that out again?

"Hi, Dad," Lydia mumbled, coming down the stairs.

Graham turned around and held out his arm to his tired daughter still in her pyjamas. "Hey, Lyd. Did you have a good sleep? You're up early." He moved his mug thinking she would sit on the arm of the chair, but instead she sat on his lap and cuddled into his chest. She didn't exactly fit like she used to. But Graham shifted to give her room and wrapped his arms around his daughter smoothing out her mop of hair in his face.

"Who else is up?" he murmured in her ear.

"Mom is." She quickly sat up. "And she said I have to move into Ally's room because Abigail and Nora are sleeping in my room tonight. That's not fair," she whined, before cuddling again.

"Well, Jack has to sleep on the couch, so Uncle Todd and Auntie Sarah can have a room. That's so much worse. At least you get the top bunk."

"I hate that bed," she complained, with a big morning yawn. "I don't want to share a room with Ally."

"Lydia, you've got to try to get along. I know it all seems so unfair to you -"

"Well, it is," she interrupted.

"I know that, because you keep telling us it is. But nothing is really fair in life you know. We got two babies when we really only wanted one more," he teased.

"Da-ad," she whined with a smile.

Graham thought for a moment before he spoke, stroking the length of her long dark hair. "Do you remember what our life was like before Ally got epilepsy? We were an everyday family who did ordinary stuff like everyone else. But then this happened to her and it affected all of us."

"I do get sad, you know, when it happens....to her."

Graham was quiet for a second. "I know, we all do. It's like we all fall down along with Ally. But that's what families do. We fall and we get back up again. Sometimes we may need to help each other up and other times we watch as they learn to do it themselves. And then we are their biggest cheerleaders. Ally can't do this alone, she needs us."

Lydia sat up again and wrapped her arms around her knees. "I know that, Dad. But it's just hard sometimes. She gets all this attention and everyone is always asking about her -"

"I bet you that boat in that boathouse that Ally would do anything not to get that attention," he said, pointing to the floating building just a few feet away from them.

"You love that boat, Dad," she said, looking at him.

"Not nearly as much as I love my kids and what we have going on here. We're a family, Lydia. For better or worse, your mom said to me. We promised each other and everyone we brought into this world that we would look out for them, no matter what."

She looked into the water and brushed the stray hair from her face. Turning to face her dad, she cuddled into his chest once again. "I don't like feeling this way. Like I don't like Ally. I do, it's just that, oh, I don't know."

"Come on spit it out. I just put my boat on the line for you," he teased, rubbing her back gently.

She sat up again. "It's just hard to watch her suffer during a seizure then act like nothing's wrong, while we're the ones who have to take care of her."

"But Lydia, she can't help that. It's not her fault and she doesn't mean to "act" any way. This is the disease and we have to sometimes fit into how it....comes." He put her hair behind her ear. "I hate it too, Lyd. I wish that it would all go away and maybe it will and maybe it won't. But whatever happens, we will still be here, for Ally and you."

She nodded, looking out onto the lake. "Mom is making breakfast."

"Eggs and bacon?"

"Pancakes and sausages."

"Well, let's not disappoint and keep her waiting."

They stood up and walked back up the stairs, smelling the welcoming aromas of breakfast coming from the cabin. Nothing more was said. It was suddenly all just right, once again.

24
Cabin Conversations

After breakfast, Lydia quietly moved her things into Ally's room. It was about noon, when Todd and Sarah arrived with two sleeping little girls. The rest of the afternoon she played with Abigail and Nora, who didn't need their usual afternoon naps. Even though Lydia was fourteen, she still enjoyed the creative imagination of three and four year old little girls, as they pretended that their dolls were going to the beach.

Ally wasn't interested in pretend, so she asked to go on the motorboat with the boys. Joanna and Sarah took out the much gentler canoe. Of course, there was a few intentional close calls between the two water crafts, causing a few battles on the lake. The water was still pretty cold, but they went swimming by the boat dock. Lydia brought her cousins down to join them. It turned out to be hotter then was forecast, allowing them to enjoy hot sunshine until the late afternoon.

Once they had all dried off, naps and relaxation were next on the agenda until it would be time to get ready for supper. Ally sat out on the deck off the kitchen. Jack and Graham went for a run together down the bay road. Joanna found a book, Sarah took a nap. Lydia, Abigail and Nora got a snack and resumed playing in their room. Todd grabbed himself a beer and went to join Ally outside.

"What are you up to all by yourself?" Todd asked, sitting beside her on the swinging bench.

"Nothing, just looking and thinking."

"That sounds about right," he said, taking a swig from the bottle.

Ally studied the amber bottle that her uncle held. "Will I ever be able to drink beer?" she asked. "I mean, because of all the drugs I'm on. What would happen?"

"Well, first your mother would have an absolute fit and your dad would never allow you to leave your house again," he answered, very matter of fact.

"Uncle Todd, I'm not kidding. What would happen?" she asked again. "Answer me like a doctor, not my dad's brother."

Todd glanced over, seeing she was serious. "Well, Ally, it's not recommended to mix alcohol with any drugs, ever. Drinking might increase some of the side effects that could risk a seizure. The alcohol changes the chemistry of the medications. Didn't you learn about this in science?"

"Yeah probably, but I may not have been listening," she said, twisting her long brown, hair into a bun on top of her head. "So is that what's happening to your blood now?" she asked, turning towards her uncle.

"I'm not on any drugs and I don't plan on driving until tomorrow so I'm fine if my blood gets a little beer into it," he answered, tugging at the wet label on the bottle. "What is it that you're exactly asking me, Ally?" he questioned, taking another sip and putting the distracting beverage down onto the small wooden table beside the swing.

She debated whether to ask. But she trusted her uncle and knew he would be honest with her. "I just want to know if I'll ever be normal again?" She looked out into the distance as if normal was a faraway place across the lake.

"You know Ally, I don't think normal exists for anyone. I see a lot of bad circumstances and people are constantly getting bad news about their health. It happens," he answered.

"Is it hard telling people they're going to die?"

"You ask me that on my day off," he teased, slapping her knee.

"I'm not a baby. I want to know," she said, looking down as emotion came close to the surface. "Could I die?"

"Hey, Ally," he said, tenderly putting his arm around his niece. "Where is this all coming from?"

She sat up taller. "I'm not kidding, sometimes it feels like..... everything is sad and unimportant. It feels like this thing is going to take over me and it's going to kill me." She looked at her uncle. "Is it?"

Todd analyzed what she was really saying as he battled between being the supportive uncle or a medical expert. "Tell me about what your neurologist has told you?"

"Just does these stupid tests where I have to touch my nose with my finger and then follow her finger around with my eyes. Then she asks how I'm feeling. We talk about school and piano. Then they adjust my drugs and she tells me the side effects."

"And do you ask her these questions you're asking me?"

"Well, she said I shouldn't drink alcohol or have a baby right now. Like I needed a specialist to tell me that."

She hesitated playing with her medical bracelet. "But my parents are with me at my appointments, and I don't want to scare them so I don't say what's bothering me. And I don't want to search the web in case I see something I don't want to know. So, I'm asking you as a doctor and my uncle, could I die?"

He took in a deep breath and debated what to say. Was this her curiosity asking questions or did it go much deeper than searching for mere answers? He moved to face Ally. "Your type of epilepsy shouldn't cause death. But of course if you are in a dangerous situation and have a seizure, it could be fatal. That's why it's important that you have people you trust around you," he advised. "There are things you can do to decrease your risks like avoiding heights and not swimming alone." He hesitated a second seeing if what he was saying was what she was asking. But Ally was looking towards the setting sun. "Ally, you should let your parents know how you're feeling."

She sighed deeply. "Mom just freaks out all the time. I want to grow up and move on with my life. I don't want this to hold me back. I'm not always going to be with people who know me. And it would feel weird to introduce myself by saying, 'Hey, I'm Ally the epileptic.'"

He chuckled. "I knew people at university that had seizure disorders. Lots and lots of people have medical conditions that they learn to live with and are very successful. But you just need to come up with a plan for yourself so that when you are on your own, you have people who know about your situation and who will look out for you."

She thought about it. It was overwhelming to think about moving out and starting university. But she also had to manage her illness, all on her own.

"You are already successful, Al. I've known some epileptics who won't get out of bed. Or they've just given up on living as normally as they can. You're not like that. You're determined and hard-headed; focused on piano and always doing your best. That's going to get you very far in life. You're that kind of girl."

She peered out into the distance again not quite sure she in fact was that kind of girl. "Okay. I just wanted to know if this was, you know, going to get me in the end."

It shocked him how blunt she was talking about her death. She obviously had been thinking about it a lot. "Not if I can help it, Al. You're a smart girl, you'll figure it out."

"Thanks, I think I'm going to take a nap before supper. I'm exhausted."

She got up and headed inside the cabin. She fell asleep in her parents' bed, the only room not occupied. A little bit of relief helped her to drift off quickly. Death was something she had started thinking about more than she cared to admit, even to herself. Her uncle was probably right, but now all she wanted was to slip into that beautiful place where nothing really mattered at all, sleep. She was gone.

Todd grabbed his beer and took another gulp. Abigail opened the balcony door. "Hi Daddy," she said. "I'm done playing now." With her little legs, she forced herself up on the swing beside her dad as he gave her a boost. Sitting beside him, she looked up and smiled with a giggle.

"Push me, Daddy."

With a push of one foot they were swinging together, making her laugh. She moved to sit on her dad's lap. He cuddled his little girl as they watched the birds fly overhead; Abigail pointed as they flew from tree to tree. Todd held her close to his chest as she was babbling about the clouds and the bugs.

The sun was setting across the lake. Todd went through the conversation with Ally in his mind as his innocent and healthy little girl clapped her hands trying to catch flies. He knew he needed to talk to Graham when they got back home.

***

Later that night, the Kornelson clan gathered around the table for a surf and turf feast. Jack grabbed the last off the buttery garlic shrimp, yanked off the tale and shoved it into his mouth. "Hey, Nora, are you going to eat that shrimp?" he asked, pointing to her full plate of food.

"Go for it, Jack," Sarah answered for her. "I guess she hasn't quite developed a taste for shrimp."

Jack reached over and cleaned off his cousin's plate.

"That boy is going to break your grocery budget, Joanna," Todd commented, watching his nephew scrounging for scraps. He nudged his brother. "Remember when we used to eat like that?"

"Yep, and tonight I still thought I could. What were we thinking barbecuing all those steaks and shrimp. I need to go for another run or I'm going to bust open," Graham moaned, getting up ever so slowly.

Joanna began to stack the dirty plates. "I believe there is dessert."

"Are you kidding?" he questioned, rubbing his stomach. "None for me, whatever it is. I overate," he answered as Sarah came back from the kitchen with pie.

Todd was wiping the ketchup from Nora's little hands and face. "You have never ever said 'no' to pie, Graham. Ever."

"Well, I will. Or I'll at least wait until later." He looked at the pies. Chocolate laced with a mocha cream and cherry, probably a peach pie. "Can you save me a piece for later?

"Not if I get to it first, Dad," Jack said, standing beside Sarah as she served him a slice of the chocolate for starters.

"Pie, Daddy," Nora asked, from her high chair.

"Okay, I'll have the same size you're going to give Nora," Graham conceded.

Todd stood up raising his hands in victory. "There it is. You caved, man!"

"I didn't cave, I just don't want to be rude. Just a small one, Sarah."

"Graham, don't overdo it," Joanna warned. "Just say no!"

"I can't. I'll share with Nora, and then I'll be done."

Ally sat quietly while eating just the cherries in the slice of pie. She was noticing her clothes were getting a bit snug and decided to go easy on the dessert. She also noticed that Lydia was unusually quiet this weekend and seemed to be avoiding her. Or maybe Lydia was just having fun playing with their little cousins. Lydia loved being the older one and orchestrating them in their activities. And the little girls loved getting the attention from Lydia. Ally put her fork down and looked at her family. Her mom and aunt were laughing about something, probably stupid. Her dad and uncle were teasing each other and talking about when they were young. There was a peaceful, familiar feeling that overcame her. She loved the cabin and being with her family. But yet it all felt so odd experiencing these strange moments of contentment mixing in with her dark thoughts. Bentley nudged Ally's leg and she sneaked him the piecrust. She watched her dad tease Nora by pretending to take her pie. And Jack offering to wipe Abigail's hands while Lydia, her mom and aunt took away the rest of the dishes.

This is a good moment, Ally thought. It had been a long time since her family had found moments of happiness like this. Effortlessly talking and laughing and working together. No one seemed to notice how special and ordinary this was; and it didn't really matter. Ally noticed and she smiled ever so slightly.

Just as the food was put away and the adults sat down with cups of coffee, it started to rain outside. Soon it was coming down in sheets that were accompanied by claps of thunder and lightning, which streaked the night sky. They all stood by the large living room window that overlooked the lake and the vast, dark distance. Nora got scared and crawled up her dad's leg and was soothed in his arms.

Graham started a fire in the fireplace as they found their spots and ended the evening talking about everything and nothing. Laughing, retelling about the day and remembering the past. They drank coffee and listened to stories by the glow of the fiery embers as rain spattering against the windows of the cabin. Everyone soon claimed fatigue and slowly they made their way to bed. Graham offered to stay by the fire until it was out. Joanna told Sarah to put her already sleeping babies to bed while she would clean up the coffee.

Ally was already in bed when Lydia had finished in the bathroom and came into her room. "Can I turn on the light, or are you sleeping?" Lydia asked, quietly.

"No, I'm not sleeping. I'll turn on the lamp for you," Ally offered, reaching over and turning the knob on the ancient lamp that had been in the cabin as long as she could remember.

Lydia put her clothes onto the chair and took out her earrings, adding them carefully into the little box that she kept at the cabin.

"Okay, I'm done," Lydia announced, coming to bed. She was about to turn off the lamp before crawling up the ladder to the top bunk, when she saw Ally.

"What's the matter?" Lydia asked, with a slight panic in her tone.

"Nothing, why?"

"Cause you're just staring and it scared me," Lydia said, placing her hand over her heart.

Ally thought of a snarky comment to say and then roll over. But she didn't this time. Instead, she patted her hand on the bed for Lydia to sit down. "Can I ask you something, Lydia?"

"What?"

"Tell me what it's like. What do you see?" she asked her little sister, searching her surprised face for clues.

"You mean when you have a seizure?"

Ally wanted to fire back a sarcastic comment, but was too tired for that and just wanted answers. She nodded.

Lydia toyed with the random buttons on the patchwork quilt. She had never talked about it before or let alone described it. "I don't know, scary, I guess."

"Does it look like, I'm going to, die?"

Lydia stared at her sister and slowly tears filled her eyes. "Ally, don't say that."

"Why?"

"Because, your seizures won't kill you. And it sounds awful to say."

"How do you know they won't kill me?" she asked, sitting up a bit more.

"Because that's what Mom told me. And even though you stop breathing for a while, you always start to breathe again."

"Is that what happens?"

"Why do you want to talk about this?" she asked, crossing her legs.

"Because... I don't know. All I know is that I wake up and I ache and my head hurts and then I wait and see where all the bruises and marks show up on my body."

Lydia rested her chin in her hand remembering all the seizures she had witnessed over the past two years. Everyone was just as awful and horrifying as the first one. Watching her sister flail and twitch, making gasping noises and turning shades of grey and blue. Her eyes bugging out of her face and her lips swelling up as her body and mind lose all control and function. Lydia closed her eyes to erase the images. She looked at Ally sitting beside her, all normal and talking and being her sister.

"It's terrifying, Ally. One second you're here and normal and then all of a sudden you're gone and looking like you can't breathe and your entire body is struggling." Lydia swallowed back the harsh memories. "I don't want to talk about it anymore," she said, as her voice choked up.

Ally reached out to her sister. "It's okay, Lydia. I just sometimes wonder."

"Wonder what?"

"What it's like, you know, for you, watching me? Seeing it."

"I hate it Ally and I wish it would go away and it would never happen to you ever again," she said. A quiet tear rolled down each cheek.

Ally pulled the covers back. Lydia crawled inside and cuddled with her sister like they did when they were little. "It's okay, Lyd. It is. You don't have to talk about it."

"Have you ever asked Mom about it?" Lydia asked, sniffling.

Ally shook her head. "No, I don't want to freak her out. She gets so...intense. I can't imagine that she'd ever let me out of the house again if I started asking her questions like this. And then she'd tell Dad."

Lydia turned on her back and pulled the covers up to her chin. "Then you can ask me, if you want, okay? Can I turn the light off now?"

"Sure. Aren't you going to sleep in your bed up there?" Ally asked, moving over, grateful that her bed was a double.

"Can I sleep with you?" Lydia asked. "I hate that bed."

"Yeah, get the light," Ally said, smiling.

An hour later, Joanna was on her way to bed when Graham came from the bathroom.

"I'm just going to check on the girls," she said, gently opening their door. The light from the hallway streamed into the room as the top bunk lay untouched. Joanna and Graham quietly walked into the room.

Noticing his daughters cuddling together under his grandmother's quilt, he touched Joanna's arm and pointed to the girls. Their long brown hair flowing together not knowing where one began from the other. Joanna smiled and looked up at Graham. Slowly they tiptoed out and closed the door.

"So glad we came," Graham whispered. He shut off the hallway light as they walked into their room.

"Me too."

25
Garden Stories

Joanna pulled weeds from around the zinnias.
Putzing in the garden had always given her a welcomed
place to ponder. One revelation that she contemplated
while cutting back the rose bushes, was realizing she had
barely had a conversation with Laura or Pauline over the
past few months. July was almost over and other than a
few Facebook chats and email forwards, there had been no
great effort to connect. Joanna stood up and stretched out
her back as she peered at the glorious blooms of the lilies
and pots of colourful annuals.

Pruning back a spent Gerber daisy, Joanna thought
about her family and friends and how they were like plants
in a garden. Sometimes flowers, like people, can be surprising when they're going to make an appearance. The
sad Russian Sage in the back corner, wasn't going to make
it, no matter how much attention it was given. While others
were faithful and would show up every year to make an
impression with joy and colour. Looking farther into the
garden, Joanna noticed that the delphinium continued to
suffer. It always did have issues. But Joanna hated to see

any of her plants yanked out and discarded. Every spring, she nurtured each plant hoping they would survive. Some plants always were more needy. She would try pruning them back, move them around; hoping they would do better if they were replanted and had a fresh start. Some plants were tiny and insecure and were overshadowed by a another one that was getting too big for its space. They all needed different kinds of attention.

Using the strategically placed stepping stones, Joanna went to the very back of the garden where the hollyhocks, original to the yard, proudly waved in the wind. These were the grand old ladies of the garden; standing united, tall and proud. Secretly they were her favourites in the whole yard.

A garden is never really finished, she surmised, wiping her brow. It grows, struggles and sometimes it doesn't make it, no matter how much tending and nurturing they require. Weeds will always threaten the other flowers with their ugly roots that spread like nasty gossip. Joanna walked through the massive flower garden that lined the back of their property. But when the flowers and plants bloomed with abundance of colour it was all worth it, she decided, deadheading along the way.

Joanna sat on the bench hidden in the back and lifted her face to the glowing sun beating down its hot rays. She heard the birds singing and the wind whispering through the trees that lined the sides of their yard. Bentley was running around sniffing out forgotten treasures. It was simple in the garden; private, secluded, beautiful and fresh. It cleared her head and calmed her down from life's complications; it was here she found perspective again.

"Hey Jo, are you back here?" Graham called out from the back porch.

She stood up and waved.

He held up the phone. "It's for you. It's your mom."

Running from across the yard, Joanna took the phone that was on mute. "What time is it?"

"5:30." He took off his suit jacket and loosened his tie.

"Oh, I had no idea it was that late. Lost track of time again. Where are the kids?"

"Why don't you talk to your mother first, before she thinks you're ignoring her," he suggested. He took a beer from the outside fridge and sat down on the couch. He needed to mow the lawn he noticed scanning the yard.

"Hi Mom. Sorry I was out in the backyard. What's up?"

"Well, I have something to tell you. I've decided to retire from the library," she answered without any emotional preamble.

"Wow, Mom, that's great. Isn't it? When did you decide to retire?" she asked, sitting on the porch steps.

"Recently," Susan answered, with a small pause. "I'd also like to ask you... something else."

Joanna turned and looked at Graham. "Okay."

Susan hesitated a second too long, but Joanna was patient and let her take her time. It wasn't often that her mother asked her for anything.

"My last day will be August 4th, and I was...I'm asking if you would host a garden party for me on that day. Just for a few friends and your sisters and their families of course. And the library board and staff I suppose."

Joanna's jaw dropped making Graham very curious.

"I think that would work for us. Yes, I'd love to do that for you, Mom."

"Nothing too fancy or too over the top, Joanna. It's just that you have a lovely garden and I thought it would be, nice."

"Sure whatever you want. Just let me know what to prepare and for how many and I'll take care of everything," Joanna said, with a surprising sense of appreciation.

"I'll take care of any costs, Joanna."

"Not to worry, Mom."

"Well, the chair of the board said he wanted to make sure I got a proper send off. I'm sure they will cover the expenses," she stressed again.

"We can work it out." There was another strange pause. "Well, that's great, Mom, I'm glad you decided to finally retire. Now you can go on trips with Dad and -"

"Well, we'll see how I like it," she answered with a touch of bitterness.

Joanna wondered if this was not her decision. Perhaps the library board encouraged her to finally retire after nearly forty years.

"I'll keep in touch. I will probably call you next week and we can work out some of the details. Good bye Joanna," she said and hung up the phone.

"She's retiring?" Graham asked.

Joanna stood up and sat down beside him, taking his beer and gulping down a big sip. She hated beer and made a horrible face.

"She's retiring," Joanna reiterated, gladly returning the beer. "And she asked me to host the retirement party for her."

"She asked?" he questioned again.

Joanna nodded wiping her sweaty brow. "Nothing fancy or over the top she said." Joanna was already thinking of how she was going to set up the backyard for the party.

"So you're going to do it, I take it?" Graham asked, putting the cold beer bottle on her arm to get her attention.

She looked at her husband. "Of course, I'm going to do it. My mother never asks, she just orders."

Joanna imagining an old fashioned garden party. "I don't care what she says, I'm going to make the best party I've ever done." She was already placing tables with white table clothes around the yard. Party sandwiches, strawberry lemonade and maybe she would try baking petit fours. She and Pinterest would be busy over the next few weeks.

"Do I have to be there?" Graham asked meekly.

"Here you are. I'm hungry," Jack said, coming from a basketball game in the park. He was rather hot, smelly and sweaty.

"Jack, my boy," Graham said, "just in time to mow the grass. We're getting ready for a tea party," he mocked.

"Don't sit on my cushioned chairs, Jack, you're dirty," Joanna quickly barked out before he had a chance to sit.

He sat on the stairs. "I don't want to mow the lawn and I'm not getting ready for a tea party, whatever that is."

"And yes you both have to be there," Joanna stressed. "I'm going to need your help getting tables and chairs back here and you'll have to mow the day before and edge the yard too. There's a lot to do and you have to help out. This is for Grandma."

Jack grabbed a coke from the fridge, "What are you talking about?" he asked, moving the toss pillows off the wooden swing, taking a seat.

"Grandma's retiring and she asked me to host the retirement party."

"Terrific," Jack muttered.

Graham gave him a high hive. "I hear you, son," he said.

Ally and Lydia came from the house. "Here's everyone," Ally said, taking a seat. "When's supper? I'm hungry."

"Yeah, me too," Lydia agreed, sitting on her dad's lap.

"Oh Lydia," Graham groaned. "Don't you think you're getting a little too old for this?"

"No," she said, leaning her head against his chest.

"Guess what girls? Grandma's retiring from the library and asked me to host a party for her," Joanna said, clapping her hands with excitement.

"Hasn't she been there for like 100 years?" Ally asked, putting her head on the teak dining table. "I'm so hungry, when are we eating?"

"Me too, what are we having?" Jack asked, crushing the empty can.

Joanna sighed. They really didn't care, did they? "Hamburgers. They're in the freezer," she answered, coming back to reality.

"Okay, I want two," Jack said.

"Girls set the table out here. Graham can you start the barbecue. Jack, go to the freezer and get the hamburgers and buns. I'll make a cole slaw or something," Joanna instructed.

Looking at her blooming and lush backyard, Joanna smiled. It felt good to get acknowledged for her efforts, especially by her mother. Throughout her childhood, she had so few memories of her mother showing interest in her three daughters' accomplishments or hobbies. It caused an unspoken divide among them; allowing a disconnect to run through their stilted conversations. Their mother's career always came first was how Joanna remembered it. Joanna was surprised that her mother even knew what her garden looked like. But she stopped the trail of silent and petty thoughts, forbidding the doubt to creep in. Her mother wanted her help and for today, that was enough. Joanna stood up and took one more glance of the yard; always a surprise waiting in the garden.

26
Lessons

That familiar blue car drove up in front of the Kornelson house. It parked right in front of the sidewalk that went up to the front porch of their home. He took the long walk to the stairs and was about to ring the door bell when the front door flew open.

"Hi Matthew," Ally said, smiling.

He awkwardly waved to her. "Hey."

Joanna came around the corner of the wraparound porch, watering the flower pots. "Hey, Ally," she said, although it came out more like a question.

"Hi Mom. Matthew and I are going meet everyone at Christine's place."

"And what's going on at her place?" Joanna asked, trying to act as casual, watering the pots of impatiens.

"We're just going to hang out there and then I think her dad is going to make a fire and we're going to have s'mores and stuff like that," she said, looking up at Matthew.

He was well over six feet tall with blue eyes and short, cropped, blond hair. He was a high school athlete and had the potential to get volleyball scholarships at several universities. He and Ally got to know each other through the jazz band where she was the pianist and he played guitar. They were often the last two talking at the end of the class when everyone had gone. They started hanging out when they realized they had a few mutual friends. Matthew moved to Mountain City when he was starting grade 10; still newer to town and eager to fit in.

"So what time will you be home?" Joanna asked, putting down the empty watering can.

"Does it matter? It's not like we have school or anything," Ally answered, trying to act cool under her mother's glaring eye.

"What time would you like her home by, Mrs. Kornelson?" Matthew asked politely.

Joanna liked this kid. "No later than 11:00."

"Mom, midnight at least. No one else has a curfew," she complained.

"No one else has epilepsy either, my dear. And I don't believe for a second that no one else has a curfew," Joanna answered back. There was no hiding or denying Ally's condition, it was part of their family. Plus, if Matthew was going to be hanging around as much as he had been the past few weeks, he needed to know this would become his reality too, and that meant a curfew.

"Do you have your pills with you?" Joanna asked.

"Yes," Ally said annoyed, shaking her purse hearing the familiar shaking of the bottles.

"Okay, midnight at the absolute latest and not a second later, do you hear me?" Joanna threatened, looking at them both. "And Matthew you have my cell number if anything is to happen?"

He nodded holding up his phone. "Right here and I also have Mr. Kornelson's too."

"Sheesh Mom, we're just going to Christine's, not across the world," Ally said as her and Matthew waved good bye and walked down to his car. He opened the door for her and he must have said something funny because Ally started laughing. Joanna smiled.

Graham pulled up the driveway, coming from his Sunday afternoon golf game with his buddies. He waved to the blue car as it slowly and cautiously pulled onto the road.

"Where are they off to now?" Graham asked, getting his clubs from the trunk of the car.

"A bonfire at Christine's," Joanna answered, sitting on the rocking chair. "How come I feel much older than I am?"

"Sitting on a rocking chair on a Sunday afternoon, perhaps," he answered, leaning on the railing.

Graham pointed down the road. "Do we just let her go with that kid every time he comes over?"

"Now who sounds old? He's a good kid who happens to be named Matthew Rogalsky. You don't have to refer him as 'that kid' anymore."

"Hey, was that Matthew Rogalsky here again?" Jack asked, bounding through the front door. "How come I always miss him when he's here? He's an amazing volleyball and basketball player. I can't believe he's dating my sister."

Graham stood up. "Wait, what? What's going on here? He's dating her?" He looked at Joanna. "When did this all happen?"

"Nothing is happening," Joanna answered. "What makes you think they're dating, Jack?"

"Well, he picks her up all the time and brings her home from school," Jack replied.

"That's because she needs rides. They're just friends," Joanna stated with a brief hesitation.

"Really? You think he's just being nice to her and giving her a ride? Whatever, Mom," he pointed out. "Hey Dad, wanna shoot some hoops?"

"Give me a second. Let me catch my breath. I just had my daughter married off in my head," he moaned, holding his chest. "Hey Jo, do you want to hear about my round?" Graham knew how much she hated hearing about every stroke of his golf game. It all sounded the same to her. She could never remember what the difference was between birdies and bogies.

She stood up and kissed her husband. "Go play basketball old man!" she teased and headed back into the house.

Soon she heard that pinging of the basketball bouncing on the driveway, a shot at the wooden backboard and then a cheer and groan. The summer had been going well, so far. Lydia was enjoying her last day at camp and was coming home tonight. Ally was working at the Burger Shack. She had her bad days, but they were all feeling equipped in managing her mood swings. Jack was growing every week, now nearly as tall as his dad and starting to fill out. And the best part was that Lydia and Ally seemed to be friends again. Joanna often found them talking in one of their rooms before bed. Or Ally brought Lydia her favourite ice cream from the Burger Shack when she got home from work.

The retirement party the week before had been a triumph for Joanna, if no one else. She had decorated with jars of flowers and old books on top of linen covered tables filled with elegant sandwiches, cakes and lemonade. Joanna loved hosting the party for her mother. Even if her sisters may have judged her efforts, it didn't rattle Joanna. She was honoured to do it.

It was a summer of learning lessons about herself and what she was capable of accomplishing and overcoming. Although they never knew how long the streak of good days were going to last, she would enjoy these moments as long as she could.

***

School was starting in one week. Back to studying, schedules and early morning choir rehearsals. Ally zipped up her hoody contemplating if she was ready to head back to school quite yet. The evening air was getting cooler as she and Matthew sat on a picnic table overlooking the beach. The sun was setting, casting dark shadows in the tiny waves and licks of the water. A family was on the other side playing in the sand and enjoying the last few hours of the daylight and saying farewell to summer.

"Do you want anymore?" Matthew asked, holding out the cardboard container of French fries. Ally shook her head, putting her hands in her pockets.

He tried tossing the empty carton into a nearby garbage like it was a basketball, but missed by a long shot as the breeze took it sideways. "Ah, I thought I had it," he said, getting up and throwing it into the garbage can. He turned around and saw deep thoughts on Ally's face.

Shortly after Christine's backyard bonfire, they realized they were becoming more than just friends. Matthew even offered to talk to Ally's parents. Nervously, he sat with Graham in the backyard one evening and asked if he could date his daughter. Ally asked her mother to stay out of it. Ally feared her mom's smothering over protectiveness would scare him away. Joanna was offended, but Graham talked his wife off the ledge and told her to go for a run when Matthew came over; he was confident he could handle a teenage boy on his own.

Slowly, Matthew made his way back to his spot beside Ally. "What are you thinking about?"

"Nothing," she replied casually. "I just stare into nowhere sometimes."

"That is not a look on your face that is thinking about nothing. I catch you staring a thousand miles away and I always wonder, what is going on inside that brain of yours?" he asked, watching her.

She quickly turned to face him. "My brain? You want to know what's going on with my brain?" she said seriously.

He looked down. "Sorry, that's not what I meant," he stammered, feeling slightly embarrassed. He did want to talk about her condition, but he never knew how to bring up the topic.

Ally didn't want to talk to Matthew about her illness. She liked that they talked about normal, everyday things. But she also wanted him to understand that epilepsy was always with her. She played with the medical bracelet on her left wrist.

Reaching out he turned it over and read 'epileptic.'

"There it is, that's me in one word," Ally proclaimed.

He turned it back over and held her hand. "Nope, that's a condition you have, but not who you are. I don't see you as that one word."

"That's because you've never seen a seizure, Matthew," she answered carefully.

He didn't know what to say.

"Matthew, why me? Out of all the girls, why me? There is a line up of them who would go out with you in a heartbeat. I see them follow you around the hallways always trying to get your attention."

"I don't care about that. They don't know me; it's weird. You listen to me. In jazz band, one time I saw you watching me when I was playing, and I realized you weren't watching me, you were listening to me play. And then you suggested a different chord progression. At first I thought, *you're a piano player, what do you know about guitar?* And then I saw you were telling everyone else how to play -"

"Oh, that makes me sound so bossy, just like my mother," she cringed, bringing her hands to her face.

"No, you knew what you were talking about and you made us all sound better. I thought, how does she know that? And then I heard you play piano and I knew. You listen and hear things most other girls don't."

She looked into the distance again as her heart took a little flip.

"That's why I picked you, Ally. You are different, but not in a way that I think you think," he said, stumbling over his words. "I've done some reading about seizures, you know."

She turned to face him. "Really? And any advice for me? Because the doctors don't always know."

He shifted, facing her. "I'm into science and find all that brain activity stuff interesting, I guess. How the synapses work or don't work. Does your seizures have like a starting point?"

She pointed to the middle of her forehead with her finger. "Right here," she said. "The frontal lobe." At least that's what the EEGs said."

He looked at her. "Does it feel weird, you know, when it happens?"

She stared towards the beach again.

"Sorry, Ally, you don't have to talk about it if you don't want to. I'm sorry I keep bringing it up."

"Matthew, I just want to feel normal, like everyone else, and I don't. And I don't remember what it was like before I was diagnosed anymore." Quick tears sprang into her eyes as she willed them away.

"I'm sorry Ally, it's -"

"No, it's okay," she said, taking his hand. "I feel normal with you." She grabbed her bracelet. "This has never gotten in our way and I don't want it to, ever. But I can't say that it won't. That's how my life is." She shrugged her shoulders.

He moved the wisp of hair that blew across her face. "Okay, Ally. But I need to tell you something."

"What?"

"I don't have a medical condition and I don't feel normal," he said, smiling.

She chuckled, "You know what I mean. You know 'normal'."

He shook his head. "Nope, what is normal anyway and who says who gets to call them normal? Come on, let's walk down to the boat dock," he said, getting up and reaching for her hand. Just then, Ally's phone started beeping, reminding her that it was time to take the evening round of drugs.

"Just a second. This is just me being normal," she said, digging in her purse for her pill pack that she prepared once a week. "I need water."

He handed her his watered down Dr. Pepper. "This do?"

She popped out the gathering of little pills from its container and tossed them back into her mouth and took a few sips.

Holding hands they walked along the beach to the other side, up the old wooden stairs built into the escarpment and then down the quiet road to the boat dock. Making their way back to his car they got in and decided to go for a drive.

Finding a lonely country road, they drove in silence listening to the radio. They chatted about starting school again. Matthew talked about playing volleyball this year with a new coach. Ally talked about piano and her dream to attend university. They talked about other friends and what classes they had the first semester and who they hoped would be teaching math this year. Matthew said his parents were putting a lot of pressure on him to get athletic scholarships. Matthew was good at everything and was overwhelmed with his decisions about the future. He didn't want to disappointment his hard-to-please parents. Ally had only met them once, and although polite, she sensed the high expectations for their son.

Driving several miles in silence Ally blurted out, "I really wish I could drive. I see everyone else driving and I can't. That's what makes me feel not normal more than anything."

Matthew slowed down and pulled off the deserted road. He got out of the car.

"What are you doing?" she asked, as he walked around and opened her door.

He gestured for her to get out of the car. "Come on," he coerced, gently pulling her out.

"Matthew, what are you doing?" she shrieked as he guided her back to the driver's side.

She sat with the steering wheel in front of her. It felt so strange. There were pedals by her feet and the mirror on her left side. Matthew sat in the passenger side and put on his seat belt.

"What are you doing?" she asked again, this time giggling with nervous excitement.

He looked around. "No one is here. So just drive."

"But Matthew, do you know how much trouble I will be in, you will be in, if I get into an accident?"

"Then don't get into an accident," he suggested, leaning over her and clicking in her seatbelt. "Put your foot on the brake, no, that one. Now move the gear shift down to the D for drive." He quickly grabbed her other hand and put it on the steering wheel.

"Okay, now slowly take your foot off the brake and put it on the other pedal. Now gently put pressure on the pedal."

She floored it, as they lunged ahead.

"Easy, I said." He couldn't help but laugh.

"That's it. Just gently put your foot down and that's it." They moved ahead a few feet going less than 10 kilometres an hour. "That's it, you're driving, Ally."

She gripped the steering wheel until her knuckles turned white. Sitting straight up, she had to remind herself to breath. "I'm doing it!" she squealed.

"Okay, but go straight. Go straight, Ally. Straightened out the wheel!"

"I don't know how. What do you mean?" she yelled out laughing.

He grabbed the wheel and guided the car back to the middle of the deserted country road. Matthew reminded her to relax as she sped up to 20kms. He kept encouraging her as they crept down the road.

Ally couldn't help but smile at Matthew. "I'm driving a car," she shrieked in a high pitched voice. "I'm driving."

"But you have to look at the road," he stressed, grabbing the wheel and slowly yanking the car away from the ditch.

Once they hit the next mile road, he told her to pull over to the side and they would switch. The sun had set and it started to get dark, ending the driving lesson.

"Okay, now keep your foot on the brake and move the gear shift back to P, for park."

She did and grabbed another lever. "What does this do?" Water sprayed across the windshield as the wipers swept across. They both jumped in surprise, making Ally laugh even harder.

"Lesson over," he laughed out loud. "Time to switch."

Getting out of the car they met in front of the headlights that were beaming through the dusk countryside. They naturally walked straight for each other. She looked way up and he looked down.

"Thank you," Ally said with tender appreciation.

He cupped her chin with his hand and moved in closer. Gently, he gave her a sweet and innocent kiss. When they slowly parted they remained transfixed in front of the head lights.

"But don't ever tell your dad," he said quietly in her ear. "He's a lawyer and could throw me in jail for what I just did."

"The driving or the kiss?" she asked, hugging him.

27
Truth Be Told

Graham stared at the computer screen, reading the same line of the email, again. He'd been having trouble concentrating all day and had struggled with browsing through a simple brief in the morning. He'd managed to spill coffee on his desk and had to ask Ben three times to repeat himself over the phone. Ben, appearing frustrated, came into Graham's office and asked if everything was alright.

"Of course," Graham flippantly had said. "Everything was great," he lied.

He had been thinking about Ally a lot lately, wondering how she was doing. Two weeks before his mother-in-law's retirement party, Todd had dropped by to talk to Graham about the conversation he'd had with Ally at the cabin. Todd hadn't wanted to get into too many details and break confidences, but Graham had recognized his brother's deep concern. And if Graham were going to be totally honest with himself, he didn't want to know the details. The summer had gone so well. No fighting, no seizures; peace had been restored to his family. Joanna was so involved in planning the garden party for her mother, he didn't want to concern her about Ally. Why rock that boat again?

Ally needed to learn to cope and manage her life of medications and seizures on her own. With school and friends and now a boyfriend on the horizon, Graham wanted to trust his oldest daughter to make good and responsible choices. If Joanna were to find out that Ally was having questions about death, he knew Ally would never be allowed to be alone again. He believed he knew his daughter; she was a smart girl who wouldn't harm herself.

Graham tapped a nervous hand on his desk as the doubt and insecurity continued to plague him. He hoped he knew his daughter, he rephrased. And he wished he could trust his wife to be reasonable. But lately, he didn't know what he believed anymore.

He shut down his computer and added files into his briefcase, weeding out the ones that didn't need his attention tonight. He wanted to talk to Ally on his own, but he didn't know what to say, how to start the conversation. He didn't want to throw her off, she was doing so well. But who was he kidding, the truth was obvious, he didn't want to talk about death with his teenage daughter. Shutting off the light to his office he walked down the hall, saying good night to a few straggling staff.

Getting into his car, he started the engine and turned up the volume, hoping the modern beat would drown out his haunting thoughts. Everything was feeling so normal at home. Why bring something up that would disturb his family's balance? At least his unplanned plan of not talking about it seemed to be working so far. At least he didn't see any indicators that she was troubled. Todd had said she was having some dark thoughts. Perhaps her emotions were catching up and now she was understanding the impact of the illness on the rest of her life. Perhaps she was just going through a phase. Perhaps, Graham hoped that Ally managed to come to terms with living with epilepsy and discovered she would make it.

He waited at the traffic light, tapping to the beat on the steering wheel. Maybe he would go for a run after dinner. Jack had a soccer game tonight. Maybe after that. He loved to run alone at night. Jack often asked to go for runs with him too. Jack was his spitting image. But Graham remembered when the recovery after a run didn't take quite so long, and the distance didn't seem quite so daunting. Jack looked like he could run forever, although he often admitted that his dad was in pretty good shape, for a dad.

Graham turned the corner to his street and then one more turn onto his driveway. He parked in front of the garage, grabbed his briefcase and wondered what Joanna had made for dinner. Walking into the kitchen, he expected to see his wife with maybe a kid or two sitting around. It was an empty room. A bad feeling ran up his spine.

"Hello?"

No answer.

"Anyone home," he called out, walking into the hallway when he noticed Joanna's car pull into the driveway.

"Graham," Joanna shouted, opening the back kitchen door.

He hurried back to see his wife full of panicked fear and ready to burst. "What happened?" he asked, knowing the answer.

Joanna took in a breath. "Ally had a seizure at work. They called me, so I went to get her. Can you help me get her out of the car," she explained, trying to breath.

Following her to the passenger side, Ally sat with her swollen eyes closed. Her bottom lip was puffy, red and bulging. She opened one eye and moved her head. "Daddy," she whispered.

"Right here, let's get you out of the car," he said, undoing the seatbelt.

"Daddy, I can't do this anymore. I don't want this anymore," she muttered through tears. "I can't anymore," she cried.

"Come on, Ally. Let's just get in the house." Helping her up, she stumbled into the kitchen like she was drunk.

"I can't do it, Daddy," she murmured, holding her aching face in her hand. Lowering herself, she sat on the floor and burst into sobs repeating that she just couldn't take it anymore. Joanna was crushed, watching her daughter collapse into hopelessness.

"Oh Graham, let's get her upstairs," Joanna begged through her own brokenness.

"Just give her a minute, Jo. Where are the twins?"

Joanna had to think for a minute. "Ah, Jack took his bike and went to, ah, soccer. He went to the soccer game already. And Lydia, is at a friend's house."

Graham looked down at Ally and kneeled beside her. "Ally, let's get you to your room and then we'll clean you up. Do you have a headache?"

"Of course she has a headache, Graham."

Annoyed, he looked up at Joanna, who was barely keeping it together. He would help her later, first he wanted to see Ally coherent again. "Let's get up, Ally, okay. You'll feel better if you're in your own bed."

She looked up and around the room. "Where am I then?"

"You're on the kitchen floor?" he answered.

"In my house?" she asked, looking at him with her eyes not yet focused.

Graham smiled. "Yes, you're at your house and we want you to go lie down."

"Okay," she said obediently. "I can't get up."

"Here we go," Joanna said, reaching for her right arm, as together her and Graham managed to slowly take the back stairs to her room.

Joanna took off her greasy, smelly work clothes and helped Ally slip on a pair of pyjamas. Graham got something for her headache and a glass of water.

"What happened to me?" Ally asked, noticing her parents sitting on her bed.

"You had a seizure."

"I did? Where?" she asked, feeling her swollen face.

"At work. Don't you remember?"

She thought for a second longer and then shook her head. "Matthew gave me a ride. I said goodbye to him."

"And then you had a seizure at work. Do you know what you were doing?" Joanna asked.

She shook her head, confused.

Joanna licked her lips. "They said you were getting some buns ready for burgers and then you fell right in front of the grill."

Ally tried to recall. "I don't remember that."

"What's the last thing you do remember?" Graham asked.

"Getting dropped off. No, wait, I do remember. Christine was talking to me at the grill and then," she raised her arms in the air as if to indicate she was falling down. Joanna noticed the burn mark on her arm.

"Oh Graham, she must have burnt her arm on the grill," Joanna said, alarming Ally.

"Oh no," Ally said crying. "I had a seizure and I'm burnt."

Graham took her arm and saw a red line across the inside of her forearm. "It's not that bad. Just get some ointment or something and gauze."

Reluctant to leave her side, Joanna headed to the bathroom and found a burn spray, gauze and medical tape. "Here, let me spray this on your arm, Ally. And let's check to make sure you're not burnt anywhere else."

"Did they tell you how she fell?" Graham asked, covering her arm with a piece of the white cloth.

"They didn't really see it. But they heard a couple of bangs so they assumed she hit her jaw and then hit the floor. Her arm must have touched the grill on her way down," Joanna explained.

"My head hurts and my jaw," Ally said, closing her eyes.

"I know, get some sleep and then we'll ice your face and you can have something to eat. Okay?" Joanna said, standing up. Graham followed and closed her blinds on the window.

Stepping out of her room, Joanna closed the bedroom door and broke down. Graham took her in his arms and held her close. The good summer they shared together had just been erased. All the ordinary days had now been disrupted again. They would have to start over, once more.

School was starting after the long weekend; just a few days away. And now Ally would be entering grade 11 with a black eye. Joanna's disappointment ran so deep, she physically felt it burning in her core. How could this keep happening when they keep doing the right things for her? How can this still be happening to Ally with all the promises of new medications, lower and higher dosages. Tests, scans and specialists. Nothing was working and Joanna was discouraged and angry.

Joanna wiped her tears and looked up to Graham. "What do you think she meant when she said she couldn't do it anymore? Do you think she wants to quit her job?"

Graham looked passed his wife hoping to hide the truth in his eyes. "She's confused, Jo. You know how she is when she wakes up. Who knows why she says the stuff she does," he casually ad-libbed, guiding her down the stairs. Taking in a deep breath, he decided to call Todd.

***

Coming down from Ally's room, Todd sat at the kitchen table with Graham and Joanna. He had just finished a shift at the hospital and was on his way home when he got the call from his brother to come over. Todd checked the burn mark on her arm and examined her jaw hoping it wasn't broken. It was fine, just bruised. They talked a while, asking the typical doctor questions and then he left her to sleep.

"So?" Joanna asked, getting a plate out for Todd, indicating he should stay for supper.

"No thanks, Joanna. Sarah has dinner ready. Her jaw isn't broken and the burn will heal."

Joanna sat down and pushed her uneaten dinner aside. "That's good. It could have been so much worse I guess. She was standing right beside the grill when she fell."

"It's been a while since her last seizure, right?"

"Not since spring," Joanna answered quickly. She remembered every single seizure like they were appointments on her calendar.

"Maybe it's worth taking a look at her meds again," he suggested.

"They just added a third medication. What's left? They keep adding more pills, then changing dosages and then changing their minds," Joanna said with exasperation. "Every time they believe this will be what she needs and every time they're wrong."

Todd looked over to Graham and then back to Joanna. "It's hard sometimes to figure out. Most patients can be managed with just one drug. Adding additional drugs may only be minimally effective, but they have to try. It's trial and error I'm afraid, until they can find the right amount of each. You just have to patiently keep trying."

Joanna looked down at her hands laying on her lap. She felt defeated and wanted to give up. Giving up on what exactly, she didn't know. There was nothing to quit. Quit the drugs. Quit on Ally. It felt impossible to look forward, so bleak and unmanageable.

"She kept saying she couldn't do it anymore and she didn't want this anymore. She's never said that before," Joanna said to Todd, as she got a plate of the stew ready for Ally. "Maybe the job is too much for her right now for some reason."

"Did she say anything more about dying?" Todd asked Joanna.

Joanna looked up with horrified shock. The look emphatically told Todd that she didn't know.

"I don't understand," she said sharply, putting the plate on the table.

Todd glanced over to Graham. He hadn't talked to his wife about Ally's concerns about death.

Graham kept looking down. Feeling their glares, he closed his eyes. The room went still.

"What are you talking about, Todd?" she demanded, crossing her arms. "Graham what did she say? Would someone answer me."

Graham finally looked up and immediately was filled with regret for not confiding this to his wife. So much for protecting her feelings.

"Ally spoke to me this summer at the lake, I thought..."
He looked at his brother who was shaking his head. "I
thought Graham would have..."

"I didn't, yet," was all Graham could manage to say.

The awkward moment lingered, making Joanna more
frazzled with the only sound coming from the ticking of the
old fashioned wall clock.

"Okay, well, I'm going to go then. Sorry. Call me if anything changes, okay?" Todd stammered, and rose to leave.
He wanted to console his sister-in-law who stood beside
the island looking down, lost in her anger and betrayal.
She seemed embarrassed, like she should have known
something important and didn't. She looked like she was
going to yell.

Graham walked Todd to the back door.

"Hey, sorry man. I thought you would have told her."

He slapped his brother on the shoulder. "Not your fault.
You didn't know. I should have, but...I'll take care of it."

"She looks like she's going to kill you, Graham. I've
never seen her like that," Todd whispered.

Unfortunately, it was a look Graham was becoming very
familiar seeing.

Todd took a step back and gave his big brother a
quick hug and slap on the back. "Call if you need me,
okay? I'm not just a doctor on a house call here, I'm your
brother, man."

Graham nodded and watched him back off the driveway.
He took in a deep breath knowing full well what awaited
him inside. He took his time to close the door and turned.

The kitchen was empty. A quick and short sense of relief came over him. He headed upstairs and saw Ally's door ajar and heard them talking. He rubbed his face with his hand and headed into their bedroom. He took off his tie and threw it on the bed. The cufflinks went onto the dresser somewhere while he pulled out the shirt tucked into his dress pants. Joanna walked in and closed the door. He turned around. His eyes went to the floor.

"Just let me explain," he said, sucking in a big breath.

She is too calm, he thought. A simmering anger was waiting at the surface.

"I suppose you better explain something to me," she said with preciseness. Arms crossed with hard eyes looking straight at him.

"Can we sit down," he offered, gesturing to the chairs in front of the fireplace.

"No," she answered quickly. "Say it. Tell me what you know and I don't."

"Jo, it happened back in, June I think."

"What happened?"

He looked at her and took in a deep breath, slowly pacing the room. "I didn't know what to do, so I just thought I would see if things would just -"

"What, go away? Get better all on its own?" she hammered out.

"Let me finish, Jo," he said, finally facing her. "Todd told me that when we were all at the cabin, Ally was asking him questions about, you know, if seizures were fatal and if they could..."

"Could what?"

Graham couldn't say the words. "If they could..." He placed his hands on his hips. "If they could take her life," he finished with a lump in his throat.

Joanna looked up placing her fingers to her temples. "This was in June? Like, more than three months ago? And now you tell me? No wait, you didn't tell me. Your brother alludes to it, thinking, no, assuming that I knew Ally was having these concerns about her life."

He didn't say anything.

"You knew this and didn't talk to me about it," she said, more of a statement than a question.

"Looking back now, I see that I should have perhaps mentioned it to you but -"

"You think perhaps you should of, huh?" she added with an angry twist.

Joanna kept breathing in and out like it was no longer an assumed function of her body. Anger, hurt and betrayal were colliding inside, stirring into an explosion. She wanted answers to relieve her pain.

"What has happened to us, Graham? That you wouldn't share something like this about our daughter? Why wouldn't you talk to me about it?"

Graham rubbed his forehead as he felt a bead of sweat forming. "Because I thought it was a phase. I thought we were having such a great summer and Ally was doing great, that it was nothing."

"Nothing means Todd wouldn't have mentioned it to you in the first place, Graham. You're telling me that you both knew about this and left me out of my daughter's struggles?" she spewed out angrily.

He paced again before turning to his wife. "When Todd finally told me, you were busy getting that garden party ready. I didn't want to worry you or for you to get all overly concerned about Ally."

"She's my daughter and you deliberately kept something this important from me. How dare you, Graham?" she accused, jabbing a finger in his chest. "And don't use the stupid garden party as an excuse for not telling me. I am her mother and she needs me."

"Do you ever listen to yourself, Joanna?" he yelled back, matching her intensity. Walking away he faced the window and then turned back. "She's not *your* daughter, she's *our* daughter and somewhere you forgot that. You're always telling her what to do, never letting her decide anything anymore. You try to control everything and everybody." He took a breath. "She's *our* daughter. This is *our* house. Those are our kids. When did this become your problem to handle alone?"

"When you decided to step aside, Graham. I needed you. I needed you to talk to me and work things out about how we were going to raise her with epilepsy. And you never said anything. It was always me left with the decisions. And not telling me that our daughter had thoughts about dying is the last straw," she yelled. "When she was spinning out of control from all the seizures and the drug changes, I'm the one who was here," she screamed through tears.

"That's not my fault. I can't be here 24/7 like you. I'm making a living so we can have all of this," he threw in her face. It was a slap; he knew it and he regretted it. Anger had gotten in the way of reason. He closed his eyes. "Sorry, that's not what I meant."

Joanna went silent, drowning slowly in the hurtful words. She turned to walk out of the room. Graham went towards her.

"Don't touch me," she demanded, taking a step away. He withdrew his arms from her shoulders.

"Don't walk out, Joanna," he pleaded. He took in a deep breath of regret. "I should have told you, but I was scared. I didn't want to upset you and I thought that if Ally wanted us to know, she would tell one of us."

"But she didn't, did she," she said, in a near whisper. "She didn't want either of us to know. So she told her uncle, who then confided in you. And what did you do about it?"

Graham wanted to answer her in the worst way. He wanted to say something that would bandage up this wound. But he couldn't think of a way out. Sorry was so inadequate.

"Joanna, listen to me. This is not about me against you. Or Ally against us," he said, pointing towards the hallway. "You have got to stop treating me like I'm always the enemy against your battle of protecting Ally."

She had enough and tried opening the door, but he closed it with one hand. "Joanna, please. I'm begging you not to walk out on me."

Turning quickly, she reached out and grabbed his shirt in her fist. "I am so angry with you for not trusting me again. You could have told me and we could have worked through this with her. But instead you hold on to it," she said, letting him go and walking to the window. She buried her face into her hands and screamed and cried. He came behind her and put his arms around her, but she walked away.

"No, don't try to comfort me and say it's all going to be okay. You don't get to make it okay, anymore. It's never going to be okay. My baby can't be normal. I carried her inside of me and I thought that she would be perfect and healthy and have a normal life. You don't know that ache a mother feels, Graham. I have to protect her and help her manage her life so she can be on her own, and I don't know if that is even possible anymore. I don't know what to believe about anything anymore."

"Joanna, I want those things for her too. Why are you always trying to exclude me from what you want? I thought we were in this together, doing life, raising kids. That was our dream, not just yours," he revealed, sitting on the window bench.

"Then why didn't you tell me what Ally was feeling when Todd told you this summer? Why did you deliberately leave me out it? Todd must think I'm so stupid that I didn't know."

"No, he thinks I'm an idiot for not telling you."

"Why don't you trust me, Graham?" she asked softly, sitting at the foot of the bed. "I can deal with Ally, no matter what comes our way. I am her mother and I will see her through anything that she will have to face." Fresh tears came to the surface because reality hit her hard, telling her that this was not close to being the last hurdle she would be facing. "Why didn't you trust me with the truth?"

He took in a quick breath and looked to the ceiling. "I didn't tell you because everything was going so great. And when I do tell you things, you take on everything like it's your burden, yours alone. It feels like you don't trust me to handle anything anymore, Joanna. We used to be a team. We used to be able to talk everything through. Now we just yell and argue."

He stood up and headed to the closet tossing his dress shirt on the ground. "You're right, maybe I don't trust you, Joanna." He reached for a T-shirt and slipped it over his head. "Maybe I don't trust that I'm going to tell you something and then you'll leave me out of the decisions about our kids. Our kids, not yours. Our house and our life." He ran his hands through his hair, so frustrated. "When did we lose sight of that?"

Joanna sat in silence.

Cautiously, he sat beside his wife and leaned forward. "Something has gone off the rails if I feel I can't tell you something and you can't rely on me that I'm here for you."

They sat in the decaying quiet, feeling each other's hurt, feeling the divide between them. The harsh words still ringing in their ears. Life was easy when it was easy, but when it was difficult, they were lost.

"I feel like I've fallen into a hole, Graham. And I keep falling and falling and there's no bottom. It's never going to end. I'm just getting farther away from what I want." Her voice was distant and hollow. She wiped a lonely tear from her cheek. More followed. Until, it broke and she couldn't keep the sobs quiet and polite. Graham reached for her and wouldn't let her go even though she tried.

"Hey, no, no, Joanna. I'm here. I'm here for you," he said softly. "If you're falling, we're all falling down together."

Graham started crying. It was sadness for their daughter, it was tears of grief for his suffering marriage. They were tears of frustration for his helplessness to fix all that was broken in their family. His guilt for not being the man Joanna needed him to be.

Joanna clung to his arm wrapped around her. Why was this all happening to them? She wanted to know. She wanted answers to everything because she was tired of feeling like she knew nothing.

"Graham, I can't keep living like this. I can't live with secrets and pretending. I don't want to live like that. I promised myself that I wouldn't have a life like that," she said, as the ache kept coming out of her. "It's like I'm not being honest with myself, I'm living a lie. I won't do that."

"Don't say that, Joanna. We'll figure it out," Graham said, gathering himself. "I promise we will. Our kids need us together. I need you, Jo. I don't want to do any of this, good or bad, without you." He heard the pleading in his voice. "We're going to get through this. I know we can."

She looked at him. "Then you have to promise me you'll be honest with me. I keep having to guess what you're thinking. It feels like I'm the one left to deal with everything. I know you work hard and I'm grateful that I can be at home full time. I really am."

"I know that and you're a great mother. I shouldn't have said what I did before," he said, wiping his face with the back of his hand.

"Why is this happening to us?" she asked, not sure she even wanted to hear an answer now.

He kissed the top of her head as he thought about what to say. "Life happens, I suppose. I don't always know what to say or what to do in these situations because....my life has been so easy, Jo. Nothing has been so hard that I can't handle it," he said.

Then he paused. "And my dad, he always knew what to do. I'd go to him for answers." He leaned forward clasping his hands together trying to keep it inside. He willed the tears to go away as he clamped his eyes tight. "I miss him. Every day. I want to go talk to him and ask him what to do about you and about Ally. And I can't." He broke and the tears came. "I looked up to him so much and I feel like I've let him down. I feel like I'm failing him and you and my family."

Joanna touched her husband's back with a gentle hand. She hadn't seen him grieve for his dad since the week of the funeral. She didn't realize he was still stuck, all these years later. Missing him and letting go was hard, but she thought that was behind them. Joanna didn't notice that Graham still missed his dad.

"Oh Graham, I'm sorry," she confessed. "Of course you want your dad here. I know you loved him and were so close to him. I'm sorry I should have been more sensitive and asked you how you were doing without him."

As they began to share words of regret and revealing their vulnerabilities, a gentle and kind healing trickled into their hurts and worries. A fragile understanding was bridging between them. Life got in the way of the life they were trying to build; or the life they thought they were living. But the heartache of losing his father, Ally's illness and raising teenagers, left them feeling tattered and worn down. But they both knew they had to rebuild what was falling down around them. There was a dim light of possibility among the shadowed darkness that lay around them. Hope was still flickering.

Graham's phone stopped their thoughts as he pulled it out of his pocket. "It's Jack."

They both looked at the clock, his game had already started. "What do we do?" Joanna asked.

"Do I tell him what happened?" Graham questioned.

They were exhausted and struggled to make even a simple decision. Joanna rubbed her aching head, willing this day to be over.

The phone buzzed again.

"I'll stay here and you can go to the game," Joanna finally suggested. It seemed like such an easy solution but they were mired in so much emotion, nothing seemed easy right now.

Graham answered the phone. "Hey, I'm on my way. What? When?" He stood up and looked like he wanted to throw the phone out the window. "It's okay. I'm on my way, Jack. Sorry. I'll explain in two minutes. Which field are you at again? Okay. I'll be right there."

"What now?"

"Jack rolled on his ankle and it may be broken. He thought we were there, so yeah, he's a little ticked off. I'll take him to the hospital."

Joanna just closed her eyes and laughed out of surrender. Could this day get any worse? Ally called from her room. "Okay and I'll go see what she wants."

They were half way down the hallway, when Graham turned to Joanna. "I know it's been tough. But I am so glad I'm doing life with you."

She managed a smile. "You make it sound like prison."

"Well, sometimes....we're going make it," he added. "Don't give up, Jo." And he kissed her on the forehead.

"Go take care of Jack. We'll talk again when you get back."

He turned and ran down the stairs. Joanna went to Ally's room and saw that she was crying. No, the day wasn't over just yet.

***

After waiting for a few hours in the ER waiting room, Jack finally got his foot X-rayed which showed a broken bone in his foot. Jack was upset that he couldn't try out for the high school volleyball team next week and would cut out of all sports for at least six weeks. They put him in a walking cast. Ice it, keep it up and get in to see an athletic therapist for rehab were the instructions from the ER doctor.

When they finally got home from the hospital it was nearly 11:00 and Graham realized he hadn't eaten all day. He and Jack ate reheated stew, lingered around the kitchen island talking about this very strange day. It was almost midnight when Graham and Joanna had Jack settled into bed, and doped up on pain medication. Ally fortunately fell asleep after she received her drugs. Lydia got home from her friend's house when Graham and Jack were at the hospital and she had gone straight to bed. Graham peeked in her room for a quick good night before it was finally his turn to call it a day. Joanna cleaned up the kitchen and took Bentley out one more time. She was exhausted and there would be no time or energy to talk with Graham again tonight.

But as Joanna was getting ready for bed, she wanted to know one more thing. "Graham, does Ally need to see somebody? Does she need help?" Joanna asked, placing her earrings on the side table.

"I don't know. I guess so. I don't want her to think that we believe she can't handle her life. But maybe she can't," Graham said, putting his toothbrush back in its holder.

He walked back into the bedroom and sat down on the edge of the bed taking off his watch. "Can we just call this day quits?" he asked, just above a whisper.

"What if tomorrow's worse?" Joanna asked, crawling into bed and feeling the relief from her pillow.

"I can't imagine worse than this," he added, turning off the lamp and lying down beside his wife. "Is Lydia home?" he asked drifting off.

She smiled. "Yes, she came home when you were at the hospital with Jack. You went to say good night to her, remember?"

He kept his eyes closed. "Oh yeah. It's all a blur."

"I know. Good night."

And the day was over.

28
Absence

Ally heard the bell ring, but nothing much before that. She looked at her teacher and saw his lips move, but didn't understand.

"Hey, Ally, are you coming?" Amanda asked, nudging Ally's arm.

"Huh, what?" She turned to face her friend. "Yeah, I'm coming."

Ally stood up and gathered her books. Was she daydreaming or was this something else? Ally couldn't figure it out. She followed her friends down the hall trying to shake the bizarre feeling. She stood behind her group of friends as they gathered in the foyer between classes. Looking down, Ally tried to remember the last five minutes. Or was it even longer, she didn't know.

Ally scanned the busy school seeing kids laughing, talking and gathering. She knew these people, but she was lost among them. She stood outside the circle as the group of girls kept talking about a party she didn't know anything about. Moving the strap of her bag higher onto her shoulder, Ally willed herself to get back in the game, to shake this weird sensation.

"Hey, Al, what's with you today? You're off in la-la land or something," Emily laughed, bringing unwanted attention to Ally.

"No, I'm good. Just a little out of it today," she remarked sheepishly.

"Whatever, Ally. So are you coming to the party on Friday? Bringing Matthew?" Emily teased. Ally looked at her, curious why she always referred to her and Matthew like they were a joke?

"Don't know, I guess. We haven't talked about it yet," she said, just as Matthew came up behind her and lay his hands on her shoulders. He was at least a foot taller than her and it suddenly felt comforting to have him hold her up in the face of these friends.

"Hey Ally, do you have a class now? I have a spare," he said, not yet noticing Ally's apprehensiveness. She turned and looked up at Matthew.

He saw something very uncertain in her eyes. "You okay?"

Turning Ally walked away, taking Matthew's hand as she led him away. Going out the front doors, she sat on the concrete steps. Sitting down, he placed an arm around her as she tried to gather her emotions, burying her face in her hands.

"What did they say?" he asked again.

Ally played with the sleeves of her shirt. "I don't know, I feel weird and everyone around me seems to be acting even weirder. Did Emily say something to you just now?"

He thought for a second. "No, she just had that 'I'm better than everyone look' on her face. I don't know how you two are friends." Then he added, "did she say something that made you upset?"

Ally didn't really know. She felt overwhelmed and just wanted to run away.

Ally shook her head. "I don't think so. I'm just having a weird day. I feel like Alice in Wonderland when she falls through the hole and everything is so confusing and strange."

"Do you want me to take you home?" he offered.

"No, then my mom will go berserk on me," she sighed. "I have chemistry next and I don't want to sit there and look at the dumb graph of letters and numbers. I feel so stupid."

He reached for her hand, "Hey, don't talk like that. You're not stupid. Did you take all your meds when you were supposed to? Did you get enough sleep?" He sat up taller, then added, "I know, you keep thinking about me too much."

Ally laughed and leaned into Matthew who held her close. "You're going to be fine. What do you need me to do?" he asked, quietly in her ear.

"Can I skip chemistry?" she asked only half joking. "Can we go up to the beach for a while?"

"Really? It's the end of September, a little cold for a swim," he teased.

"No, I just want to go and sit there to clear my head. Would I be an awful person if I skipped a class?"

"Yes, yes you would Ally. No one at Mountain City Collegiate has ever skipped a class, ever. You'd be the first."

"Hey Al, are you coming? The bell is going to ring?" Christine called out from the school doors.

"In a second, I just need some air, not feeling great," Ally said as she watched her friend go back inside the school just as the bell rang.

Then she saw Lydia. It was strange to see her twin brother and sister in her high school.

Lydia walked to her sister. "You okay, Ally? The first bell rang, you're going to be late," she said.

"No, you're going to be late, Lydia," Ally said, looking up.

"Ally, is something wrong, were you crying? Matthew is she okay?" Lydia asked full of concern.

"She'll be okay, " Matthew answered. "Just feeling a little off today, but she'll be okay. I'll stay with her, you go on to your class, Lydia."

Reluctantly she took a few steps then turned back. "Do you want me to call Mom?"

"No, don't call Mom. I can take care of myself, Lydia," she barked out. Ally stood up and turned to her sister, feeling bad for her snarky comeback. "But thanks, Lydia, for checking up on me. You're a good sister for asking. I'm fine."

"Okay, see you later," Lydia said slowly and made her way back into the school, disappearing into the crowd. The second bell rang. Ally picked up her bag and grabbed Matthew's hand, pulling him to stand beside her as they made their way to his car waiting in the student parking lot beside the school.

Ally needed to clear her head and find her balance again. Matthew was so kind and understanding and even though he could have chosen to do anything else during his spare, he chose to be with her. Ally was so grateful that he had come into her life, just in time.

They got back to school as Ally simply merged with the rest of the students in the hallway heading towards the gymnasium. She hoped that they weren't going to be doing too much running today, she was just not up for it. Ally went into the girls locker room and into a bathroom stall just as a group of her fellow classmates came in. She recognized their voices. They talked about how much they hated chemistry and how so-and-so had been gaining weight and how good looking another student had become over the summer. And then she heard her name.

"I just don't know why Matthew is going out with her," Emily questioned. "I mean, come on, she's alright and everything, but really, Ally?"

"Yeah, I know right?" Amanda added. "She's so different now. All that seizure weirdness," she scoffed, making gestures and noises of a seizure.

They all laughed.

"Matthew is so amazing looking and he's really nice," Emily continued on. "I really thought he was into me for a while and then he goes for Ally. I don't get it."

"Me either," Kate added in. "My mom said that her mom said she keeps needing to take more and more drugs. No wonder she looks clued-out half the time."

They all laughed.

"She's a druggy!" Emily cackled.

They all laughed.

And then they walked out of the locker room talking about a new show they were obsessed with watching. Talking like no one was listening.

Ally finally felt the tears rolling down her cheeks. She grabbed some toilet paper and did her best to hide the evidence of her broken spirit. How was she supposed to face her friends again? *What friends?* she thought. The betrayal cut deep and the knife kept sinking in slower and swifter than any seizure. She felt raw and empty. All the goodness that Matthew helped her see, now vanished with the cruel and thoughtless words from her lifelong friends.

She couldn't think anymore. An instinct grew inside as she left the stall with her bag and walked into the gym. Ally walked passed the group of girls who in unison turned to see who was leaving the girls' locker room. Ally made eye contact with each of them as the painful truth filled the large room, no words of explanation required. Nothing could unsay the words that Ally still heard ringing in her head. There was no misunderstanding, Ally saw the lingering guilt in their eyes. Ally went straight to her teacher who was standing in front of the bleachers.

"Ms. Hollins, I'm not feeling well today. I've been having a few strange episodes this morning. I think I need to skip gym class today."

She looked at Ally nervously. Ally knew that whenever she talked to her teachers about how she was feeling, they always let her sit out for fear she would seizure on their watch.

"Sure, no problem, Ally. She passed her some work sheets from her clip board. "Why don't you go to the library and work on these questions about good eating habits and hand them back to me at the end of class."

Ally took the papers and left the gym. Walking down the hall, she tossed the work sheets into the garbage and made her way across the school to the music room. As she had hoped no one was in the room but the band instructor. "Mr. McDonald, can I play piano?"

He wasn't going to pass up the opportunity to hear Ally Kornelson play the piano. She was more talented now than he would ever be.

"Sure, do you have a spare?" he asked, gathering up some folders.

"No, gym class. But Ms. Hollins said I didn't have to participate today," she said, making her way to the piano. Ignoring Mr. McDonald she turned on the electronic piano and started to play Vince Guaraldi's jazzy theme of Linus and Lucy. It was busy and complicated and Ally could pound out the left hand hearing the familiar theme keeping it steady and rhythmic. She thought he asked her if she was feeling okay. But she didn't answer. She was lost in a place where the world made sense to her. The music, the notes, the beat all so confusing, but here she understood who she was. She improvised the parts she didn't know and kept playing when she felt stuck.

Mr. McDonald watched her in awe at his office door. Ally didn't care, she felt alone anyway. When she was done with

Charlie Brown, she started playing Glenn Miller's, 'Boogie Woogie Bugle Boy'. She had learned how to play it when she was eleven years old. Her fingers flew on the keys hitting every note, nailing every down beat, all for memory. It swirled around her, making her forget the day that was unraveling.

When she heard a bell ring, the music stopped. "Thanks, Mr. McDonald." She got up and walked out of the music room.

Getting through English Lit., Ally managed to walk out of class before that group of friends had a chance to catch up to her with their lame explanations. Ally heard them calling her name, but she kept on walking straight out of the school. Plugging in her ear buds, she never looked back.

That was until she got home when she walked into the kitchen and found her mom talking on the phone. Joanna saw her daughter's face. Ally walked towards her and the painful tears poured out of her as she fell into her mother's arms.

"Ah, Hannah, I'll have to call you back. No, she's fine, I think. I'll call you later," Joanna said, tossing her phone down. "Oh, my poor baby," Joanna soothed. "What happened? Oh Ally, it's okay. It's going to be alright."

Lydia walked in a few minutes later and she saw her mom hugging her sister who was sobbing. Lydia placed her backpack on the chair and joined the embrace.

Minutes later, Ally went to lie down. Lydia explained to her mom what she had heard happened at school. It wasn't a big school and most of the kids had all grown up together, so word got around fast. And when Ms. Hollins had found out what had transpired in the locker room, all the girls were brought into the principal's office. This was not a familiar crowd to be sitting in the office. So as they were seen by students passing by, the gossip had spread about what they said about Ally.

Joanna was devastated and wanted to call each of their mothers. But she tried not to overreact in front of Lydia as she explained in detail what happened to Ally. Joanna focused on forming the meatloaf instead, hoping to keep her anger hidden from her daughter. Lydia went to do her homework while Jack watched TV, resting his foot that was still in a cast for another week.

Graham was right, Joanna realized putting the meatloaf in the oven. Joanna's first instinct was to tell Ally what she should do. She didn't listen very well. Joanna wanted to fix it for Ally and make her pain go away. Setting the table, Joanna struggled with her instincts to protect, and thought about what she should say to Ally to help her feel heard and understood, not managed.

After dinner, Graham and Joanna sat with Ally in her room. They listened as she told them what these friends had said about her. They sympathized and let her know that they were upset she had to go through this situation. They explained that sometimes true friends are revealed and what an opportunity for her to see who they really were.

"Life is about how you react to circumstances," Joanna said. "People are going to misunderstand and say stupid things to you and it reveals their lack of character, not yours. Show everyone your strength and devotion to doing the right thing and that you can rise above ignorant words."

"I don't want to do anything, Mom," Ally said, hugging her pillow. "I don't want to go to school tomorrow."

Her dad sat closer to Ally. "I know it's hard. But imagine how much harder it's going to be for them."

Ally thought about what her parents said. But she didn't care. She didn't see good in anything. It was all getting too difficult to see the happy, positive side to her life. So she simply nodded at their words of advice and said she just wanted to go to bed.

***

The next few weeks didn't show any signs of improving. Ally was experiencing more absence seizures but didn't realize what was happening to her. She had more blood work done and her medications were once again adjusted. The situation with Ally's friends didn't improve either. For days they avoided each other until Amanda approached Ally and offered an apology. Slowly, the girls made their amends, but it was never to be the same again. Christine stood by Ally the entire time and proved her genuine friendship, just like her mom had predicted. Matthew did his very best to support her among her troubles with balancing precarious medications and uncertain friendships.

Ally often wondered how long he would stick around, believing she was not the girlfriend he deserved. She told him several times that she couldn't always be there to cheer him on during his late night volleyball games. So much of their time together was focused on her, that she wondered if this is what he had in mind for his girlfriend.

But he had remained steadfast and constant every time she challenged his intentions.

But the biggest test came one Friday night when Matthew and Ally went to see a movie. On the drive home, everything was normal. They talked about school, teachers and the movie. It was the Thanksgiving weekend and the leaves on the trees had turned brown and gold and were falling on the ground. The winter chill was creeping into the air, so Matthew kept the car running as they talked on her driveway. It was dark outside with the only light coming from the outdoor lantern on the front lawn.

"I know, it's weird to think that we're almost done high school," Matthew said, looking out the windshield as the oak leaves touched down and floated on the window.

"I know, I'm thinking about that too." Ally thought about it all the time and wondered if she would be able to actually live an independent life.

"We may end up at the same university. That would be kind of cool," he said, looking at her in the shadowy darkness. He noticed she was smiling and happy. "Although my parents seemed to have it all planned out for me. They hardly ask me anymore what I want to do, or where I want to go," he said, turning and looking out his window. "So have you decided that you really want to pursue a music career after high school?" he asked, seeing the leaves twisting under the streetlights. He looked over to Ally who sat quietly not answering.

"Ally?"

There was no response.

"Are you okay?" he asked, as panic and the signs of a seizure collided.

"No, no, Ally," he screamed, trying to find the interior lights of the car. "Ally, what's happening?"

The light came on and he looked over and watched as her body stiffened and her eyes rolled back. Then her hands and arms began shaking. He yelled again and reached for her as her head unconsciously moved and contorted to one side. He was afraid and alarmed and he panicked.

Then she started to make horrible choking noises. Matthew was convinced she was going to die. He got out of the car, ran to the house and banged on the front door.

"I need your help." He tried the door and ran inside. "I need your help. It's Ally!"

Graham came rushing from the den. Joanna ran down the stairs.

"Where is she?" Graham demanded, bolting out the front door.

Matthew swallowed hard and followed Ally's dad. "In my car. I didn't do anything, I swear it. We were just talking and then she didn't answer me," he screamed, walking around the car.

He watched Graham fly into action, releasing Ally from the seatbelt she had gotten tangled in and slightly tilted back the seat as she finished the remains of the seizure.

"How long has it lasted?" Joanna asked, standing beside Matthew.

Panic was racing through him as he continued to hyperventilate. "I don't know. I was talking to her and then she wasn't answering me and then I looked over and I didn't know what was happening to her," he said, beginning to cry.

Joanna saw the helpless and horrified fear in his shadowed eyes. She recognized that look of wanting to look away, but not being able to stop watching the seizure. Joanna touched his arm, taking him out of the moment.

Graham stood up. "Are you going to be okay? Because I need to get her inside. Can you help me or not?"

"Does she need to go to the hospital or something. What do I need to do? Is it over? Is she okay now?" he asked nonsensically.

"Matthew," Graham said, grabbing his arm. "She's fine. You didn't do anything wrong. She just needs to get into the house. We'll just give her a few minutes. Do you want to stay or go? It's up to you, Matthew," he added, seeing how visibly upset the young boy had become.

Tears sat at the surface as fear outweighed his sadness. Ally sat in the car, lifeless and weary. Joanna moved Ally's hair away from her face. Crouching down beside her, Joanna talked to her as if Ally was listening. In a few minutes, Ally started muttering and tried to sit up.

"What do you need me to do?" Matthew finally asked, gaining his composure.

"Just help me get her out of the seat and we'll see if she can walk," Graham suggested before turning to Ally. "Hey, we're going to get you out of the car now and into the house, okay," he said to his daughter.

"Okay," she said softly.

Graham managed to get her legs on the ground as they helped her out of the seat. She staggered and leaned into her dad.

Joanna grabbed Ally's purse and turned to Matthew. "Come inside, okay."

"Maybe I should just go home," he said, watching Ally slowly make her way to the front steps.

"I need help," Graham called out.

Matthew walked over and supported Ally's left side as they made their way inside the house and up the stairs to her room. Gently laying her down, Ally fell like dead weight onto the bed. Graham and Matthew took a step back as Joanna got Ally comfortable among her pillows and blankets. Gesturing that they leave the room, Matthew followed Graham down to the kitchen, where they sat down at the table. Matthew was still shaking, realizing he had witnessed a seizure.

Jack came into the kitchen. "What's going on? Hey Matthew?"

"Ally had a seizure in Matthew's car. She's fine and Mom is with her. Where's Lydia?" Graham asked.

"Oh man. She's in bed already," Jack said.

Matthew sat in obvious distress. Graham noticed Jack staring at Matthew, making it even more awkward. Matthew was Jack's hero and he was now falling apart in their kitchen.

"Jack, you head on to bed too, okay," Graham said, giving his son a quick hug.

He nodded and went up the back stairs.

Graham turned his attention back to Matthew. His hands were shaking. "Let me get you a drink, Matthew. And then we can talk."

Graham got a coke from the fridge and set it in front of him.

Matthew looked down, staring at his shaking hands. "Is she going to be okay now?"

"Yes, she will wake up soon and then realize what happened and then she'll be okay again," he answered, looking at Matthew processing what he had just witnessed.

He finally peered up at Graham. "Is this what a seizure is like for her?"

Graham popped open a can of ginger ale. "She usually falls and hits her head and bites the inside of her mouth and lip. Because she was sitting she probably won't have any bruises this time."

"I didn't do anything, Mr. Kornelson... to cause this," he said, with a shaky voice. "I swear we were just talking," he explained emphatically.

Graham tried to hide a slight smile behind his drink as he gulped it down. "Thanks for telling me that, Matthew." He put the can back on the table. "You didn't cause anything to happen. So far no concoction of drugs has kept her seizure free. I know it wasn't you, relax."

They sat in quiet contemplation. Matthew opened the coke and took a long drink.

He took in a deep breath and then let it out. "For some reason I never thought this would happen, and I don't know why. She seems so, okay, whenever we're together.

Yeah, she talks about it and is down sometimes, but I never imagined this happening."

"Neither did we, but now this is part of her life. It's not who she is, but this is her reality, Matthew," Graham said, testing to see where this would go.

Matthew took another drink and contemplated his next response. "I really care for Ally, Mr. Kornelson. I do. She's so interesting to me and she's not like the other girls. I try to get her to see that I'm not into girls who are all about image and status and stuff like that. Ally is different and I don't know if it's because she has epilepsy or it's just who she is."

"We'll never know, Matthew. But this is who she has become in spite of dealing with epilepsy. Maybe she would have been one of those other girls you're referring to, or maybe not. But you need to be honest with yourself and with my daughter, Matthew," Graham said, leaning forward on the table. "I know you guys are still in high school and I'm not reading into anything here, really I'm not. But man, that's my little girl up there and you witnessed a very personal and difficult situation for her and our family. You need to figure out how you're going to deal with it and help Ally cope. You owe her that."

Tears came into the young man's eyes as he looked at Graham. "I'm not leaving her. She means a lot to me and I feel awful that this is what she goes through," he said, trying to keep the tears back.

Graham reached out and grabbed his shoulder as the tears came. "It's okay, Matthew. What you saw was really difficult. And it doesn't get easier. It somehow unfortunately just becomes a little more normal, if you can believe that."

Matthew dried his eyes with the sleeve of his shirt and simply nodded.

"You're a good kid and I appreciate what you've said about Ally and how much you respect her," Graham added, just as Joanna came down the back stairs realizing she was interrupting a moment.

"How is she?" Graham asked.

"She's awake now. Fortunately she didn't bite her mouth so she's not bleeding or anything like that."

Joanna turned to Matthew. "She wants to see you. I told her I would see if you were still here. She knows what happened."

"Can I see her?" he asked, looking to Graham.

"I think that it would be good for you to go talk to her. She can actually be kind of funny coming out of a seizure. Not that it's a laughing matter, but she can be quite hilarious trying to make sense of things," Graham offered, easing Matthew's tension.

"Go on up if you want. And if you don't, I can tell her you'll call her tomorrow," Joanna suggested.

"No, I'll go. I want to see her," he said, slowly standing up. He took in a deep breath and straightened out his shirt. He went up the stairs.

Joanna sat down at the table. After a minute she looked at her husband. "Is he going to break her heart?"

Graham shook his head. "Not tonight he won't. But Joanna I think he knows what he's gotten himself into and if he's not man enough to deal with this, then -"

"He's just a kid, Graham."

"So is Ally. She doesn't have a choice to live with this, but he does. And I hope he realizes that sooner than later. He's a good kid, but I don't know if this is what he's ready for."

"I guess we'll see," Joanna said, looking at the back stairs.

29
Distractions

Autumn was Joanna's favourite time of year. She loved the changes of the colours and the cool temperature and the anticipation that Christmas was right around the corner. But Ally's seizure with Matthew had proven to the tipping point for the Kornelsons to find any joy in the holiday season.

Joanna's mother decided to host Thanksgiving dinner, her first gathering since she had retired. Although, there were great intentions, the day together had turned out to be the forecasted disaster. Ally was feeling awkward and awful all day. And Joanna's sisters couldn't understand why she was having such a difficult time coping, believing she should be used to it by now. How could her life possibly be such a hardship, they questioned, while clearing the dinner dishes.

Without thought, Joanna tossed the handful of dirty forks into the kitchen sink with more force than she intended. "Really, Pauline, you think because we have a cabin and a nice car, we have no problems? Are you kidding me?"

"That's not what she said," her mother corrected, putting the leftovers into the fridge. "Stop being so dramatic. You look exhausted, why don't you lie down or something."

"That is exactly what she said, Mom. And I'm not going to lie down," Joanna answered back, staring at her older sister who had been pushing her all day.

Joanna was indeed exhausted. It had been increasingly difficult in dealing with Ally's setback. Managing her family's constant struggles was getting more and more challenging. Lydia and Jack still needed to carry on with their lives as Ally had to keep starting hers over again.

"Joanna, what I'm trying to say is that you have a life that many people don't have. When your life is stressful you have the option of taking off to the cabin. You take winter vacations every year. You can have whatever you want whenever you want it," Pauline explained, her words dripping with hidden jealousy.

Joanna grabbed a towel hanging on the stove handle as tears of defeat and fatigue came to the surface. "You know what I really want, Pauline. More than cabins and cars and fancy things, I want my daughter to have a normal brain. That's what I want, and guess what? I can't have it. All those *things* aren't really important if someone you brought into this world has to deal with a medical condition," Joanna explained taking a breath. "I come to these gatherings and get judged and ridiculed because of the family I married into. I have never thrown what I have or don't have in your faces the way you have with me," she stated with a lump in her throat.

"Please, can we just stop this talk -," Susan said, standing beside her youngest daughter.

Joanna tossed the towel down. "No, we can't, Mom. We can't just talk about anything in this family; never have. Pauline just keeps bullying me for who I married and what I have. I had no idea material possessions were so important to you, Pauline."

"Joanna," Laura injected, "I think that you've had a tough few weeks and you're saying things right now that you don't mean."

Raising her arms in surrender, she paced the kitchen. "A tough few weeks, are you kidding me, Laura? I've had a few tough years watching my daughter's life come undone. I am trying to keep her and my family surviving all of this. But none of you care about that. All you see is a life you think I have."

Joanna faced them. "My daughter has epilepsy. My family is falling down a path that I can't get off of and you have the audacity to say 'you're so lucky you have a cabin, you have a rich husband.'"

Laura looked at her mother and Pauline standing in the small room speechless and looking down. "Joanna, I guess we just didn't know how to help you or what to say to you."

Joanna wiped her eyes harshly and looked at her mother and sisters staring at her. "Nope, you didn't."

Pauline pursed her lips together and huffed in frustration. "It always looked like you were handling everything so perfectly like you always do. How did we know this was hard for you? I offered advice and you told me that Graham's brother was -"

"That's because Graham's brother is an actual doctor, Pauline. Don't you get it?" Joanna took in a quick breath. "And how could anybody possibly be 'perfect' when you're living with someone who has a serious and complicated illness?"

Laura, who always tried to be the voice of reason, cut Pauline off before she could cause any more damage. "Joanna, it's just that -"

"No stop, I don't need to hear anymore today if that's okay with you. When you look at me you still see your annoying little sister who has it all. I'm done. I'm too tired to argue about this."

Pauline huffed in an air of anger. "You know Joanna, don't throw your pity around. I took care of you when you were little and you never appreciated what I did for you all those years. And now you're complaining about your sad life having to take care of your family in your big, expensive house. I've had to work my entire life, since I was fourteen I've had a job. So sorry, but it's your turn to understand what it's finally like to have a hard life," she accused, pointing her finger at Joanna.

Graham walked into the kitchen and saw the distraught look on his wife's face. He looked at his in-laws and then back to his wife. He held out his hand for her to come to him. "No one talks to my wife like that again. Do you understand me?" he said with a quite commanding presence.

"Graham, we are her sisters and have every right to say -"

He held up his hand for her to stop. "Would you please stop talking? I don't care, Pauline. I don't. I care about my wife and how she gets treated by her sisters. I care that when we leave this family I have to restore her confidence that you keep tearing apart. I'm sick of it and it will stop today."

He guided Joanna out of the kitchen and straight into the car; the kids were already in the back seat. Graham had heard the conversation in the kitchen escalating. He had enough of his wife having to defend their life.

Pulling out of the driveway, they didn't look back. Joanna wiped her tears away as she was filled with relief. Graham took her hand. They drove home.

***

Although the Kornelsons were facing some pretty awful days, grace had also found a place in their home. Graham and Joanna had found that middle ground they had nearly lost. They became that team again, when one needed a helping hand or a pep talk during days of defeat. It wasn't perfect, but it was better. The kids no longer were allowed to divide and conquer them to gain the upper hand. After the disastrous Thanksgiving with Joanna's family, Graham and Joanna made genuine efforts to ask their kids how they were coping and made open communication with each other a priority. Ally had two more seizures and another specialist appointment was apparent. Joanna found it hard to stay positive for her family and optimistic for the future, but something was different. Her family was finding a place of gratitude and a bond was forming like a protective shell to safe guard them as they continually coped with what life was dealing them.

Joanna looked into the mirror while sitting at her dressing table. Her hair was perfectly made up and so was her face. She needed earrings and hairspray and she was ready for the banquet. But she shuttered inside. The last place she wanted to go tonight was another foundation fundraiser dinner. Graham's office had bought a table and they were obligated to attend.

The week had been long and difficult. Ally's neurologist had suggested another drug change. This one more drastic; weaning her off the two she was currently taking and adding a newer drug. Joanna read about this anti-seizure medication and on paper it looked like the winning cure. But experience with drug changes told her otherwise.

So now they would wait to see what was in store for Ally and what road of uncertainty they would all go down. Adding the earrings and another layer of lipstick she was ready. One more pump of hairspray and she headed downstairs to find Graham.

"So pizza is in the freezer," she reminded the kids who were flaked out in the family room, searching Netflix.

"Yeah, we know," Lydia said, staring at the TV. "There it is, Sherlock," she announced to Jack who had the controls.

"Sherlock!" Graham exclaimed. "Do we have to go to this fundraiser?" he asked Joanna.

She would love to stay home on this Saturday night with her family too, she thought slipping on her high heels. "I promise we don't have to stay a minute longer than absolutely necessary," she confessed. "But we need to go."

With great reluctance, Graham rose from the comfort of his chair and they headed off to the gala event.

The salad was creative and the entree of roast beef, a scoop of potatoes and ginger glazed carrots certainly was better than the frozen pizza they would have had at home, Joanna decided. But she wanted nothing more than to get out of the tight fitting dress and let her hair free from the bobby pins. Graham and Joanna were fixtures at community banquets and fundraising events. Although not much in the way of working a room, they knew enough people to make these social outings somewhat enjoyable.

Grace talked about her latest home renovation with promises to get Joanna's expert opinion, although she never did. Grace was filled with promises of lunch on her terrace and weekend brunches, but Joanna knew she was all talk. Todd and Sarah were sitting at a table with other doctors and hospital staff. Once the guest speaker inspired and motivated this local crowd about what one can do if one just believed in oneself, Joanna and Graham would be gone. They both hated to linger longer than needed. Checking her phone, there were no texts from the kids. She took that as a good sign.

Joanna remembered that she used to look forward to getting dressed up and having a night out at these dinners. But she had grown weary and found it difficult to carry on small talk or to even want to be in public these days. Life seemed so uncertain with Ally's condition that it always felt like the next shoe was ready to drop.

After a brief standing ovation for the speaker and final farewells, the room began to clear out. Graham was called over a few tables away to be introduced to someone Ben wanted him to meet. Joanna grabbed her small handbag as someone tapped her shoulder. Turning around, a woman slightly older than herself offered an artificial smile.

"Hi, are you Joanna Kornelson?" she asked rather stiffly.

"Yes."

"I'm Deloris Rogalsky." She paused. "Matthew's mother."

Joanna reached out her hand. "Oh, it's nice to meet you. I'm glad you came over. We've really enjoyed having Matthew around. He's a really great young man."

Deloris licked her red, shiny lips. "Yes, thank you. We are proud of him and all that he has accomplished, athletically. We have great hopes for him. And his future."

Joanna felt a tug of confusion. "I can imagine. We have the same hopes for our daughter as well. But with music. She wants to be a concert pianist."

"Yes, that's what Matthew has mentioned." She looked down, with an urgency to quickly say more. "Matthew also came home from your place a few weeks ago, rather distraught. It was upsetting. To see our son have to go through, that."

Joanna balanced herself evenly on her stilettos, steadying herself. "Yes, it is very difficult and you should be very proud of him. He handled it very well and showed great -"

"That's just it, Joanna," Deloris quickly added. "He doesn't have to deal with difficult situations in his life like that. He needs to focus on getting a volleyball scholarship. Top schools are interested in him."

"Yes, he has told us that too. And I'm sure he will make it," Joanna added stiffly, not offering this woman a way out. If she had something to say, Joanna was going to make her say it.

Licking those annoying thin, bright lips again, Deloris took a half step closer. "Matthew doesn't need distractions like what he experienced with your daughter."

Joanna's back stiffened and her eyes matched her growing rage. "My daughter's name is Ally and she is not a distraction."

Deloris wanted to react but her husband came and stood beside his wife, causing her to stop. "Stan, this is Joanna Kornelson, Ally's mother."

He didn't smile or offer his hand. He uncomfortably glanced at Joanna, back to his wife and then looked away.

These two people raised a gracious, understanding young man? Joanna thought, clearing her throat. "Your wife was saying that Matthew has a bright future ahead of him this coming year with a few universities interested in picking him up," she said politely.

"Yes, that's right," he answered mechanically.

"It's great to have kids who are focused isn't it? Ally as well. She's quite an accomplished pianist already. She's played at competitions in Winnipeg and has great ambition to pursue a career in music." Joanna knew she was over the top and obviously bragging. But she had to. She had to prove to this pathetic couple that Ally was not a disease. She was a girl who liked their son. Joanna cringed at the thought that Ally was being perceived as a distraction.

"Yes, I'm sure she is, but will she not be limited?" Deloris asked, tilting her head.

"Limited?" Joanna questioned with faulty innocence. "By what?" she spat out without blinking.

Deloris swallowed hard and didn't flinch. "I think we both know what I mean."

"No, I don't think we do," Joanna shot back, politely smiling.

"Deloris, this isn't the time," Stan quietly muttered.

"We don't want our son to be distracted or have to go through what he had to the other night, ever again. That wasn't fair to him. He was unprepared and very bothered by it."

Joanna closed her eyes and took a second to regroup as the audacity of this woman's intolerance slapped her in the face. "Obviously you've done a very good job of protecting your son from any hardships or *distractions* in his life. But I need to be clear, we didn't ask for Ally to have epilepsy nor did we want her to suffer the way she has. But sometimes these *distractions* get in the way and you learn to deal with them. Not hide and pretend awful things don't happen to people in your life."

Graham came behind Joanna and placed his hand on the small of her back. He felt her tension. "Hi, I'm Graham Kornelson. I think we've met before," he kindly said to Stan, reaching out to shake his hand. "You're a loans manager at the Royal Bank, right?"

"Yes," he offered, shaking Graham's hand.

"I'm a partner at -"

"Graham these are Matthew's parents," Joanna hastily interrupted. "They were just explaining to me that Matthew has great potential this coming year."

"We've enjoyed getting to know him. He's a great kid."

"Yes he is. Very kind and supportive," Joanna said, looking at Deloris a little longer than necessary. "But we should go. Nice meeting you," she offered with strained politeness and walked away with Graham at her side.

"What was that about?" he asked, helping her with her coat.

"I'll tell you in the car," she said as they said good bye to a few more acquaintances at the door.

Once in the car, Joanna let out a deep moaning sigh. "They called Ally a distraction for their son. Can you believe it?"

"You didn't look like you were talking about what a lovely fall we were having," Graham commented, heading down the highway.

"I'm not joking, Graham. She was mean and catty and I couldn't believe how narrow minded she was."

"Not everyone is going to be able to handle a girlfriend with seizures, Jo," he said, staring out the windshield.

"Now you're taking their side?" she asked, feeling the anger all over again.

"I'm not taking sides. But we've been fortunate that we've had people who have treated her fairly, for the most part. It's not always going to be the case, Joanna. Not everyone is going to be understanding of her circumstances." He took her hand. "I'm being realistic," he added.

Joanna hated to face that reality. Living in a smaller community they had the benefit of people knowing who Ally was. Like Roger and Dean at the Burger Shack giving her a summer job. And the teachers allowing her leniencies with assignments and tests if she was having a rough patch. What will happen when she moves away and goes to a university where no one knows her? Joanna closed her eyes at the thought and relived the conversation with Matthew's mother. No one had been so bold, placing Ally in the discard pile like she was not enough or too damaged. *Well, maybe he didn't deserve her daughter*, Joanna decided.

"Stop thinking about it," Graham requested, breaking into her angry thoughts.

"How do you know that I'm thinking about it?"

"Because you're squeezing the blood out of my hand," he said.

She laughed. "Sorry. But that woman ruined my whole day now. I felt like we've come so far and now I feel just set back. Who does she think she is for saying Ally is not good enough for her son? Does she even know Ally? She doesn't obviously, she doesn't know us or her. Does she know her son, because he is nothing like his parents."

"You can tell Matthew your issues with his parents, because his car is in front of our house," Graham said, pulling into their driveway.

Joanna huffed.

"I'm kidding, Jo. You can't say anything to him or Ally about meeting his parents. He can't help what his parents say anymore than you can help what your family says to you." Graham preached. He took off his seatbelt, giving Joanna a few more seconds to let it sink in.

"I know you're right, and I won't say anything. But I'm still upset about it," she explained, getting out of the car.

"I am too. But that's life and this is our family," Graham said, guiding his wife into the house. "And what goes on out there doesn't have to affect what goes on behind this door," he added, opening the kitchen door and letting his wife enter. Hearing the TV, they walked into the family room and found Matthew and Ally on the couch; Ally had fallen asleep leaning against his arm. Lydia and Jack were reclined on the chairs, with plates of pizza crusts and bags of chips scattered on the coffee table. Joanna couldn't have been happier.

30
Going To Be Some Changes Made

Another bleak and harsh winter found the Kornelsons struggling. There was no winter getaway for Graham and Joanna. And Christmas had passed with a blur of people, food and confusion. Ally continued to seizure and continued to slide down a slope of sadness and grief as she watched her normal become something of a distant dream. The doctors told them at least the seizures weren't weekly or even daily. Joanna tried to find comfort in that. And wondered if that's what they were waiting for.

Joanna's pep talks no longer offered the same hope to Ally. And the twins became lost in the shuffle of managing seizures and temper tantrums. It was feeling futile for them all. Ally wrote her final semester exams but with great effort. Her teachers understood and compromised where they could. Fortunately, Ally was a very good student and she still managed to excel academically in spite of missing so many days of school.

Joanna encouraged Ally to go out with her friends or to still attend youth events at the church, but she had lost interest. On occasion a friend or two would come over or Matthew spent an evening or dinner with their family. The only joy that Ally clung to was sitting at the piano and practicing. She found solace and familiarity in that room at the back of their house. It may have been a library or a study back when the home was built a century ago. But Ally claimed it as her refuge and practiced as long as she could stand it.

By the end of March with the renewal and spring coming, the Kornelson family were preparing to watch Ally suffer through another drug change recommended by their neurologist. Joanna studied her new drug schedule to make sure she got it right. At least they were able to start the transition during spring break so Ally wouldn't have to miss school. But Lydia and Jack felt short changed when they were told there would be no spring break vacation like all their other friends. Jack was also feeling pockets of neglect when his parents didn't attend several of his hockey games, and made him travel with other families. Lydia's interest in dance had dwindled as her parents' time had gotten more and more focused on Ally, once again.

Joanna's guilt ran through her like oxygen. She saw the unfairness but didn't know how to balance it. She and Graham would meet with the twins and hear them out and tried to get them to understand that Ally had been struggling the past few months and needed them more than ever. And then they promised to make it up to them once Ally had regained proper therapeutic levels of the new medication. Although, Joanna's motherly instincts had hinted, not to hope too much.

"Mom," Lydia yelled down the stairs.

"What happened, is she -" Joanna panicked running up the stairs.

"Ally's hollering at me again and I am so mad at her, she took -"

"Lydia, you can't just yell for me to come running like that. I thought she was having a seizure. You scared me half to death." Joanna could feel her heart going back to normal.

She could also feel she wasn't in the shape she used to be. Running had stopped being a daily priority. She was lucky if it was weekly. Too exhausted to go out at the end of the day or not enough energy in the morning, after a bad night with Ally would keep her up for hours.

"She keeps taking all my stuff," Lydia said between clenched teeth. "And I know she does it on purpose, Mom."

"No, she doesn't. What did she take?" she asked.

"My black shirt I wear for choir."

Joanna sighed. "I'll get it back and I will talk to her. Could you please go set the table, then take the casserole out of the oven."

"Casserole, yuck," she complained, lumbering down the stairs.

Joanna sighed again and headed for Ally's room when she heard the screaming. Opening the door, Joanna watched Ally grabbing her clothes from the closet and dresser drawers, tossing them all over her room. Hollering and crying, Ally was having another temper tantrum as her emotional world had been thrown into turmoil.

"Ally, come on, stop that," Joanna said sternly, grabbing Ally's arms. She tried to get away. But Joanna resisted her urges to flail and lose control.

"Nothing fits me. I'm so ugly and stupid. I hate my life," she kept repeating, trying to destroy her room.

"Ally, stop!" Joanna demanded, not giving up her fight. "It's okay, let's talk about it. But throwing a fit won't help. Now stop!"

"No, I hate my life, I hate my life, I HATE MY LIFE!" she screamed.

Joanna guided Ally to her bed as screams and tears of displaced outrage gushed from her daughter. "I want it to go away," Ally cried. "I want to be normal again, I hate my life."

Joanna barely held her emotions together. This was the fourth outburst in a week, and Joanna was growing weary and feeling like a failure herself.

"Ally, it's going to be okay. We're going to do this together. You're not alone," she cooed. They were now merely heartless sounding words that had been repeated too many times.

Ally calmed down as Joanna brushed her matted hair from her face. "Matthew wants to take me out tonight and I have nothing that fits me. I'm fat and ugly and I don't want to go out."

Joanna sighed, believing this was a problem she could help solve. "Let me help you find something that you can wear, okay? I know you have clothes that will fit. We'll go through your summer things," she offered, getting up and beginning to match outfits together.

Ally didn't like any of her mother's attempts. She just lay on the bed and said 'no' to every idea offered. Joanna kept trying until finally a pair of black leggings, a long flowing top and scarf would suffice. But then Ally decided she didn't want to go out in pubic anymore.

Pursing her lips together, Joanna sat back on the bed. "Ally, I think you need to go out, even if it's just for a few hours. Matthew hasn't seen you all week and he keeps calling you."

"I don't care anymore. I wish he'd stop calling me," she said into her pillow. "I just want to sleep."

Joanna took in a deep breath tucking the hair that came loose from her ponytail. "Then you need to tell him that. You can't keep putting him and your friends off, Ally. They want to be with you and if you push them away, they'll give up."

Ally sat up. "That's a horrible thing to say. You're my mother, you're supposed to make me feel better, not worse about myself." She flopped back onto her pillow and covered it over her head.

The words stung deeper than Joanna was willing to admit. She would think of herself later, right now Ally had to face reality. "Listen Ally. Come on Ally, take the pillow off your head when I'm talking to you."

She wouldn't budge.

"Fine, I'll go," Joanna stated and got up.

"No, don't leave me," Ally whined, grabbing her mom's arm.

"Ally, I know this is tough. But you can't just shut people out. They are your friends. They have bad days too. But you have to show some effort for them too, you know. And sitting in your room all the time isn't going to make you feel better either."

"But Mom, I don't want to be in public and see people. I played in the festival again just like you made me and that was hard enough. I don't want to go out."

Joanna did force her to play piano in the local festival promising Ally that if she was picked to go on to Provincial level, she didn't have to go this year. Ally was selected to compete at the Provincial piano competition which she swiftly declined allowing the alternate to go in her place.

"You can't just stay home. You have to keep making the decision to make the best of each day. You have to go back to school next week."

Ally had realized that but was not prepared to even think about that catastrophe waiting to happen.

"Get out of your pyjamas and come down for dinner. You'll feel better once you've eaten. When is he coming to pick you up?" she said, rubbing Ally's back.

"Seven. He wants to go to a coffeehouse."

"Sounds fun, coffeehouses are a great place to see people and relax, listen to music."

"Then you should go if you think it's going to be *fun*," Ally remarked back, hugging her pillow closer.

Joanna was exasperated. Clamping her lips together to keep in her bitterness, she heard Bentley barking, telling everyone that Graham was home. *Finally*, she thought.

"Get dressed and come eat. Dad is home," she instructed, getting up and heading down the back stairs.

Finding the wine glass she left behind on the kitchen island, Joanna took a sip. She noticed the table was not set, nor was the casserole cooling on the counter like she had asked Lydia to do more than half an hour earlier.

"Lydia," she screamed, slamming the wine glass on the granite counter top breaking the stem. Red wine splashed everywhere. "Lydia!"

Graham walked in just as Joanna screamed for her daughter to come into the kitchen.

"What did you do?" he asked, picking up broken glass off the floor, trying to keep Bentley from licking up the wine.

"What?" Lydia asked, walking into the kitchen watching her mom take out a very burnt casserole from the oven.

"I asked you to set the table and take the casserole out of the oven. Now it's ruined," she screamed.

Lydia gulped hard, seeing her mother's temper. "Jack wanted to show me a video he found and then I forgot."

Joanna looked up to the ceiling begging for just a bit more patience, but none was to be found. "Well, set the table because we're eating this," she yelled at Lydia, showing her the blackened casserole.

"I am not eating that!" Lydia fought back.

"Yes, you are. And I will not take any more talking back from you. I asked you to do two things and you couldn't do that."

"I'm ordering a pizza," Lydia announced, reaching for the phone.

"Don't you dare," Joanna threatened. "You screwed this up and now you have to eat it, do you hear me," she yelled, as Graham came to her side.

"That's enough," he said to Joanna, throwing the broken pieces of glass into the garbage. "Lydia put the phone down. You do not get to decide if we are ordering pizza or not."

"She has been mean to me all day. All my friends are gone on spring break vacations and I'm stuck with her and Ally screaming at everyone," she cried.

"Oh, are we yelling at everyone again?" Jack asked, casually walking into the kitchen.

"Jack that isn't helping," Graham said, getting a spoon and scraping off the black cheese that coated the casserole. He dug deeper into the charred chicken and potatoes. "Joanna this is not edible."

"I don't care," she said, grabbing a stack of plates and nearly tossing them around the table. "That's what we're eating. I'm not exactly thrilled to be stuck here at home with you either, Lydia. So don't think this is just about you not getting your way. When do I get my way?"

"Joanna," Graham scolded. He loosened his tie. This was the third day in a row he had come home to a house of yelling and blaming.

He saw the weary fatigue gripping his wife. She was exasperating her children as much as she was trying to keep everyone happy. It wasn't working. He would be taking the rest of the week off, he decided. His family had once again found their breaking point. He opened a cupboard and found a bag of chips and he tossed it to Jack.

"You two eat that until I've had a chance to talk to Mom. Go watch TV."

"Graham -"

He held up his hand to Joanna until the kids had closed the swinging kitchen door behind them. "Listen, I know you're exhausted and this has been an awful week. I will take the rest of the week off and give you a break. I don't think either of us expected Ally to be going through such a horrible transition."

Joanna's exhaustion turned her into a weepy mess as she fell into her husband, nodding in agreement. She cried softly, feeling like a hopeless failure who couldn't get through to her daughter. "I feel like I'm losing Ally. She doesn't listen and I don't know if I'm saying the right things to her anymore," Joanna said, through her tears. "And then Lydia and Jack are so bored and impatient."

Graham listened quietly as she continued to offer him a laundry list of all that had gone wrong this day. When she was done, he poured her another glass of wine and one for himself. They each took a sip and Joanna breathed again feeling better for having someone to listen to her, instead of her kids talking back and rolling their eyes.

"So this is what is going to happen," he gently said. "You are going to apologize to Lydia for yelling at her. Even though she didn't listen to what you told her to do. You scared her by slamming down the wineglass and then talking to her like that. And then Jack can order pizza and chicken, then we'll all take it down a notch for tonight. There's a hockey game on TV in one hour and we can just stay home and be together, okay?"

"Ally's going out with Matthew tonight."

"Even better. Once less kid to mother for a couple of hours," he said smiling, then taking another sip of wine. He kissed his wife and headed out of the kitchen. "Jack, order pizza and a bucket of chicken. We have a hockey game to watch. Lydia, your mother wants to talk to you. Get into the kitchen, please."

Joanna took in a much needed cleansing breath, and blew it out looking up and closing her eyes as a sense of relief washed over her. It wasn't the wine, but her caring and wonderful husband's presence. Gently she placed the wine glass down as Lydia slowly opened the swinging door. She looked at her mom. Joanna held out her arms. Lydia inched closer. Mother and daughter embraced and with tearful words, apologized.

Matthew and the food arrived at the same time, which easily convinced him that maybe they should stay and watch the game first. Ally hated watching hockey but preferred that to going out to a busy, happy coffeehouse. When the game was over, Matthew and Ally decided to stop by the coffeehouse with the promise of not being home too late. Joanna didn't care, she was grateful that Ally was leaving the house even for a little while.

When Joanna finally got to crawl into bed that night, she was glad another bad day could be put away. *Hopefully tomorrow would be a better day,* she thought easily drifting off. *Maybe tomorrow would be better.*

31
Losing Ground

There would be few happier days for Joanna and her family. Ally continued to spiral down on the new medication. Joanna's expectations kept slipping to easier goals, from wanting Ally to perform piano at Provincials and school concerts, to simply getting to school each day, to wanting her to finish grade 11.

By June, Graham and Joanna were basically home-schooling Ally who had been terrified to walk down the hallways at school. She cried and hid in the girls' bath-room, only Lydia was able to get her out of the stall and to their mom, waiting in the principal's office. They had decided the best decision for Ally was let her work on assignments at home and write her exams in the privacy of the guidance counsellor's office.

Joanna was emotionally hanging on by a thread. Ally had a terrible time getting to bed and falling asleep, reminding Joanna of the times when Ally was a new born and she got her days and nights mixed up. Ally suffered from unex-plained fear and doubt about leaving the house or talking to people. She only wanted to watch, The Brady Bunch, reruns from her laptop. Graham spent his evenings talking with Ally or getting up for her at night if she was having a nightmare and he wondered when this transition period would end. Graham came home throughout the day if Joanna couldn't handle her outbursts or an untimely seizure.

Jack and Lydia had learned to be self sufficient and often ate dinner alone as Ally needed her parents upstairs. They got themselves to school, did their homework together and arranged for their own rides with friends. Nana Ellie would pick them up after school and bring them to her condo where they barbecued hamburgers. Uncle Todd took Jack to his baseball games and practices when he was available. And Aunt Sarah stepped in by inviting Lydia to take her younger cousins to the water park or to stay for a sleepover. Ally didn't go back to the Burger Shack that spring. It was too much pressure. She tried, but had panic attacks just before her shift, causing the understanding owners to quickly find a replacement.

Graham fell into the seat of his car, relieved that is was the end of a crazy and horrible day at the office. Divorce, bankruptcy, estate issues all kept him busy as he tried to guide, advise and gather information for other people all day long. Finding answers to their problems; solutions for people who had gotten themselves into trouble.

It was another hot day. He started the car to get a blast of AC. Putting on sunglasses to hide his weary eyes, he waved to Ben who was leaving the office. No one really asked about Ally anymore Graham realized, watching his business partner get into his Lexus. It was probably because Graham's standard answer was always, 'we're doing fine'. Fine was a great place to be; so average and ordinary, just like everyone else. Telling people, 'by the way, our life is falling apart', left them awkwardly speechless or they had a story of their own. So Graham's answer simply became, 'fine, everything is all good'.

Putting the car into gear Graham headed home knowing it had been a trying day for Joanna. Maybe they would go to the cabin this weekend. Although Jack had started working at the golf course making him even more unavailable. Maybe he would at least try to go for a run tonight. It had been awhile since he felt that his home was stable enough to take time for himself over these past few months. If he wasn't at work, he was soothing someone's tears away. Going to church had become infrequent causing church goers to ask how Ally was doing. Again, how do they answer that without getting bad advice or shallow responses?

Plus, they were just tired. Collectively they had grown exhausted of living with seizures and fits and personal turmoil. Graham no longer believed this was normal for Ally, even for a girl who was on a dozen pills a day. The promise of this new drug was making Ally crazy and they saw her slipping away from them as they obediently followed the doctor's instructions. They had demanded an appointment with their exceptionally busy neurologist. When Dr. Shaw returned their phone call, Graham had explained that this cocktail of drugs was no longer an option for them. Epilepsy was the illness but their battle had turned to the horrible side effects of the drugs. He explained Ally's crazy mood swings and constant irritability. They had an appointment for next week.

Graham pulled into the driveway and saw Jack throwing hoops in front of the garage. He took off his tie and threw it onto his briefcase. He wasn't sure why he brought it home since he never found time to catch up on files in the evenings.

He got out of the car as Jack threw him the ball. Going for a three point shot, he missed the basket as Jack retrieved it, making a perfect layup shot. Jack threw the ball to his dad again. But this time, Graham just dribbled it, walking closer to the garage. "Isn't it too hot out here to be throwing hoops, Jack?"

"It's hotter in there," he said, pointing his thumb towards the house, then wiping sweat from his forehead.

"Who this time?" Graham asked, dribbling the ball.

"Lydia and Ally were going at it. And then Mom stepped in and now I think it's just Mom and Lyd," he explained, trying to steal the ball. Graham gave in and with a brisk chest pass, tossed it to Jack.

"I better go check it out."

"Good luck, Dad," he offered, swishing another basket.

Graham walked in hearing Lydia crying and talking at the same time. When Lydia saw her dad, she ran and hugged him while complaining about her mother again. Graham saw the wine glass on the counter. It must have been one of those days he realized looking at the rest of the kitchen. Breakfast dishes were still on the table, with full grocery bags left on the counter.

Graham successfully calmed his household down again before offering to barbecue the store-bought beef and veggie kabobs. When supper was over and everyone appeared satisfied, Graham announced he wanted to go for a run now that the evening had cooled off from the daytime heat.

"I want to come too, Dad," Jack said, picking at the red onions left on his plate.

Joanna closed her eyes, remembering what the freedom of running felt like. "Me too?"

Lydia gestured that she was not staying home with her sister, by pointing at Ally and shaking her head.

"Why don't you girls ride your bikes beside us as we run?" Joanna suggested, gathering the dinner plates.

"Do I have to," Ally moaned, putting her head down on the table.

"Yes, Ally, that's a great idea," Graham seconded, rubbing her back. "I go so fast I don't think you'll be able to catch up with me."

He saw Ally's slight smile. That was a good sign. "You're old Dad, you can't run fast anymore."

Graham tossed his used napkin in her face. "I'm not old. I can keep up with this punk," he said, playfully grabbing Jack's muscular thigh.

"Actually, you do run pretty fast, Dad. You're not old, but you're old-er," he clarified, downing the rest of his iced tea.

"Okay, everyone bring something inside and we'll all head out," Joanna said, more excited than she had been in weeks.

And they were right. It was a perfectly calm evening as they ran through the residential streets lined with trees acting like a protective canopy. Joanna ran on their treadmill when she didn't want to be away from home but nothing compared to running outside. The endorphins ran through her brain and she was feeling like her old self again. Turning a bit to see Ally, she wondered if she was feeling the same?

Hard to tell under the sunglasses covering her eyes. "Hey, Ally, having fun?" she asked, through each pounding step.

Ally half smiled and kept going. "It's okay."

Joanna looked forward and tried to keep her spirits up. How she had prayed that Ally would find normal again and be who she once was before all this started three years earlier.

"Hey, now, here comes a nice image!" called out one of the pastors of their church. He was washing his car on the driveway and waved at them passing by. "Oh, that is a great sight to see," he added. "A happy family enjoying this beautiful evening together."

Joanna wanted to stop in her tracks. *Really, that's what he saw in them? Happy? Nice? Enjoying being together?*

"Haven't seen you folks around," he quickly said as the Kornelsons continued their pace. "How's life?" he asked with a big toothy grin.

"Been at the cabin. Going again this weekend I'm afraid," Graham offered, slowing down his stride just a bit. "Life's great, isn't it?" he half asked, with a hint of sarcasm.

"It sure is. Well, God bless you folks," he offered, waving them off.

"We're going to the cabin?" Joanna asked smiling.

"Yes," Graham answered picking up the pace. "Yes, we are."

***

The next week Graham and Joanna took Ally back to see Dr. Shaw. This was to be their last appointment with her since Ally had just turned seventeen in April. She would now be sent to the adults' neurology clinic with a new neurologist. When Ally didn't understand Dr. Shaw's questions during the appointment, she told Dr. Shaw to talk slower and use easier words that she could understand. It became apparent to Dr. Shaw that this last medication added was not the right medication for Ally. She would be taken off the drug immediately and see how she managed back to just two drugs.

More changes, Joanna thought to herself. They politely shook hands with Dr. Shaw and made their way through the winding hallways back to the parkade. With another medication schedule to follow, Joanna was hoping this would finally be the end of it and they could get back to whatever normal was left for their family. She didn't know what that would even look like.

The long, hot summer progressed into more days of peace and civility from Ally's fits of anger and tantrums. Ally began to hang out with her friends a little more often and Matthew was coming around again, so excited to see Ally getting back to herself. And even with the positive changes, Joanna had noticed that Ally wasn't quite who she once was; she was quieter and more contemplative.

She used to be silly and outspoken, witty and clever. Now she used her words carefully always with an air of caution.

Joanna sat on the front porch and waved to Matthew and Ally as they drove off to meet up with friends. Lydia biked to Nana Ellie's for a sleepover while Jack and Graham had gone out for a round of golf. Joanna put her head back on the rocker and sighed, taking in the late summer air. It felt like a storm had passed through their home leaving them basically intact, but seeing them changed. But it wasn't all bad changes. They had grown closer as a family this summer. So much talking and gaining understanding about themselves. Spending hours together under their roof finding solace and protection from a world that didn't understand them. Hiding away at their cabin when they needed the world of nature to revitalize them once more.

Ally would be starting Grade 12 in a few weeks. One last year of high school and Ally would be grown up and gone. Hard to believe the years had passed by so quickly. So many moments, too many to remember. How Joanna wanted Ally to have good memories of her childhood. Even in the bad times, she wanted to find the good in every moment they shared.

Savouring this time alone, Joanna found a loneliness creep in. For months she had been dealing with so much stress it was strange to find herself sitting on her front porch with peace and quiet as her company. Had she really survived the past few months? Did that all really happen to her family? There were too many times to admit, her frustration had turned into anger at the expense of her kids and husband. Now with some perspective and healing, Joanna vowed to be the mom she wanted her kids to have. Ally had been drowning in her own life's medicated turmoil while the twins were forced to watch it all unfold.

Joanna had always questioned her mothering. Was she doing and saying enough? Did she do too much for her kids or not enough? Where was the balance? She constantly compared herself to her mother and sisters. She looked at her friends and wondered about all of their mothering ways. Was she enough for what her children required? It was something she may never get answered. She would just keep trying to do her best and then hope for the best.

Joanna added a pillow behind her back and pushed the gentle motion of the rocking chair. Closing her eyes, she dared herself to think about the future, Ally's future. It was often her last thought before she fell asleep and the first thing she thought about when she woke up. What would happen to her daughter next year when her friends would be leaving for different schools and opportunities? It terrified Joanna to think that all their hopes and dreams for Ally couldn't be possible. Ally had dreamed of playing piano all her life.

They had recognized Ally's musical talents early on and gave their daughter every opportunity to cultivate her love of music by registering her in children's music schools, choirs and piano lessons. And now what? How could those brief ninety seconds that the seizures lasted, change the entire landscape of Ally's future?

She had to stop looking beyond today. It was too painful, it was too far into the future that held too many unknowns. She told herself that she needed to focus on what could be accomplished for Ally now. She told herself she needed to focus on what she could control, and not what was out of her grasp. She had to believe that the future would be bright and promising. It was all that was left to believe in. Joanna wiped away one falling tear.

32

Hope & Promises

Halloween was approaching, and the scary part was they were not seeing the improvement they had been promised. The doctors assured them that the severe mood changing anti seizure medication was completely out of her system. Perhaps she was feeling other outside pressures such as school, piano and friends. Wasn't that every teenagers issues? Joanna told the doctors that this was different; Ally was still not herself. It was one thing to want to stay home from school, but it was quite another that Ally couldn't get out of bed. And if they forced her too, she would cry and scream in panic. One evening Ally admitted that she had no future, that all was hopeless. So why get out of bed? Nothing seemed to make her want to get up. She had quickly agreed with Matthew that perhaps they should take a break. She was relieved she had told Joanna one day. It was one less person she had to deal with.

It took all of Ally's strength to make it through the day. Sleeping was her new hobby. Showering and caring about her appearance seemed trivial. Again, Joanna and Graham tried to get her to see the bright side; to look at what was good more than what was bad. One Sunday afternoon, Joanna insisted that Ally go for a walk with her and when she simply refused, Joanna put socks on her daughter's feet and physically hauled her out of bed. The walk had been just around the block but it was already too much for Ally, who came home and went straight back into bed.

When Ally refused to go to another doctor's appointment to make sure her therapeutic levels were accurate, Joanna was at the end of her rope. All the begging and pleading and compromise had all proven to be futile and useless. Ally was slipping away into a place Joanna couldn't go. She was continually listening to the song, Aquarius, and it had started to scare Joanna. The constant sadness and weariness took a toll on the others; laughing and being together seemed out of place now.

Jack continued to excel in sports as he and Lydia had started grade 10. Lydia babysat for several families. She was showing interest in becoming a teacher. But while she was helping her mother get supper ready, Lydia had mentioned possibly going into nursing. Preparing supper together had become Joanna and Lydia's special time. It was easy to talk when hands were busy getting dinner on the table. Ally was always in her room, while Jack's schedule kept him at practices after school and games several evenings a week. They had found yet another new normal.

On a dreary November afternoon, Hannah invited Joanna and another friend Eve for coffee. They chatted about family and got updates on each other. They swapped recipes and holiday plans. They laughed and casually talked until Eve asked Joanna how Ally was getting along.

Joanna's smile faded away. She didn't know how to answer anymore. Her daughter couldn't get out of bed. Her daughter didn't play piano anymore. Seizures seemed to be the least of their concerns now. Ally had become an unrecognizable stranger in their home. Was that what they wanted to hear?

"So she hasn't had a seizure for a while?" Hannah asked, serving the pumpkin coffeecake.

"Christine says she's been having trouble coming to school, is everything all right?" Eve kindly questioned, sipping her tea.

Joanna didn't want to answer. She wanted to get up and leave. She wanted to hide in her bed like Ally. But she needed to talk about it. In fact, Joanna knew she had to tell someone what was happening.

She took in a deep breath as tears came to the surface. Her broken heart and shattered dreams for her daughter could no longer be a kept secret inside their family walls.

Joanna took in a quick breath. "Ally has changed so much. And in ways we didn't expect. She's lost all her friends, her ambitions." Joanna wiped her tears. "She doesn't want to leave her room and she's just...sad. All the time."

Hannah refilled the tea pot with hot water and took a moment before delicately asking the question. "Have you taken her in to see a doctor about depression?"

"No, she's not depressed," Joanna quickly corrected. "It's just been a hard few years, that's all. She'll get through this. I just need to keep being understanding and let her get strong again," she explained. "But thank you for your concern. It's nice to be able to talk about it and feel heard for a change. So, thank you."

But Hannah, who was kindly insistent, looked at Joanna. "You are a great and devoted mother, Joanna. But let me say that even the best mothering in the world can't heal a person who is depressed. And from what you are saying, it sounds like Ally is suffering from some level of depression. I have been there too, Joanna. When I had my third miscarriage, I didn't want to get out of bed and couldn't if I tried. I'm not an expert by any means, but I recognize the signs, because I was there."

Joanna looked away from her dear friend. She knew she was offering her the truth as no one else would, but Joanna was not yet ready to hear it. "I don't know what to do," she cried softly.

Hannah sat down across from Joanna. "Call someone she can talk to, professionally. Get her to a doctor and see if they can put her on an antidepressant. The longer you ignore depression, the worse it digs into your soul," Hannah explained.

"Lots of people are on medication, Joanna. And a lot of people need to see a counsellor to help them get back on track again," Eve added. "There is no shame in either. You can't keep trying to hold on to this by yourself and fix it."

Joanna gathered herself together and took in what they were saying. Taking a sip of water, she finally nodded. "It's not that I disagree with you because I don't, at all. I know people as well who needed...but it's just hard," she tried to say in between sobbing breaths, "it's just so hard when it's your daughter and your family going through it.

I always thought that illness and depression happened to other families." She paused. "Even after all these years since Ally was diagnosed, it's hard to accept that this is our family, my family."

They sat quietly as Joanna continued to foster ideas and claim the acceptance that she had been denying. "I thought that the epilepsy and all the drug changes was enough to deal with. I don't think I can, we can handle another crisis."

Hannah took Joanna's hand. "But that's where the counsellor will help Ally find coping skills to manage her feelings. You can't white knuckle yourself out of depression. I tried it and I know others who have. You can't always win on your own. But you can win."

***

Later that night Joanna slipped into the den where Graham was going over some briefs. Reluctantly, she suggested to Graham that perhaps they needed to get help for Ally, more than what they were doing for her. That maybe Ally's struggles were not just about the drugs or the epilepsy any longer. Maybe this had become something else entirely and she needed help but didn't know how to ask for it. Graham soon agreed and admitted he was exhausted trying to fix Ally. Graham called Todd and asked for advice.

By the end of the week, Joanna had managed to get Ally to see their family doctor who put her on a low dosage of a mild antidepressant. They were once again warned about the possible side effects that could last from four to six weeks.

"I don't want any more side effects," Ally said to Dr. Strueber.

"I know Ally, it isn't fun starting a new medication. You may have a few stomach aches and perhaps some headaches. And not everyone gets side effects. But I promise you, everything will begin to calm down."

Joanna cleared her throat. "We've heard that before, so sorry if we seem doubtful and skeptical."

Dr. Strueber sat away from the computer and folded her hands on her lap. "I know that. And as doctors, we look at the science and believe that it makes sense and that it will work. And when it doesn't, we try other medications, methods and hope that they will work. Sometimes it becomes more of an art than a science. But Ally, you have been very brave throughout this whole ordeal. Many of my patients who suffer from chronic illness also end up with depression. It's hard to learn to cope and manage something that just happens to you. I want you to start taking the antidepressant right away and then I want to see you again in a month. And I believe with time you will notice a difference."

Ally offered a small, half-like smile and got up to leave. Joanna thanked her and they filled the prescription for another drug full of hope and promises.

33
Awakenings

Ally woke up. At least her eyes did. Because she knew she saw light coming from her bedroom window. She touched her lips and they felt fine. Her tongue took inventory of her mouth, no bite marks. Nothing hurt, her body wasn't harmed. Reaching for her phone, it told her that it was 10:43 in the morning. Lying down again, she felt her heart palpitating. What happened?

Regrouping, she scanned her drug infused brain for answers, for truth. Was this the aftermath of a seizure? She couldn't recall. What was different? Something felt different, assuming this was the getting over a seizure moment. But this wasn't that moment. Sitting up she tucked her long hair behind her ears and grabbed her phone. 10:45AM, Saturday, November 28. Then she smelt bacon. What was going on? She was convinced she had a seizure but nothing was coming back and her body felt good for the first time in a long, long time.

"Mom," she called.

Her door opened. It was her dad. He was wearing that plaid, long sleeved shirt that he wore on Saturdays. "It's snowing," was all he said. But he looked again. "You okay, Al?"

Pulling her legs into her chest she grabbed her blanket. "I think so, but I'm not sure," she answered rubbing her eyes.

Graham walked into her room and sat on the edge of her bed.

"Did I have a seizure?" she questioned, looking around for evidence.

"When?"

"Like now? Or last night or sometime?"

He shook his head and touched her cheek with the back of his hand. "No, you went to bed like normal. You did have a couple of nightmares, but you fell back asleep. You're good, kiddo."

She looked at her dad. "I smell bacon," she said like it was a very strange sensation.

"That's because Mom is making breakfast," he answered, smiling at her curious questions.

"Is that normal?

He chuckled. "Is what normal?"

She hugged her blanket closer. "This, this feeling I have?"

Graham paused, leaning on his elbow. "What feeling is that, Ally? It's Saturday morning, Mom is making us waffles and bacon. It just started to snow. Jack has a volleyball game this afternoon. Uncle Todd and Aunt Sarah and Nana are coming over to celebrate Jack and Lydia's birthday tonight. It's a normal day."

"Oh," was all she managed to say. "Okay, this is normal then," she said, more like a question.

Graham sat up again. "This is normal, Ally," he said, smiling and held out his arms taking his daughter into a hug. "Let's go eat."

She got out of bed, grabbed her housecoat and headed downstairs with her dad to join her family for breakfast. It all felt so strangely wonderful.

***

Joanna and Ally walked out of the clinic into the crisp and cold winter air. Their doctor had been right. If Ally could get over the stomach pain and headaches, she would suddenly feel like the ever present darkness would somehow go away. Christmas was just three weeks away but today Ally felt like she had received her gift. She was no longer lost. The world was just beginning to make sense for her. The nonsensical fear that no one understood was disappearing. It felt wonderful.

"So you feel good, Ally? About what Dr. Strueber said to you?" Joanna asked, putting the Jeep into gear and backing out of the parking lot.

"I do," she answered, still curious about her happiness. "I do. She was right. I don't feel like I'm covered in this shadow that surrounded me. One pill, that's all it took."

"Well, I also think your meetings with Marcus has helped as well, don't you agree?" Joanna added, adjusting the heat.

Ally looked out the window. She had been seeing a counsellor that her Uncle Todd recommended. He was so interested in her ideas and how she thought her life was unfolding so far. He listened and made her think. He made her answer questions and she shared her fears and doubts.

"Yeah, he's kind of cool. Easy to talk to I guess," she finally admitted.

Joanna and Graham had also been meeting with the counsellor; and she had to agree with Ally. He was easy to talk to as they discussed how to help Ally find coping skills to manage her life on her own.

"Okay, I'll pick you up after school and take you to your appointment with Marcus," Joanna said, pulling up in front of the high school. "You all right, Ally?" she asked, noticing her stare out the window.

"Yeah, I am. Is that normal to feel, just all right?" she asked, looking at her mom.

Joanna grabbed her mitten covered hand. "Yes, Ally, that's normal," she said smiling.

Ally was asking what was normal a lot over the past few weeks. It was like she had forgotten how to function over the past six months or perhaps even longer. But now, she was excited to rediscover her life again. Patiently, they answered Ally's questions and reassured her that the doubts could be left behind.

"Okay, thanks, Mom. See you later," Ally said, getting out of the car and walking through the snowy sidewalk back into the high school.

***

"Ally, it's going to take time to figure out these pieces, but I believe that you can get them ready in time," Mrs. Buhlin said. "I'm so pleased that you want to audition."

"I want to go to university just like all my other friends. It's what I have wanted for so long and I'm not going to let anything get in the way, anymore," Ally said, marking the pages in her Bach music book.

Months ago, it had looked like Ally was finished, not just with piano, but with life. It had been difficult on those like Mrs. Buhlin, who supported Ally over so many years to see her suffer so much. Back when Ally first started taking piano lessons, she barely was able to reach the keyboard. Ally was curious and interested in learning what the black dots in the music books sounded like when she played them on the piano. Ally got frustrated when it didn't come out the way she wanted it to, but was driven to learn a piece and play it well. She listened to what the adjudicators had to say and she improved. Her discipline was remarkable for a young person who never had to be coerced or bribed to practice. Ally had always been full of determination, always. It seemed that her strong will and her steely drive helped Ally out of the horrible circumstance she didn't ask to endure. But here she was, back again, asking to get prepared for an audition at the University of Manitoba Music Faculty, only a few months away.

"I think that your Mendelssohn is magnificent and you can easily have that one perfect and ready. Also, let's work on this Bach fugue and for fun, let's prepare a Gershwin piece or a Duke Ellington so that they can see your range," Mrs. Buhlin said, writing down and scanning the array of music books sitting on the lid of her grand piano. "You are going to be so ready, my dear. I am going to see to it."

Ally smiled as she began to attack Bach. She would be ready. Her dreams had waited for her all this time she was had been lost. They had always been there, waiting to be found, and picked up again.

Ally knew that this was her destiny, she was made to communicate through music. It was never forgotten, it was just set aside until she figured out what it was going to take to get back to herself.

With hard efforts, loving support and kindness to herself, Ally's spirit had awakened again. It awoke to nothing spectacular or miraculous. She had just discovered her life again. Her basic, ordinary, everyday, boring, normal living. And it was extraordinary.

She heard Mrs. Buhlin singing out the rhythm of the piece and moving her hands to the tempo. Just as she had done since Ally was little. Ally smiled at her teacher's simple movements to the music; it felt so familiar.

It was so good to be back. All the way back to normal.

34
Christmas Time Again

Ally had no idea the brunt of dysfunction her mother must have endured over the past few years. It was the Sunday before Christmas and Joanna's family had all arrived carrying presents, salads and cookies. Again, the Kornelsons had braced themselves to get through her mother's family gathering that never went well.

The women gathered in the kitchen fussing over last minute preparations for the dinner. Graham gathered with Harry, Russ and father-in-law, John, in the living room. Jack and his three male cousins, Tyler, Brandon and Owen, found sports to talk about and headed into the family room to check out his latest car racing games. Tina looked at Ally and Lydia and went to sit with her dad in the living room. Shrugging it off and grateful their strange cousin didn't need entertaining, Ally and Lydia went into the kitchen to see if they were needed there.

Soon, they were gathered around the large dining room table as bowls of potatoes, stuffing and vegetable dishes were being passed around. It was civil, maybe even festive.

It was promising. Until the dessert was being served. Joanna went to prepare the coffee.

Susan entered the kitchen closing the swinging door behind her. "Joanna, Ally was just talking about her plans," she stated, placing the empty bowls in the sink.

"What plans, Mom?" Joanna asked, adding cream to the pitcher and placing it beside the sugar bowl on the tray. "You mean university?"

"Yes," she said a little stressed. "Now, Joanna, I know she is very talented and determined -"

"She is, Mom. And can we leave it there, please."

Her mother huffed like she did when she was being listened to. "Joanna, let me finish."

Joanna turned from the coffee maker and crossed her arms. "What do you need to say, Mom?"

She pursed her lips together. "She has gone through so much in the last while. Do you think it's a good idea now to push her into this?"

"No one is pushing her. She wants to do this all on her own," Joanna said, pouring the coffee into the butler and adding it to the tray. Grabbing it, she was about to carry it into the dining room.

"What if she's not ready and she doesn't do well and doesn't get into the university? She will be devastated. You always expected so much from that girl, Joanna," Susan said, tugging on her new Christmas sweater. "I need to tell you that I don't think this is a good idea putting so much hope into her. What if she isn't, controlled?"

Joanna placed the tray down and took a second to regroup. "Mom, I know my daughter. I know her very, very well. And I know how determined and courageous she is. I cannot imagine going through what she has experienced. And yet, she found this amazing strength to rise above it all. All of it. The drugs and tests and all those seizures, Mom, that she had to endure," Joanna paused, as her emotions escalated. She knew how much her mother hated emotions. "You're right, she may never be seizure free and we will be anxious every time we get a phone call from Ally wondering if she had another seizure. But we will not limit her or stand in her way to see her achieve her dreams. I'm not that kind of mother."

Susan was stung and perhaps deservedly so. But all she saw in Ally was suffering and didn't understand how much healing and work Ally had put into getting better.

"Well, then I guess that's settled." Susan huffed, wiping crumbs off the counter with her hand.

"I guess it is," Joanna announced with finality and walked out with the tray off coffee.

Ally had gone upstairs to get her pills from her room and decided to come back down through the kitchen. She had paused just in time to hear the exchange between her mother and grandma. A minute later Ally joined the rest of her family back in the dining room who were about to enjoy holiday pies.

"There you are, Ally," her grandma said. "I was wondering if you were okay," she added with forced nurture.

"I am fine, just needed my pills, Grandma" Ally replied.

"So university Ally, let's get back to that," Uncle Harry said, digging into his generous slice of apple pie. "That's really exciting for you. Are you looking forward to moving to Winnipeg?"

Ally glanced at her grandma, then her mother. "I guess so. I'm really looking forward to my audition mostly," she said, making designs on the whipped cream covering her pie.

"So you'll be moving to Winnipeg, then?" Pauline asked in her sharp manner. "Really?" she added, sipping her coffee.

Joanna placed her fork down ready to defend, but Ally spoke first. "Yes, of course I will be moving to Winnipeg. Why shouldn't I, Aunt Pauline?"

She swallowed hard. "I'm not saying you shouldn't, Ally. I just wonder with everything you face, how are you going to manage?"

Graham tossed his napkin down, but Ally once again spoke up. "I manage. Just like everybody else does. I know my circumstances and what I don't know I'll figure out." She paused as everyone stared at her. "What is so hard to understand?" she asked with a touch of sarcasm.

Laura poured cream into her coffee. "It's just that you've been through a lot and your parents are here. How are you going to handle university life?"

"Yeah and all that pressure. I hear university is hard," Harry added, with a mouthful of pie.

Joanna covered her mouth with her hand and looked across the long table at Graham whose eyes were burning.

"You all act like no one has ever moved away from home before," she said, cutting a forkful of pie. "And I'm not the first epileptic to ever go to university either, you know."

The word left a shocking awkwardness in the room. Especially because Ally was the one to say it. She looked at the family sitting around the table. This family who didn't really know one another; who didn't understand each other. They sat politely together at special occasions, only as friendly strangers. Ally saw the hypocrisy. She felt the untied ends that didn't link sister to sister or mother to daughter. Husbands sat in its silence. Children pretended to be unaware of the dynamic that danced around them.

"My parents didn't give up on me," Ally continued. "I'm here today because my mom didn't give up on seeing that I had a life to live, the life that was given to me. This is what I have and who I am. My dad picked us all up when we fell down. He wouldn't let his family fall apart. And because of them, I am here. They helped me through horrible circumstances, and we are still a family even though we all suffered a lot."

Joanna welled with tears. Graham sat back stunned by the eloquence of his daughter.

"We suffered, but we survived it because that's what a family does for each other. They didn't give up on me and refused to let me settle for anything less than what I deserved, ever." Ally paused placing down her fork. "I may fail, but I know how to pick myself up again. I know I can always come home because my family, the five of us, don't fall down alone. We all fall down, together."

The dining room was still.

Joanna quietly rose, excusing herself and headed upstairs to her room. She was proud and overwhelmed. She loved her daughter, she loved her family. She was amazed that all that insight was somewhere hidden inside of Ally all these months. Her daughter was going to be fine.

Graham found his wife upstairs and stood behind her. "Hey, why the tears?" he asked, embracing her. "She finally said what we've wanted to say to them for years." They laughed.

"It's just that I'm so proud of her, so proud. We have our daughter back," Joanna said, wiping away her tears.

"Yes, we do. She's back. And she's right, it's because you didn't give up," he said, kissing Joanna.

"And you didn't either, Graham. Even when I was awful to be around," she reminded, giving him an embrace.

He kissed her forehead. "Not that awful, difficult and controlling definitely." They laughed. "Now, let's go and open some awesome $10 gifts!"

Ally walked into their room and joined in the hug.

"Oh Ally, we're so proud of you," Joanna said, embracing her tightly.

"I'm your daughter, Mom. And I'm proud of that," she said, clinging close to her parents.

"Um, hello," Jack said, standing in the doorway with Lydia right behind him. "Can the hug fest resume later. You left us down there and now it's just weird."

"Oh, come here, you two," Graham said, reaching out an outstretched arm to his twins. "Let's leave them all to feel weird a bit longer." The twins walked into the room, both finding a place under the protective arm of their dad.

"I like this family," Lydia finally said. "I haven't always, but it's good again," she added, looking at Ally.

"You're right, Lydia, it's good again," Joanna agreed.

35
Acceptance

Not again, **Joanna thought coming out of the** grocery store and into the unpredicted spring snow storm. *March is such a confused month,* she concluded looking up at the sky as the heavy snowflakes pelted her face. One day it feels like spring has finally arrived and then without warning, winter promises to stick around a little while longer.

Joanna pushed the shopping cart through the sloppy mess to the back of the Jeep. After loading up the grocery bags, she put the cart away and slipped and fell in the slushy, sloppy, watery snow. *Could this day get any worse,* she thought, trying to stand up on the slippery parking lot. Yes, she knew it could get worse. But this day just wouldn't give her a break. It began at breakfast with a heated discussion with Graham before he left for the office. Then she tried to be patient standing in all the long line ups at every store she went to today. Lunch was a soggy veggie sandwich. And having to drive through cautious, slow traffic made everything take that much longer, frustrating Joanna to get the errands crossed off her growing list.

Turning up the heat in the car, Joanna dried off her hands and wet hair. She still had three more stops before she headed back home, where a pot of chilli was in the crock pot waiting for her family; that also included Todd, Sarah, their girls and Nana Ellie.

It had been a while since they had been together. So Graham had invited them over for tonight, and only told his wife about them all coming for supper during breakfast this morning. After the initial surprise and reprimand of her husband for leaving it until the last moment to let her know company was coming, Joanna actually didn't mind at all. Graham's family was easy to be with and nothing about them made her life stressful. It was the only telling her at the last minute part, that agitated Joanna. But now, pulling out of the parking lot, she was racing against the clock. And with the new layer of snow, it wasn't making it any easier to get it all done on time.

She looked down at her list. After her lunch with friends, she picked up the dry cleaning and dropped off Lydia's nearly overdue library books. Then she went to the sporting goods store to get Jack's new hockey stick they had ordered, and then she got a few extra bottles of wine at the liquor store. Now, she could stroke off getting groceries. Next, it was off to the hardware store for a new snow brush, and back to the liquor store because Graham just texted, asking her to pick up his and Todd's favourite scotch. Then she would head over to the fabric store for Lydia. She had taken up sewing with Nana and they had run out of thread to finish a skirt they were making together. And then, finally home.

A few hours later, the list was complete and Joanna drove through their slushy street, and stopped by the mailbox to get their mail. What was one more stop? Grabbing the envelopes and flyers, she crammed them into her bag and turned the corner, finally making it home. Joanna gathered the shopping bags from the trunk and trudged her way into the house. The twins obviously walked home from school and had made a mess with their shoes and soaking, wet coats left on the floor.

"Hey, you two, come clean up your mess," she called out. "And where's Ally?"

Joanna brought in another bag of groceries and the wine, as Jack and Lydia hung up their coats. "Here Jack, help me out with this. Lydia start unpacking, please. Uncle Todd and Aunt Sara and Nana are coming over tonight." She reminded them, before heading back to the car for another load. Coming back Joanna asked again. "Where's Ally?"

"I don't know, I didn't see her after school," Jack answered, taking the bag and his new hockey stick from his mom.

"I didn't see her either," Lydia said, putting milk jugs into the fridge.

That's odd, Joanna thought. How quickly her mind went to the scary place of seizures whenever Ally wasn't accounted for. Closing the door with her foot, she put down the last of the shopping bags.

"I'll text her and see if she needs a ride," Joanna said, pulling off her gloves with her teeth and getting her phone from her bag that she abandoned in the mudroom.

"Don't bother," Jack said, "Matthew just pulled up."

The blue car slid sideways up the driveway. After a few minutes, Ally came through the front door, and headed into the kitchen, dripping snowy water all along the way. She threw her backpack on table.

"I am never talking to Matthew Rogalsky, again," Ally declared.

Joanna sighed, putting her phone back into her bag and walked into the kitchen. "Why aren't you talking to him this time?" she asked, folding the empty shopping bags. "And you made a mess all over the floor, Ally. Take your shoes off and wipe it up," she ordered, before checking on the simmering chilli.

"Are you guys dating again or what?" Lydia asked. "Everyone at school can't figure you two out," Lydia added, sneaking a few grapes.

"We are not dating and I don't want to talk about him. He makes me so mad," she huffed, grabbing too many paper towels, mopping up the kitchen floor and then the hallway, talking on and on about how Matthew made her angry. No one knew what she was saying as they carried on with their tasks. This wasn't the first or last rant they would hear about her frustrations with Matthew.

"And then he said," Ally continued, coming back into the kitchen, "he was so torn because all these universities are offering him all these scholarships and he doesn't know which one to choose." She tossed the messy towels into the garbage.

"Well, good for him," Joanna said, trying to find order in her ambushed kitchen. "Here Jack, can you hang this dry cleaning in your dad's closet, please?" She looked up at the wall clock. "They're going to be here in less than an hour. Go clean up your video stuff when you're done hanging the clothes, Jack."

"Lydia, can you grate some cheese and put it in that dish set I have. It's in the butler's pantry. And then I need to chop up tomatoes and onions and avocados. Oh yes, and the corn chips," Joanna rambled on, as she continued down her mental list of things to get done.

Ally sank into the kitchen chair. "Doesn't anybody care about me?" she moaned. "He was bragging and hurting my feelings," she said, reaching for the bag of chips.

"Not before dinner, Ally," Joanna said, taking it back. "Be happy for Matthew. He's worked hard to get those chances. Has anybody else had letters?" Joanna asked, washing the tomatoes.

"Yes, lots have. And Christine and Amanda applied to the same dorm I did, so that will be fun. If we all get in," Ally said, sitting on the counter. "Why is the family coming over?"

Joanna sighed. "Because we haven't seen them for a while and just because, we like them. Now clean up your stuff. I think we'll just do a buffet or is it easier for Abigail and Nora if we sit at the table?" Joanna wondered, as her mind raced the clock.

An hour later, Joanna had nearly finished all her preparations when Graham got home, minutes before everyone else arrived. Soon, they were all piled into the kitchen, all talking at once and happy to be together. Sarah and Ellie helped out with cutting up the buns, dumping salsa and sour cream into bowls. Joanna ordered them all to find a seat as chilli, chips, veggie platters and all the fixings were placed on the table. Pouring juice for her nieces who found their places on either side of Lydia, Joanna realized this wasn't company, this was family. She smiled, recalling all the minor stresses that made her forget about what was really important about this day, her family.

Dinner was casual and fun as they laughed and joked, eating steaming, hot bowls of chilli. They talked about making extra rooms in the open loft of the cabin this summer, making it easier for them to all be at the cabin at once.

Todd and Sarah mentioned they wanted to take a vacation next month to celebrate their 10th wedding anniversary. Joanna offered to take the girls before Sarah had time to ask.

Nana nervously announced she had a special friend. "It's lonely going to concerts and movies by yourself or with just another couple," she explained, with deep reservation. The room went a little too quiet.

"Well I'm not surprised, Ellie, you are a striking woman and it was really just a matter of time before some gentleman realized that," Sarah said, breaking the awkward moment.

"We are all happy for you," Joanna added, encouraging everyone to say something.

"My grandma is dating?" Lydia stated emphatically.

"Let's not get ahead of ourselves," Graham advised. "But, yes, Mom, we're happy for you. You deserve to be happy again. But we need to meet this young man before things go any further." He hugged his mother just as Todd embraced them both.

Ellie wiped her eyes. "Thank you boys, I wasn't sure how you'd feel about it. So much change going on around here already. With Ally graduating soon and moving on."

"Yes, Ally, any word about getting accepted?" Sarah asked, wiping Nora's hands and face, so she and Ally could go find the Barbie dolls.

"No, not yet," Ally answered. "Still waiting." She walked out of the kitchen with Nora trailing behind, glad to avoid talking about her acceptance letter that had yet not arrived.

Lydia and Abigail helped plate up Nana's brownies with chocolate sauce and ice cream as Joanna prepared coffee.

"Not to worry, she'll get in," Graham said confidently, clearing the table.

Sarah got the coffee mugs from the cupboard. She looked outside. "It can't be snowing harder now. I hate this weather, you never know how to dress the kids for school," Sarah complained.

"I know," Joanna answered, pouring the coffee when they heard a bang.

Panic ran through the kitchen as they all leapt for the door, Todd leading the way.

"It's okay, I'm okay," Ally said, coming from the closet in the family room. "I was just trying to get a box of Barbie dolls down for Nora."

They all collectively sighed.

Heading back into the kitchen, a deep sense of relief ran through Joanna who remembered thinking earlier in the day, if the day could get any worse. And she knew how it could.

Sitting down at the table, Graham started asking his mother about her new friend when Joanna's cell phone started ringing. Heading to the mudroom, Joanna found her bag. Digging out the phone from the side pocket, she saw it was a text from Hannah asking about going shopping next week. Joanna would reply later. Then Joanna noticed the stack of mail she hastily shoved into her bag earlier in the afternoon. Shuffling through the envelopes and flyers, Joanna scanned them with excited hands. Then there is was, a letter from the University of Manitoba.

"Ally!" she called out, walking back into the kitchen from the mudroom.

"What is it?" Graham asked, sneaking a second brownie.

"Ally!" she called again, holding up the letter.

"Is it what I think it is?" Graham asked again.

Ally came into the kitchen and felt the anticipation in the room. Then she saw her mother holding the letter. The letter addressed to her, Ms. Allison Kornelson.

Swallowing the lump in her throat, Ally looked at her parents, before taking the envelope from her mother. She looked down at it again. This is what she had been waiting for all these weeks. She auditioned at the university in February, got a tour of the school and was told she would receive a letter sometime in the next month. It all seemed so long ago that she played piano for the panel of music professors. And now, her future, her dreams were all waiting inside the white envelope.

"What are you waiting for Al? Rip it open," Todd said, leaning on the island.

"Don't rush her," Ellie scolded. "You just take your time, dear."

Ally swallowed again and then slowly peeled open the top of the envelope and took out the folded paper.

'Dear Allison. Congratulations, we are pleased to inform you, that you have been one of 60 students accepted into the Marcel A. Desautels Faculty of Music.....'

"What does it say?" Lydia asked, bouncing up and down with excitement.

Ally smiled. She looked up and saw her family. This was their dream too. For her to not give up when epilepsy threatened to hold her back. Through all the seizures and drugs and all the times she wanted to quit, these people held her up as she coasted on their hope that she would one day find normal again.

"I'm in. I'm accepted. They accepted me and I'm going to university!" she screamed, hugging her dad first.

Ally read the letter again, and she still couldn't believe it. In a few months she would be graduating from high school, and then she was on her way to getting her music degree. It had all paid off. The lessons and practicing. The festivals and all the performances in between. She stared at the letter again that was signed by the dean of the faculty inviting her to come to the university. She had made it. She had done it.

Her eyes filled with tears as pride and relief filled her soul. Through all of these difficult years that her family had gone through, Ally was so proud that this was her family standing around her now. They endured all of it together; and together they had thrived.

Ally looked up from the letter and turned to see her mom watching her. Their eyes locked.

Ally mouthed the words, "Thank you, Mom. I won."

Joanna embraced Ally, as tears of joy ran down her cheeks. "And I knew you would, Ally. I always knew. You would win."

Based on true events....

When my daughter, Jessica, was twelve years old, I found her at the bottom of our stairs suffering from her first seizure. I thought she was dying. And I knew, my life had changed forever. The normal path of our everyday was over and a new one had begun. I didn't want to go down the road of seizures and drugs, medical tests and doctors appointments. I was desperate to keep this untimely diagnosis from defining her, or our family. And yet, denying and covering up our realities caused symptoms of the disease that cannot be found in medical journals. Hiding inside our hearts and our home was a festering rage, growing uncertainty, anger and a cluelessness of how to carry on. Nagging doubt changed who we were and we ran out of options but to come to terms with becoming that family who was diagnosed. I hated accepting our reality, making it worse as I stewed in my many disappointments for our future.

Not everyone in our lives was able to find supportive words or be there when we needed them to understand that we were suffering. I felt out of control and so inadequate to raise a daughter with a medical condition. I grieved for our ordinary life and I ached for Jessica's suffering as I watched us come apart at the seams.

Rehearsed answers and pleading prayers felt hollow and not enough to heal us. There was never a defining moment that I knew we would be okay. There was no glorious light that shone from above that gave me peace. Epilepsy was in our home causing a level of tension that covered us and burdened us as the seizures kept happening and the volatile drug changes continued.

Over time, I accepted that we may not get our miraculous epiphany. All we were given was a single moment to have the faith to continue. I slowly understood we needed to take a single minute to decide that we are going to get through this; a minute to realize we were still going to be a family. One moment to regain perspective and decide, we could do better. We started to string these moments of acceptance into days of hope, and then into months of recovery, and into years of perspective.

I look back and can see a family that healed, together. We still struggled, but I knew that when one fell we could pick each other up. And from acceptance, we grew closer and wiser. We came together and faced every seizure as a supportive family. We cried, we talked; we got over it and we moved on. Slowly we found a thin balance of watching out for each other. We were mindful of how our family was different.

But tragedy can bring out the best in people; those who were willing to courageously walk the difficult times with us. Jessica had a great supportive group of friends and teachers. And yes, her first day at her very first job, she did have a seizure. Her bosses, Ron and Sheldon, were incredible the seven summers she worked for them. Later, Jessica worked at Safeway and was very supported by the store manager, Gerald. Her long time piano teacher, Patti Schroeder, nurtured and cared for Jessica's talent as well as her spirit. The professors and staff at the University of Manitoba, Faculty of Music (yes, she did go), were caring and so determined to see that Jessica succeed and she earned her degree. Dr. Judy Kehler Siebert, taught Jessica amazing life lessons while sitting at the piano. Judy let her cry, talk and never let her become less than who she was meant to be. I believe they had a piano lesson on occasion! Our parents and extended families took care of Alayna and Riley, so we could take Jessica to her many doctors appointments and tests. Loving friends sat with us while we cried for our daughter. They offered sound advice, prayers and constant concern for us. I am blessed because of these friends.

I will never claim to be a medical expert or understand much at all about a complex illness like epilepsy. I am even hesitant to offer advice or to know what another mother may be feeling when their child gets a diagnosis. We all absorb experiences differently. What I do know for sure, we all want to be understood. We want our feelings to be validated and heard.

In finding the courage to tell our story with any great honesty, I knew I had to be real and show that we didn't do it all right and we fell short so many times. We constantly doubted our decisions and each other. But grace, forgiveness and a washing of humility over my shattered spirit gave me the courage to raise my daughter to be strong and independent. Telling my story through the eyes of the fictional Kornelson family, healed many of my broken dreams. Revisiting trauma can be a scary journey, but I'm glad I did. I realized I was stronger during those dark days than I remembered.

It is my hope that all who read this book will find an understanding of those who must live with a chronic illness and the families who stand by and attempt to keep life from falling apart. It is for mothers who cry out in disappointment and grief. For the fathers who all have dreams for their families and must watch them slip away. It is for those kids who innocently find bravery to endure unforeseen roads ahead. It is for them, for us, that I wrote this book.

Blessings,
Monica

About the Author

photo by Diana Persson

Monica Friesen resides in Morden, Manitoba, the same community where she was born and raised. She lives with her husband Robert and dog, Truman. She has three grown children, Jessica, Alayna and Riley. *And We All Fall Down; One Family's Struggle With Epilepsy*, is based on her personal experiences of raising a daughter with epilepsy. This is her first novel. Monica can be contacted at freezen@mts.net.

Printed in Canada